THE CITY MAPS OF EUROPE

16th Century Town Plans from Braun & Hogenberg

JOHN GOSS

RAND McNALLY

CHICAGO · NEW YORK · SAN FRANCISCO

ORNAM. T. ORB. TERR.

CIVITA
TES OR
BIS TER
RARVM

ARTIVM INVENTRA

PIDOR AVCTOR

CONSOCIAT. HVMANI GEN. ORIGO.

ARCHITEC. RVDIM.

DOMICIL. TER. OCIN.

LIBER PRIMVS.

CONTENTS

INTRODUCTION 5

LIST OF THE MAPS ILLUSTRATED

SELECTED FURTHER READING 128

PUBLISHER'S NOTE

The 60 cities in this volume have been
ordered alphabetically with place names
appearing in their indigenous language.
Where relevant, the English equivalent is
given in brackets. Within the captions the
cities are referred to using
their English names.

Rand McNally
The City Maps of Europe
16th Century Town Plans from Braun & Hogenberg

Published by Rand McNally
in 1992 in the U.S.A.
Copyright © Studio Editions Ltd., 1991
Text copyright © John Goss, 1991

All rights reserved. No part of this publication may
be reproduced, stored in a retrieval system, or
transmitted, in any form or by any means, electronic,
mechanical, photocopying, recording or otherwise,
without the prior permission in writing of the
copyright holder.

Designed by T.K. Designs Ltd., Farnborough, Hants, UK.
ISBN 0-528-83524-6
Printed in Hong Kong

Library of Congress
Cataloging-in-Publication Data

Braun, Georg. 1540 or 1–1622
    Rand McNally, the city maps of Europe: 16th
century town plans from Braun & Hogenberg / John
Goss.
       p. cm.
    Maps are facsimiles from the author's Civitates
orbis terrarum.
    Published in Great Britain as: Braun & Hogen-
berg's city maps of Europe, a selection of 16th century
town plans & views.
    ISBN 0-528-83524-6
    1. Cities and towns, Renaissance – Europe – Maps.
2. Cities and towns, Renaissance – Europe – Aerial
views. I. Hogenberg, Franz, d. 1590? II. Goss, John,
1947– . III. Braun, Georg, 1540 or 1–1622. Civitates
orbis terrarum. IV. Rand McNally and Company. V.
Title. VI. Title: City maps of Europe, 16th century
town plans from Braun & Hogenberg.
G1799.A1B75   1992 ‹G&M›
912.4—dc20
                                      92–12722
                                           CIP
                                       MAP

INTRODUCTION

" . . . A good prospect alone will ease melancholy . . .
What greater pleasure can there be now than . . . to peruse
those books of cities, put out by
Braun and Hogenbergius?"
Robert Burton, *Anatomy of Melancholy* (1621).

The *Civitates orbis terrarum* of Georg Braun and Frans Hogenberg, one of the great books of the world, is a celebration of the European city. The work gives collectors as much pleasure today as it did in its early years, as proven by Burton's famous comment. Published in six volumes over forty-five years from 1572 to 1617, it is one of the first modern atlases of its kind; in great detail, it depicts some 530 mostly European cities as they were 400 years or more ago.

The *Civitates* (to use the shortened, familiar form of the title) is of considerable interest, incorporating the work of prominent artists, engravers and cartographers in a series of horizontal perspectives, oblique plans or bird's-eye views, and true plans, the form perhaps most familiar to the modern reader. Georg Braun, co-compiler with Frans Hogenberg, favoured the oblique view, being of the opinion that "towns should be drawn in such a manner that the viewer may look into all the roads, and streets and see also all the buildings and open spaces".

Into this most remarkable series of engravings, Braun and Hogenberg incorporated an astonishing wealth of detail. By means of these pictures, the compilers presented to the reader an impression of the economy, status, wealth and even the social structure of the towns and cities mostly of Europe and of the immediately neighbouring regions of Asia and Africa. Where space permitted, the subject was additionally enlivened with details of the surrounding countryside, wooded, arable and pasture lands, vineyards and orchards, gardens, lowlands partly inundated by flood- or sea-waters.

Waterways, at the time of first publication during the late sixteenth and early seventeenth centuries, were the most important means of moving large quantities of goods – grain, timber, salt, stone and so on – from one place to another. Careful attention was therefore given to the correct depiction of river-going and sea-going boats and other vessels, for example, those of Dutch merchants plying in and out of the harbour at Danzig, or barges floating down the Rhine, the Thames or the Wisła rivers.

Sometimes, different sorts of traffic are included in the engravings: laden waggons, and carriages for the use of nobles, or simply the pedlar on foot. Different occupations may also be depicted and local costume often shown to gloriously colourful effect. It does not matter in the least that most of the figures depicted are out of proportion to the townscapes; rather, they serve to impart a sense of long perspective so that the viewer is drawn into the centre of the markets of Hamburg, the lading of casks of robust clarets on the quays of Bordeaux, the lively intercourse between merchants in Venice, or the discussion taking place between two figures in their academic robes outside Oxford.

But why, and how, were such perspective, or bird's-eye views and plans made? The perspective views and plans which make up the *Civitates* enabled the mapmaker to convey *vertical* dimensions – the elevations of important buildings and their architectural features – while also retaining a *horizontal* dimension, but one which favoured perspective over true scale in most cases. The plan and the view were thus combined to form a map-view or plan-view, presenting the true ground plan but featuring many of the buildings in elevation. By portraying a city in such a manner, the mapmaker could impress and inspire the reader with grandeur, power or wealth so displayed, simultaneously demonstrating his skill in the art of perspective plan-making.

A curious feature, not often remarked upon in considering the plans and views in the *Civitates*, is that, in nearly every instance, a relatively tranquil scene is depicted, tranquil, that is, in the sense that whatever activity is seen to be taking place in the subjects, it is a peaceful, everyday kind of activity: agriculture, viticulture, shipping, trading, or merely displaying local costume to the reader. This is even so in the case of many of the towns of Austria, Hungary, the Spanish Netherlands, and so on, all at one time or another during the compilation and publication of the six volumes wracked by civil and military conflict. Compare these tranquil scenes with the violent depictions of contemporary events which Hogenberg and others published as *geschichtsblätter* illustrating the horrors perpetrated during the religious wars in northern Europe in the struggle for the independence of the Netherlands from Spain, from about 1561 onwards. The contrast between the two series is stark indeed.

It seems almost as if there were a kind of censorship exercised in the production of many of the engravings in the series. What we have, then, in the *Civitates* series is an almost ideal picture of the European town and city of the late sixteenth and early seventeenth centuries.

That some collectors consider the series one of the finest costume books in existence should come as no surprise, for so detailed are the depictions of local and regional costume in many cases as evidenced by the figures included in the foregrounds of so many of the engravings. There is hardly a sign of distress, disquiet, unrest, conflict in the manner in which the inhabitants display, sometimes disport themselves. Not only are there wealthy aristocrats and merchants, as it were taking their bows on presenting their cities to the reader, but in the middle ground of many of the views artisans, labourers, peasants, farmers, small traders and skippers are seen busy about their various occupations: vines are seen cultivated in the Rhine and Loire valleys, in Gascony and in Burgundy; corn is being harvested in southern Spain; flax and cotton are prepared for despatch abroad in Cadiz, Barcelona and Marseilles; wealthy merchants of Danzig profit from the lucrative rye trade with Amsterdam; and the proud burghers of Nuremberg rejoice at having secured their profit from some trade with countries to the south and east of the Alps.

In many instances, the artist, Georg Hoefnagel, together with his travelling companions, may be included in many a French or Spanish scene on an open road, or is seen lazing by the wayside on a balmy day. The prehistoric cromlech outside the French town of Poitiers, moreover, testifies to the visits made by Hoefnagel himself in 1561 and by Braun later in 1580, for there, for all to see, are their names carved on the ancient stones.

The year 1572 in Cologne saw the appearance of the first volume of what was to grow into a six-volume series of engraved views, plans and panoramas of the then most important towns and cities in Europe and certain other places outside Europe which had had contact with Europeans. The common title of the complete work, *Civitates orbis terrarum*, appeared only as the title of the first volume, issued in 1572. The subsequent volumes, which came out in *c.*1575, 1581, 1588, *c.*1598 and finally in 1617 had their own titles, variants on the theme of the first. Each volume was issued in Latin, German or French editions.

The complete work as published between 1572 and 1617 contains some 363 plates depicting some 531 towns and cities, maps and heraldic plates. There is a close generic resemblance between the title of the *Theatrum orbis terrarum*, the great world atlas of Abraham Ortelius (a contemporary of both Braun and Hogenberg), first published in Antwerp in 1570, and the *Civitates orbis terrarum* of Braun and Hogenberg. The latter work is often considered as the rightful companion to the former by collectors; very often, especially in the case of the German text editions of both works, the Ortelius atlas and the Braun and Hogenberg town books are found in a uniform binding of brown morocco embellished with gilt and silver tooling.

In a letter to Ortelius, dated 31 October 1571, a few months prior to the first publication of volume I of the *Civitates*, Georg Braun wrote: "For various reasons some learned men here in Cologne think that Master Frans's [*i.e.* Hogenberg's] Book of Cities would commend itself more to purchasers if the proper names of places, churches and gates were given in the native language; so as to satisfy both the learned and the unlettered: the learned because they will have the Latin descriptions on the back [in the manner of the captions appended to the selected plates in the present book], the unlettered because each will see his own native town depicted with places named in a form familiar to him. I think the usefulness of this arrangement is evident when pictures of cities are sold separately, but the citizens would like them less if they could understand nothing of what they read."

Braun's purpose was to describe the shape and situation of the towns and cities illustrated, the occupations of their inhabitants, what trades and industries flourished there, sometimes including fulsome praise, perhaps to stimulate sales of the books in those places, at other times criticising the physical state of certain places. Many descriptions, especially those of towns in France and southern Spain, demonstrate a detailed local knowledge, which were very likely written by Hoefnagel himself from his own observations. Most of the plans are enlivened with costumed figures or vignettes of local people, sometimes by the original artist, or taken from such illustrated costume books as Abraham de Bruyn's *Omnium poene gentium imagines* (Antwerp, 1577) or the famous *Trachtenbuch* of Hans Weigel and Jost Amman (Nuremberg, 1577). These figures, often theatrical in character, are a great tribute to the compositional skills of the engraver in that, although drawn on a much larger scale than the rest of the design, they almost never introduce a discordant note. This particular feature of the work is said to have had the additional purpose of preventing the Turks from using the engravings during their campaigns on the southeastern flanks of Europe, as their religion prohibited the portrayal of the human figure.

The *Civitates* answered a considerable public demand. With a few notable exceptions very few printed books contained more than a mere handful of urban subjects, a great many of which were non-representational and entirely imaginary in content. For the most part, town plans and views had been issued separately as elaborate, multi-sheet publications intended for display on the walls of great houses or palaces. It goes without saying, therefore, that the *Civitates orbis terrarum* was a new kind of book, the first systematic city atlas.

Its chief editor, Georg Braun (1541–1622), was strongly influenced by Abraham Ortelius. He was a cleric in Cologne and spent most of his life in that city. Little else is known about him, except that he wrote several now-forgotten theological texts. During the compilation of the *Civitates*, Georg Braun corresponded with town officials, artists and company officials as well as with the most important mapmakers and engravers of his time. He even appealed to his readers, in the preface to volume II, to send in paintings or drawings of their towns or cities if they were not already represented in the work, or to provide more recent depictions of cities already included in earlier volumes. Braun is also thought to have written, or at least edited, most of the descriptive texts printed on the versos of the engraved views and plans of the six volumes.

Prominent among Braun's engravers was Frans Hogenberg (1535–90), of Mechelen, in Belgium. After his death in about 1590, many of the *Civitates* plates were made by Abraham Hogenberg, who is assumed to have been the son of Frans. Among other important engravers who worked for Braun on the project was Simon van den Neuvel, who contributed to the second and third volumes of the series.

It was through his friendship with Ortelius that Georg Braun became acquainted with the Antwerp artist Joris Hoefnagel (1542–1600). The latter played a vital, if until recently relatively underestimated, part as an artist in the overall design of the series. Hoefnagel, born into a wealthy family, travelled widely throughout Europe, in particular to

England, France and Spain, spending some time in Andalusia. Hoefnagel lived in Antwerp until 1576, settled in Cologne and also worked in Austria, Bohemia, Bavaria and the Tirol. In the company of the map-maker Ortelius, Hoefnagel made extensive travels throughout Italy, collecting material for publication by Braun. Hoefnagel's talent was based on his enthusiasm for knowledge. It was through his observation of detail that he conveyed the structure of the towns and cities and the way of life of their inhabitants. He was also a master of the pure landscape and of local custom. After his death in 1600, his son Jakob continued his work on the plates for the *Civitates*.

Another important contributor to the series was the Dane, Heinrich von Rantzau (1526–99), commonly known as Rantzovius, his Latinised name. He enthusiastically supplied (*communicavit*) maps, descriptions, plans and views of towns and cities in northern Europe, particularly of Denmark. It is also presumed that von Rantzau wrote the texts for the Danish towns included in the *Civitates*.

Other sources of information were the older woodcut views used in Sebastian Münster's *Cosmographia* of the 1550s. It has also been established that, directly or indirectly, Hogenberg used the unpublished manuscript surveys of towns in the Netherlands by Jacob Roelofs (*c.*1505–1575), better known as Jacob van Deventer after his native town in the Netherlands.

Many other subjects in the six volumes were taken from entirely anonymous artists or were based upon existing engravings or woodcuts by over one hundred artists and engravers.

The copy of the *Civitates* from which the selection of plates for this work was made is possibly one of the finest coloured sets of the work to have survived, so remarkably fresh are the colours, even after four hundred years or so. It will be seen, too, that the colours show a remarkable uniformity throughout the plates, from those selected from volume I to those from volume VI. As we know that the full work was published over a number of years, from 1572 to 1617, we may rightly ask how such a cohesion of colouring was achieved. The only answer would be that the complete set was coloured at some time just after the appearance of the final volume. There is nothing unusual or untoward in this, since volume I, for example, in its Latin-text edition, was still being printed as late as the 1620s.

Naturally, given the span of years over which the six volumes appeared, some images from the earlier volumes in a set collated, bound and sold in 1617 may be less sharp because of plate wear. But such faults – if such they be – were concealed by the skill of the early seventeenth-century colourist. Indeed, some of the best coloured sets which have been sold in recent years have almost invariably been complete sets of the six volumes with early seventeenth-century colouring and uniform contemporary bindings.

The great popular success of the work as a whole, or of those individual volumes that contained an abundance of plans and views of certain countries or regions, inspired a particular fashion for townbooks which lasted until well into the eighteenth century.

Of all the collaborators on the *Civitates*, Georg Braun was the only one who lived to see the series completed with the publication of the sixth volume in 1617. After Braun's death in 1622, the plates of the great work lay unused until they were purchased by the Amsterdam map-maker and publisher Joannes Jansson in 1653. Jansson reprinted some 230 of the plates, largely unaltered, or with very minor changes.

Some years later, in the 1670s and 1680s, many of the original Braun and Hogenberg plates passed to another Amsterdam publisher, Frederick de Wit, who also issued a series of town views. Later still, the plates came into the hands of the Leiden publisher and print-seller Pieter van der Aa, who issued a sixty-six-part series of illustrated folio volumes during the 1720s the *Galerie agréable du monde*; these contained many of the by now very worn impressions from the Braun and Hogenberg plates.

After this, several of the plates came into the hands of yet another Amsterdam publisher, Pieter Mortier who, in partnership with Johannes Covens issued them in composite collections of maps, plans and views during the 1750s. The later history of the plates remains a matter of conjecture but, as late as the middle of the nineteenth century, they seem still to have been in the possession of the firm of Covens & Mortier. Their ultimate fate is unknown.

PLATE 1

AACHEN

Aquisgranum, Vulgo Aich, ad Menapiorum fines . . . M.D.LXXVI.
1576.
Volume I, number 12. 320 × 325mm.

Based on a plan by Hendrik Steenwijk. Aachen, known by the French as *Aix-la-Chapelle*, has long been a frontier city. The Romans named it *Aquisgranum* after the god Apollo Granus, who was worshipped in connection with six hot sulphur springs. Aachen rose to greatness during the time of Charlemagne who, between 777 and 786, built a great palace, the *Aula Regia*, there, raising Aachen to the status of second city of his empire.

For a brief period, Aachen became the centre of Western learning and culture. From the coronation of Louis the Pious in 813 until that of Ferdinand I in 1531, Aachen saw the inaugurations of some thirty-two emperors and kings. Despite the ravages of the Norsemen during the ninth century, it was not until the twelfth century that Aachen was enclosed by defensive walls, built between 1172 and 1176 by Frederick I. The outer ring of wall – seen clearly in the plan – was completed by 1300, the older circumvallation marking the limits of the *Altstadt*, the so-called *Barbarossamauer*. In the fourteenth century, Aachen, by now an imperial free city, played an important part in keeping the peace in the lands between the two great rivers, the Rhine and the Maas.

Civic rights within the city walls were, however, restrained by the presence of the royal advocate, or *vogt*, and in 1470 an uprising led to the admission of the trade guilds to the municipal government. During the sixteenth century, Aachen began to decline in importance and prosperity: it was too near the French frontier and too far from the centre of Germany to be either safe or influential.

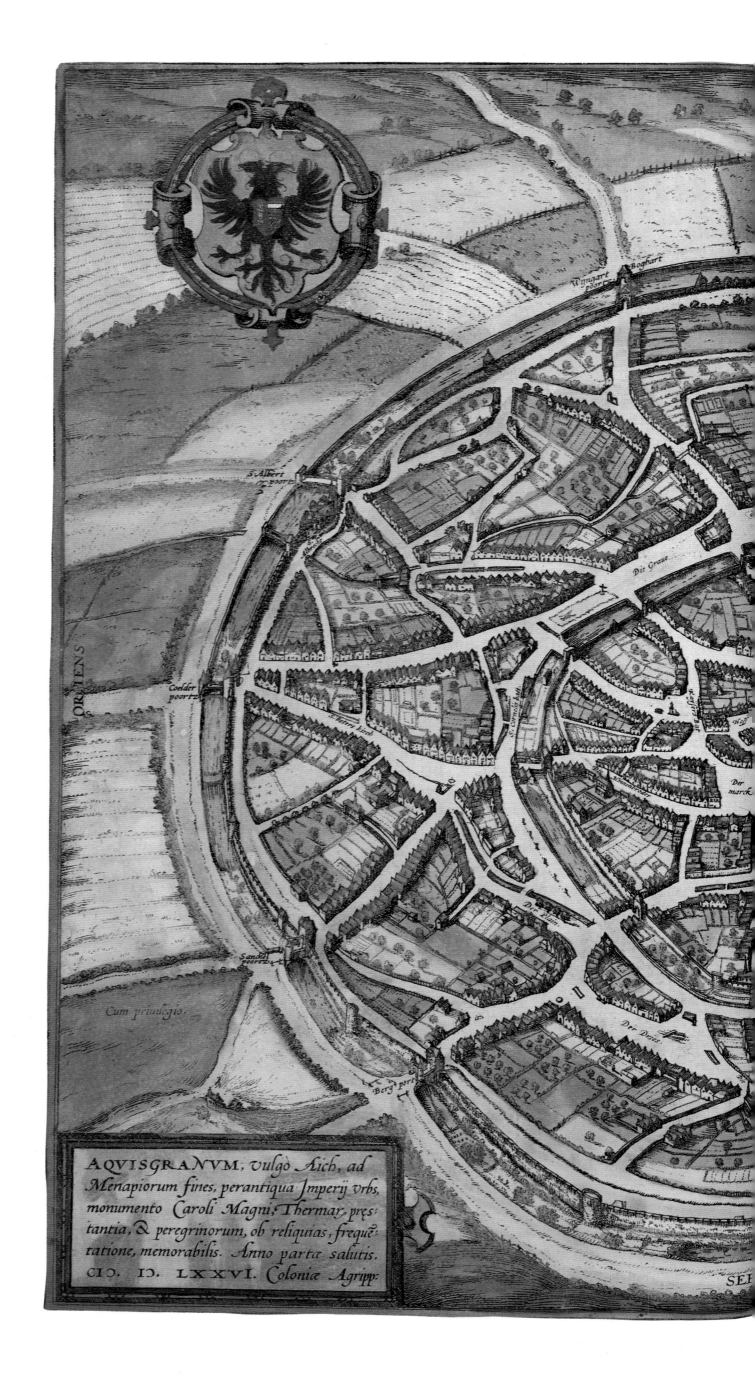

The coronation of Maximilian II in 1562 thus took place in Frankfurt am Main (*q.v.*), a precedent maintained until the collapse of the Holy Roman Empire.

The engraving, made in the 1570s, shows a city which was on the verge of decline. Aachen nevertheless contained some thirty-three churches at the time, including the great *Sankt Follian*, built in the twelfth century, and the *Sankt Paul*, with its remarkable windows. The imperial palace occupied the old centre of the *Altstadt* almost at the very centre of the engraving. The view is taken looking south.

PLATE 2

AMSTERDAM

Amstelredamum, nobile Inferioris Germaniae oppidum. 1572.
Volume I, number 20. 340 × 485mm.

After the woodcut plan of Cornelis Antoniszoon, 1544. The plan shows Amsterdam as it existed in the middle years of the sixteenth century. The engraving depicts that almost uniquely Dutch form of urban site: a river, in this case the Amstel, dammed near its mouth and its flow controlled by channels to the sea with an outer harbour created from the downstream portion – the *Damrak* – and an inner harbour from the upstream portion – the *Rokin*. The dykes containing the channels acted as routes for land traffic to and from the warehouses built on the *berms*. The *Dam* itself, seen in the centre of the plan, provided a central open space for public buildings such as the old *Stadhuis* and a church nearby.

Anthoniszoon's picture shows an Amsterdam still largely surrounded by the mediaeval town walls established and extended since the original damming in 1240 which created the *Damrak* and the *Rokin* as the original harbours. Thirteenth-century Amsterdam was merely a small fishing port, well behind such towns as Delft, Leiden (*q.v.*) or Haarlem in rank and importance. Extensions were made in 1367, 1380 and 1450, and a formal defensive system was begun as late as 1482. Essentially, this is what we see in this engraving – a wall which effectively contained the city until the great extensions laid down by the so-called *Driegrachtenplan* of 1607 were made. Parts of the old wall are still visible today – the *Schreierstoren* near the IJ, the *Waag* on the *Nieuwmarkt*, the former *Sint-Anthonispoort*, and the

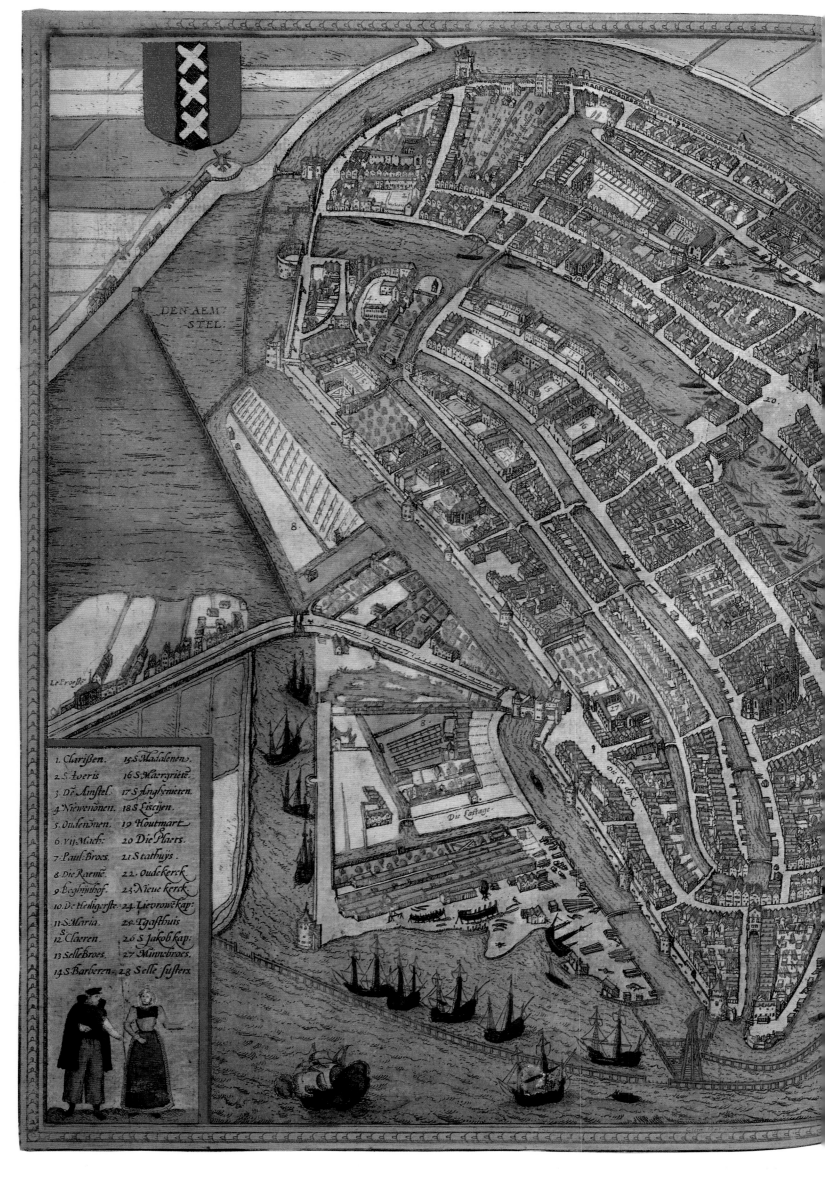

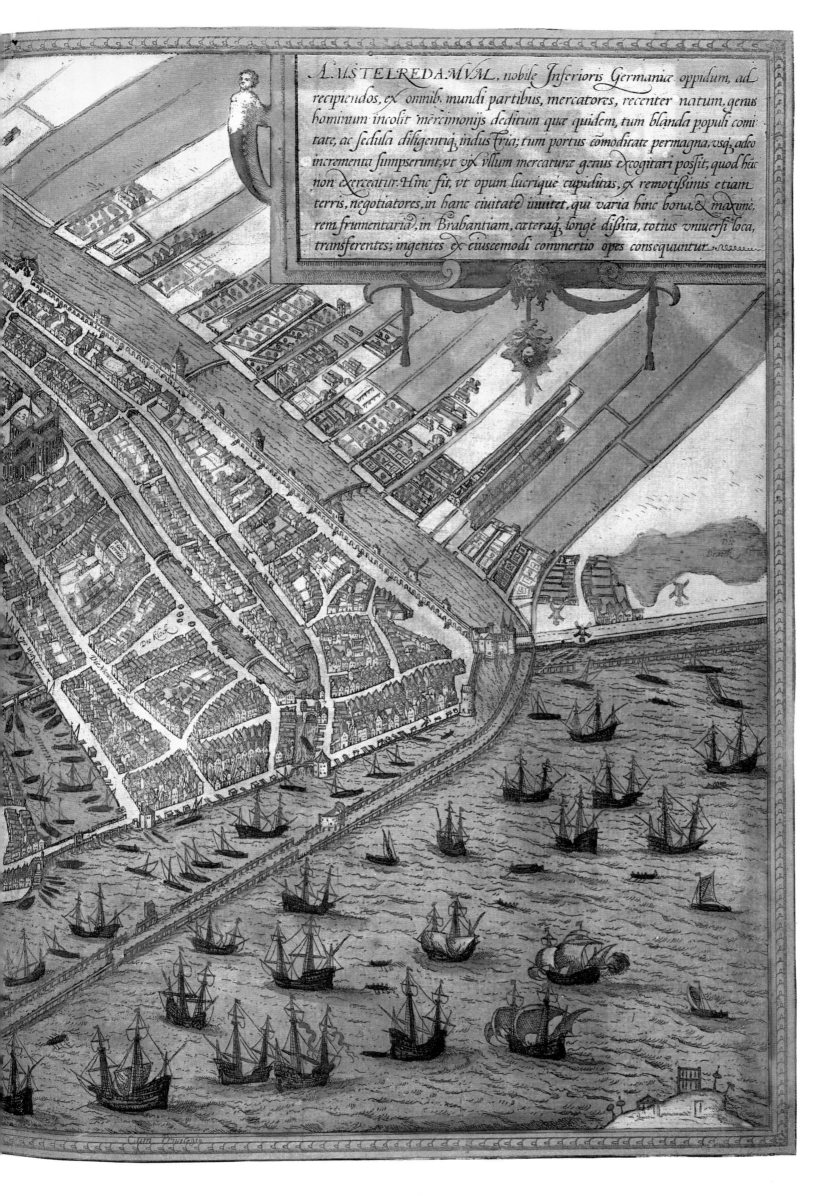

Munt. Incidentally, by the outer harbour, or *Damrak* as it is shown here, may be seen *Opt Water*, the quay on which, in later years, many map and chart sellers were established during the long years of Amsterdam's primacy as a trading city and the centre of a worldwide trading empire.

When this view was first published in the *Civitates* in 1572, Amsterdam was beginning to see an increase in trade handled by the port following the effective Spanish destruction (*q.v.*) of Antwerp by the soldiers of Philip II of Spain in 1576. By 1600, Amsterdam had assumed the rank once held by its southern rival, handling trade from the Baltic, and southern Europe and from farther afield. By 1600, Amsterdam had thus laid the foundations of what was to become a great trading empire rivalling the other maritime powers of Europe in the East Indies and West Indies alike. The shipping depicted in this engraving, however, gives some idea of the commercial bustle of the former fishing hamlet on a dam near the mouth of a small river.

PLATE 3

ANTWERPEN
(Antwerp)

Antverpia. 1598.
*Volume V, number 27. 450 ×
708mm.*

After Georg Hoefnagel,
*c.*1560s. It was not until the
late fifteenth century, when
the Zwin, the channel
leading into Bruges, silted
up, causing the decay of
that city, that Antwerp rose
to prominence. At the end
of the fifteenth century, the
foreign trading guilds and
their merchants who had
been based in Bruges settled
in Antwerp. A house for
English merchants was
mentioned in 1510; note the
Engelse beurs, off the *Korten–*
and *Langengoddaert* and the
Engelse Kaey at the northern
end of the waterfront.

In the 1560's Spaniards,
Danes, Italians,
Englishmen, Portuguese
and Germans, as well as
merchants of the Hanseatic
League, also resided in the
city, a total of some 1,000
foreign nationals in all.

In August 1520, the
German artist Albrecht
Dürer, described a
procession through
Antwerp, from the *Onze
Lieve Vrouwekerk*: "On the
Sunday after Our Dear
Lady's Assumption I saw
the great Procession from
the Church of Our Lady at
Antwerpen, when the
whole town of every craft
and rank was assembled,
each dressed in his best
according to his rank . . .
There were the Goldsmiths,
the Painters, the Masons,
the Broderers, the
Sculptors, the Joiners, the
Sailors, the Fishermen, the
Butchers, the Leatherers,
the Clothmakers, the
Bakers, the Tailors, the
Cordwainers – indeed
workmen of all kinds, and
many craftsmen and dealers
who work for their
livelihood. Like the
shopkeepers and merchants
and their assistants of all
kinds were there . . . all the
religious orders and the

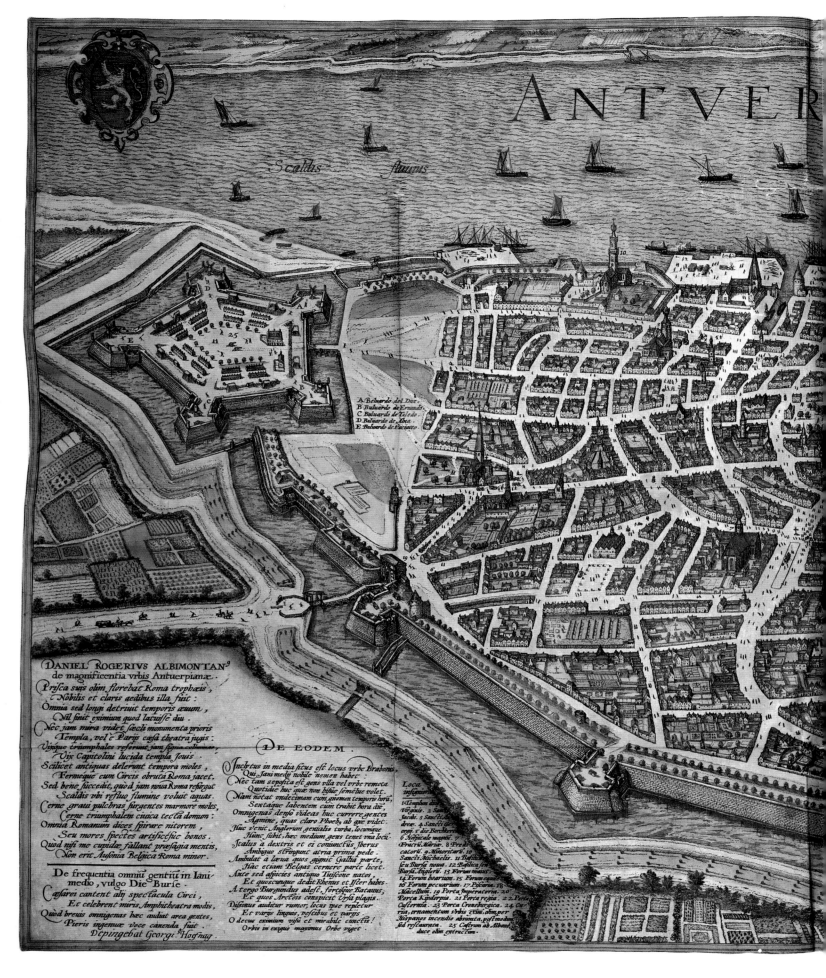

members of some foundations, very devoutly, all in their different robes . . . "

It was at the zenith of Antwerp's prosperity in the 1560s that Hoefnagel painted this magnificent view of the city of his birth. The view offers what might be called a textbook of the principles of fortification at the period. The city was defended by a line of fortification and a moat built by Charles V in 1545 and strengthened by Philip II in 1567. The citadel – the star-shaped structure at the southern end of the city – was built, according to the key, at the orders of the Duke of Alba in 1567, to the designs of Luca Paciotto. It was the first complete bastion system, which could still resist a siege even if the city wall were breached. Note the expanse of open ground between the citadel and the built-up area of the city. An enemy would easily be seen, crossing it to gain access to the citadel.

Sadly, the primacy of Antwerp was about to be dealt a savage blow. The city did not escape the religious troubles which affected the Netherlands in the latter half of the sixteenth century. In 1576, Spanish soldiers plundered the city and some 6,000 citizens were massacred. Eight hundred houses were destroyed and Antwerp never recovered from the damage.

In 1585, a further blow was dealt to the city when it was taken by the Duke of Parma after a long siege. He expelled all the Protestants, merchants and artisans among them. The Treaty of Münster of 1648 which finally granted recognition to the independence of the United Provinces also stipulated that the Schelde be closed to navigation. It remained so, almost without exception, until 1863.

PLATE 4

AUGSBURG

Augusta iuxta figuram quam his a temporibus delineata. 1563.
Volume I, number 39. 330 × 475mm.

Probably after Hans Rogel. Augsburg, called *Augusta Vindelicorum* by the Romans, derives its name from Caesar Augustus who, on the conquest of Rhaetia by Drusus, established a *colonia* here in about 14BC. It was sacked by the invading Huns in the fifth century and later came under Frankish rule. Augsburg was almost certainly laid waste during the wars of Charlemagne against Tassilo III of Bavaria, later falling into Swabian hands.

Augsburg rapidly rose to fame and wealth on account of its commerce, becoming, like Nuremberg (*q.v.*), a centre of trade between northern Europe, Italy and the Levant, beyond the Alps. Its powerful merchant princes, the Fuggers and the Welsers, rivalled the Medici of Florence (*q.v.*) but could not adapt to changes in commercial orientation in Europe brought about by the discoveries in the New World in the fifteenth and sixteenth centuries.

By 1276, Augsburg was an imperial free city which privilege it maintained until 1806, when it was annexed by the kingdom of Bavaria. The plan shows the moated upper and lower town; the main axis (the *Maximilianstraße*) is determined by the processional route between the tenth-century cathedral at the eastern end and the burial church of the two earliest bishops, Ulrich and Afra, built 1474–1500, at the western end. Along this route was established a series of markets, the oldest dating from the tenth century, connected to the city gates by a network of cross and diagonal streets. Along the *Maximilianstraße* the leading families built

their palaces and houses during the late fifteenth and early sixteenth centuries. These merchant banking families were among the richest in the known world. Jakob Fugger (1459–1525) was probably the wealthiest of them all. His wealth was derived from trade, finance, mining and many branches of industry that were then in their infancy. In modern terms, Fugger's wealth has been estimated at one hundred billion Deutschmarks. Fugger was the founder of the oldest social welfare settlement, the famous *Fuggerei*, built in 1519, which housed impoverished elderly citizens. In plan, the *Fuggerei* resembled an Italian palace, with inner courtyards.

PLATE 5

AVIGNON

Avignon. 1575.
*Volume II, number 13. 310 ×
475mm.*

Probably after Sebastian
Münster, 1575.

Avignon, the *Avenio* of the
Gallic tribe of the Cavares,
became one of the chief
towns of Gallia
Narbonensis in the Roman
Empire. During the several
Barbarian and Saracen
invasions up the Rhône
valley, Avignon was
annexed by Burgundy,
Arles and later still the
domains of the counts of
Provence, Toulouse and
Forcalquier. Towards the
end of the twelfth century,
Avignon became a republic,
but in 1226 it was
dismantled by Louis VIII as
punishment for having
supported the Albigensian
heretics and, in 1251, was
placed under the counts of
Provence and Toulouse. In
1309, Avignon became the
residence of Pope Clement
V, remaining the papal seat
until 1377. In 1348 the city
was sold by Joanna,
Countess of Provence, to
Clement VI. Following the
return of Gregory XI to
Rome, Clement VII and
Benedict XIII, two
antipopes of the Great
Schism, resided there, the
latter being expelled in
1403. Until it was annexed
by the French National
Assembly in 1791, Avignon
remained in the hands of the
popes, who ruled through
legates despite several
attempts by the kings of
France to unite the enclave
with their dominions.

The view shows the huge
fortress-like *Château des
Pâpes*, begun in 1316 by
Pope John XXII and
finished by 1370,
dominating Avignon and
almost dwarfing the
cathedral of *Notre-Dame des
Doms* at the upper centre.
Shown still intact is the
celebrated bridge of the

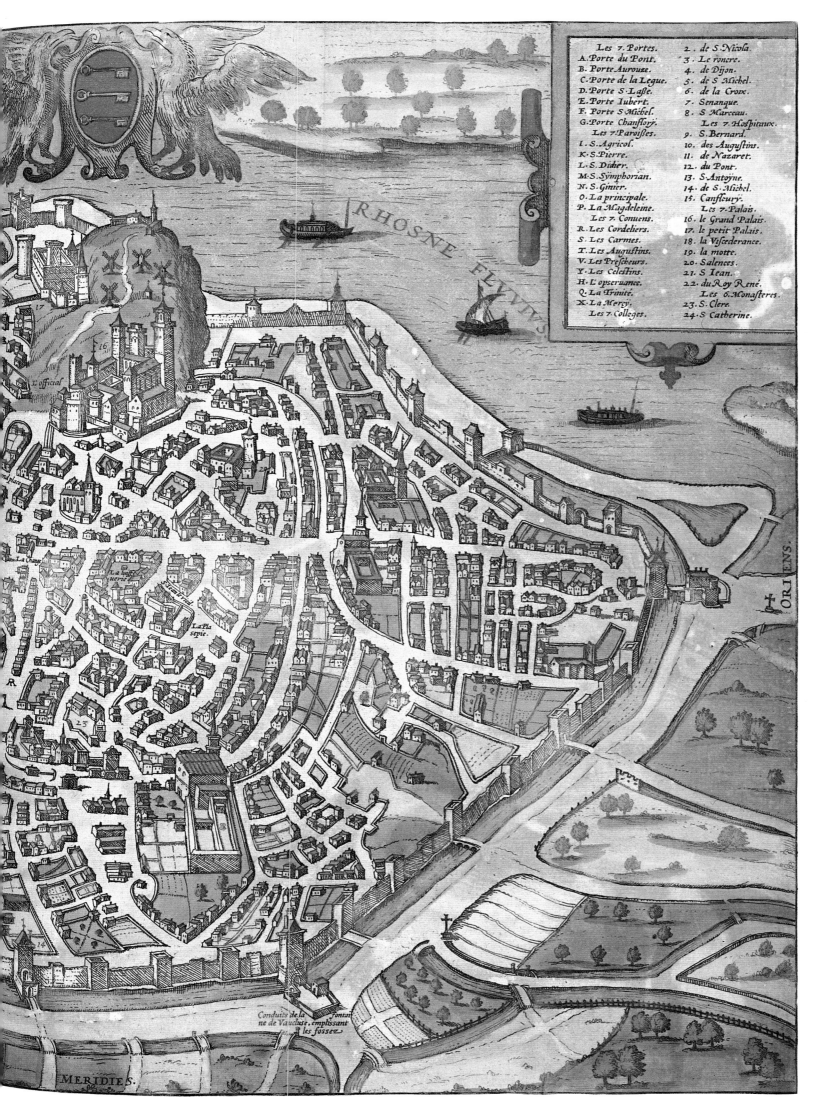

Les 7. Portes.	2 . de S. Nicola.
A. Porte du Pont.	3 . Le roncre.
B. Porte Aurouze.	4. de Dijon.
C. Porte de la Legue.	5. de S. Michel.
D. Porte S. Laße.	6. de la Croix.
E. Porte Iubert.	7. Senanque.
F. Porte S. Michel.	8. S. Marceau.
G. Porte Chanfloyr.	9. S. Bernard.
Les 7. Paroißes.	10. des Augustins.
I. S. Agricol.	11. de Nazaret.
K. S. Pierre.	12. du Pont.
L. S. Didier.	13. S. Antoyne.
M. S. Symphorian.	14. de S. Michel.
N. S. Ginier.	15. Canfleury.
O. La principale.	Les 7. Palais.
P. La Magdeleine.	16. le Grand Palais.
Les 7. Conuens.	17. le petit Palais.
R. Les Cordeliers.	18. la Viscederance.
S. Les Carmes.	19. la motte.
T. Les Augustins.	20. Salences.
V. Les Prescheurs.	21. S. Iean.
Y. Les Celestins.	22. du Roy René.
H. L'opseruance.	Les 6. Monasteres.
Q. La Trinité.	23. S. Clere.
X. La Mercy.	24. S. Catherine.
Les 7. Colleges.	

RHOSNE FLVVIVS

ORIENS.

MERIDIES.

Conduits de la fontai-
ne de Vaucluse, emplissant
les fossez.

popular song, the twelfth-
century *Pont Saint-Bénézet*,
of which only a few of the
original eighteen piers now
remain. At the eastern end
may be seen the small
Romanesque chapel of Saint
Bénézet. Avignon is shown
surrounded by the ramparts
built in 1356, one of the
finest examples of their
kind, enclosing an area of
about 180 hectares and
surrounded by a moat.
They are surmounted by
machicolated battlements,
reinforced by thirty-nine
towers, and pierced by
seven gateways, several
dating from the fourteenth
century. Also numbered on
the engraving are the city's
seven quarters, seven
colleges, seven hospices and
seven palaces.

17

PLATE 6

BARCELONA
AND EÇIJA

Barcelona. Barcino, quę vulgo Barcelona dicitur [with] ***Eçija . . . 1567.***
1572.
Volume I, number 5. 440 × 465mm.

After Georg Hoefnagel, 1567. By tradition, Barcelona was founded by the Carthaginian, Hamilcar Barca, in the third century BC. The Romans established a *colonia* there which, in the second century BC, became the most important trading port in the western Mediterranean. A bishopric was founded in 343 and, in the fifth century, Barcelona became the capital of the Visigoths. With the union of the kingdoms of Aragon and Catalunya in 1149, Barcelona acquired wealth and fame. Its merchant ships, which sailed into the North Sea and the Baltic and down to the Levant, rivalled those of Genoa (*q.v.*), Venice (*q.v.*) and Ragusa.

In 1258 the king of Aragon empowered Barcelona to issue the *Consulado del Mar*, a maritime law which became an accepted code for European maritime states. The city was represented abroad by consuls and was one of the earliest to adopt the practice of maritime insurance. However, by the time of the union of Castille and Aragon in 1479, maritime supremacy had passed to the ports of south-western Spain, so that the merchants of the American trade transferred their wealth and business at the expense of Barcelona. The citizens attributed their subsequent misfortune to the bias of the Castillian government, and many even sought annexation by France.

The cathedral, dominating the central part of the view, was built on the Monte

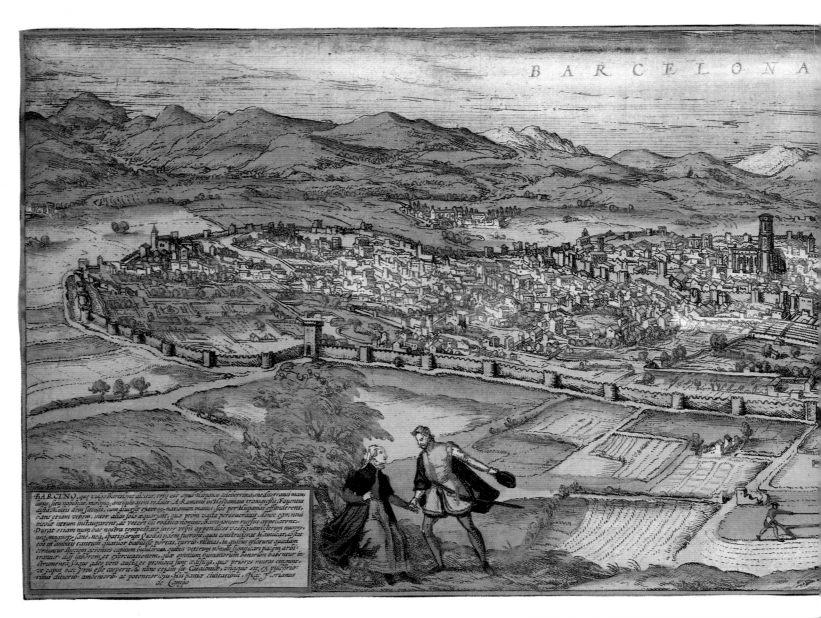

Taber between 1298 and 1448. The university was established in 1430, confirmed by papal *bulla* in 1450. A hospital was founded in 1401, and important commercial buildings such as the *Casa Consistorial* (1369–78) and the exchange (*Lonja* 1383) all date from the prosperous period prior to the union of the two royal houses. The arsenal (*Atarzanas*), visible near the waterfront, dates from about 1243. Here also was the palace of the kings of Aragon.

The port itself began as an open beach sheltered by hills. In 1438 Don Alfonso V granted a licence to build a mole – the *Moll de Santa Creu* – but it was only in the seventeenth century that extensive works in the port were undertaken. The fertile and abundant *huertas*, or market gardens, can be seen in the foreground.

Eçija, to the south of Seville, appears in the lower half of the engraving. From early times, the town's shoemakers enjoyed a high reputation in Spain. Here also woollen cloths and flannels – alluded to by the penned sheep in the foreground – and linen and silks were made. The fertile plain also grows corn, vines and cotton.

Eçija, called *Estija* by the Moors, is the ancient *Astigis*, the Roman *colonia* of *Augusta Firma*, which, according to both Ptolemy and Pomponius Mela in the first century, rivalled Cordova and Seville. Eçija is also known locally as *El Sartén*, or "The Frying Pan" of Andalusia, on account of the high summer temperatures.

PLATE 7

BASEL

Basilea. 1575.
Volume II, number 40. 355 ×
368mm.

After Sebastian Münster,
*c.*1538. Basel, often
erroneously called Basle,
was founded in 374 by the
Roman emperor,
Valentinian. It became a
bishopric in the fifth
century and, from then
until the fourteenth
century, its history is
closely entwined with that
of the spiritual and
temporal powers of the
bishops until their ousting
by the burghers, their
rivals. An earthquake
nearly destroyed the city in
1356. In 1501, after much
indecision, it was admitted
into the Swiss
Confederation, later
becoming one of the chief
centres of the Reformation
in Switzerland and in 1525
forced its bishop to remove
to Porrentuy.

Strategically situated on the
great bend of the Rhine
where the borders between
Switzerland, Germany and
France meet, the city has
long enjoyed a flourishing
transit trade; some idea of

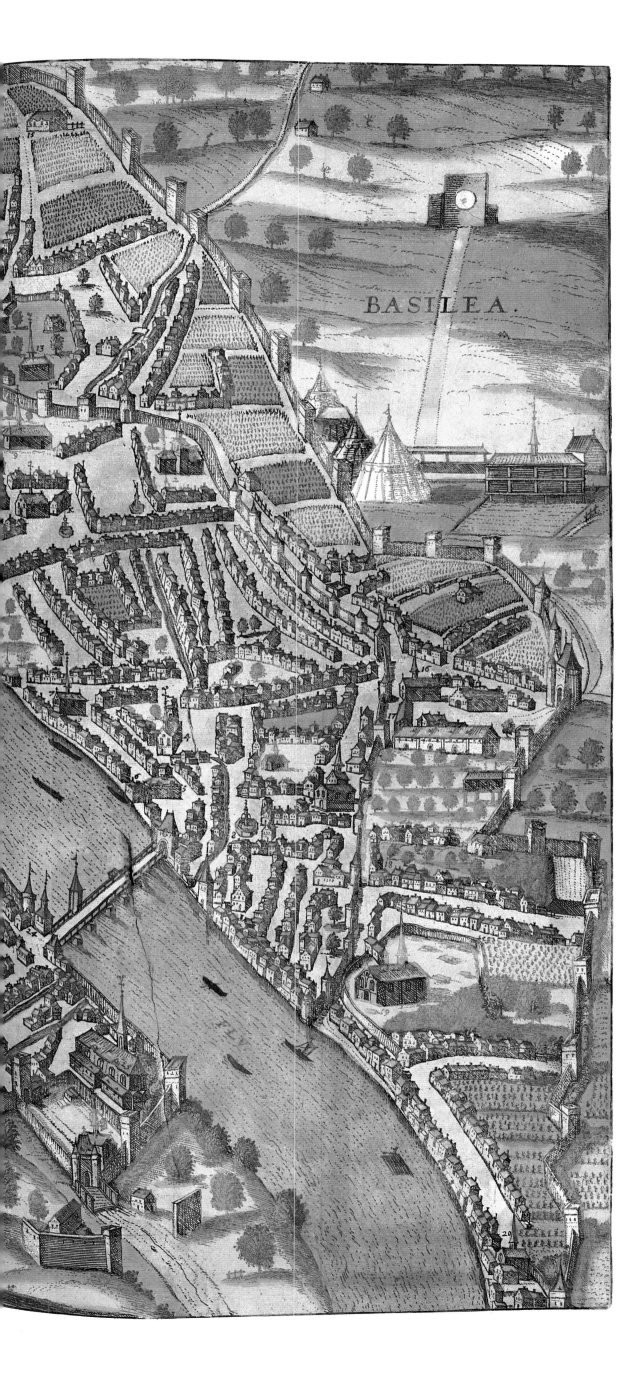

BASILEA.

this may be gathered from the busy river traffic depicted in the engraving. The most prominent building is the cathedral, or *Münster*, consecrated in 1019 but almost entirely rebuilt after the earthquake of 1356. The public meetings of the ecumenical councils of 1431 to 1449 were held there. A university, the oldest in Switzerland, was established by Pius II in 1460.

Erasmus of Rotterdam, the great humanist, lived in Basel from 1521 to 1529 and was buried here in 1536. Hans Holbein, the artist, also lived here between 1528 and 1531. In 1575, Basel was described as "a royal city without impropriety, so fair and smooth are its streets, so orderly is the arrangement of its houses and its numerous beautiful gardens. It is only near the Rhine that there are numerous dirty taverns and wretched inns. Basel has healthy and pleasant air, courteous and friendly citizens and also many handsome churches . . . "

PLATE 8

BERGEN

Bergen. 1588.
*Volume IV, number 37. 326
× 475mm.*

After Hieronymus Schol.
Bergen was founded on the
Våg by Olav Kyrre in 1070
and became capital of
Norway during the
thirteenth century.
Growing into an important
trading port, the town
became one of the four
principal stations of the
Hanseatic League, the
influence of whose
merchants may clearly be
seen in the buildings
depicted here.

Schol's view shows the
timber-built town as it
appeared at the end of the
sixteenth century. The key
at the upper left of the
engraving lists the most
important features and
buildings. The letter A
indicates the castle, with its
thirteenth-century
Håkonshall, and the more
recent *Rosenkrantztårn*; D
marks the house of the
German merchants nearby;
E shows the *Bryggen*, or
Deutsche Brücke on the
waterfront where the
German merchants had
their *Rhotstube* or meeting-
house, and so on. Many of
these buildings were
destroyed in the fire of
1702. Note also the
defences of Bergen such as
the timber palisade and the
Bergenhus, the fort shown at
the entrance of the Våg. On
the busy waterfront, with
its timber cranes, vessels are
loading and unloading and a
small boatyard is shown
near the merchants' house.

PLATE 9

BOLOGNA

Bononia alma studior. mater. 1588.
Volume IV, number 49. 326 × 492mm.

After Claudio Duchetti, 1582. The plan shows a more or less rectangular inner city dating from Roman times, (189 BC) and orientated on the points of the compass; its streets, arranged at right angles, are surrounded by the streets of the outer city, the whole is enclosed by fortified walls erected in 1206. Note that the streets leading to the gates of the outer city radiate not from the outskirts but from the centre of the ancient city. It is in this part of Bologna that some of the city's oldest churches are found: *San Stefano*, *San Giovanni in Monte*, and *SS Vitale ed Agricola*, for example. The largest of the churches (shown with a pitched roof in the engraving) is the *San Petronio*, patron saint of Bologna. It was begun in 1530. Nearby is the *Palazzo Communale* and the *Palazzo del Podestà*, both dating from 1245. Also of note is the church of *San Francesco* (1236–63), the first Gothic church in Italy, built by Marco da Brescia.

Bologna's university was founded in the eleventh century; part of it may be seen as the court-yarded, red-roofed building to the upper left of the church of *San Petronio*. It was built by Carlo Borromeo in 1562–63, and called the *Palazzo dell' Archiginnasio*. The university acquired a European reputation for its school of jurisprudence under Pepo, the first known teacher of Roman law here, in about 1076. There were as many as 3,000 to 5,000

BONONIA ALMA
STVDIOR. MATER

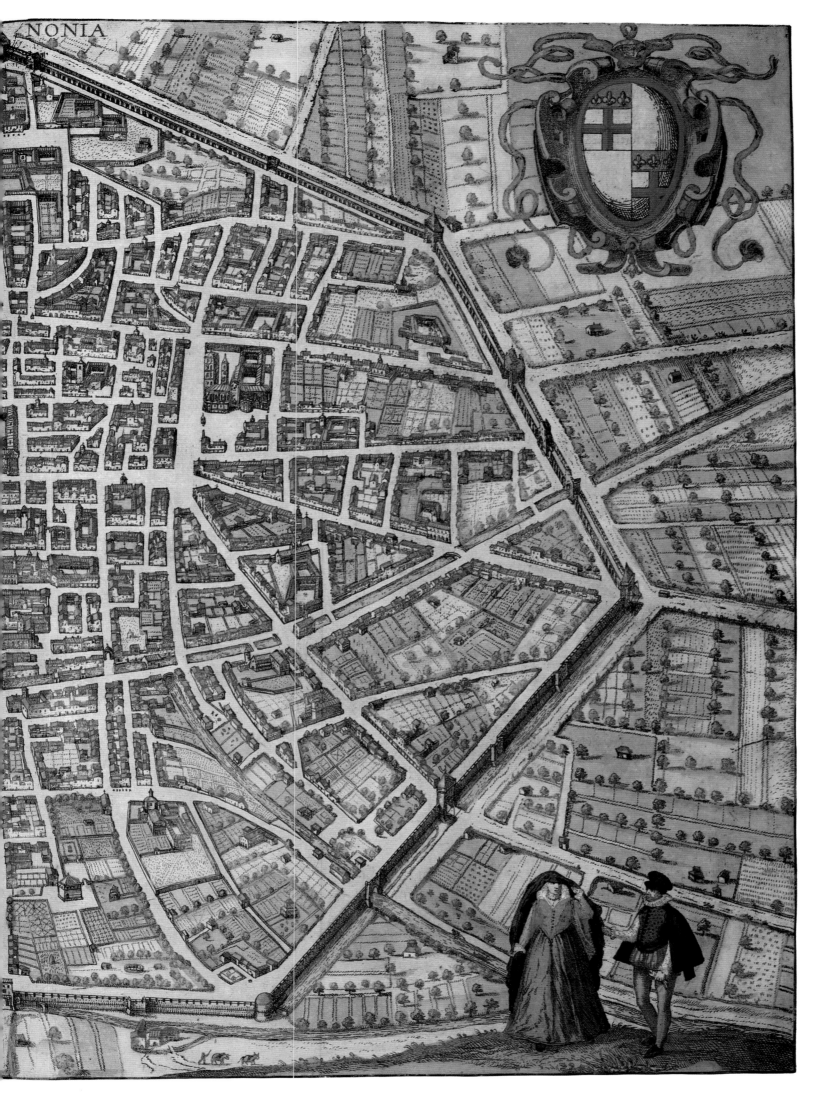

NONIA

students at Bologna during the twelfth to fifteenth centuries and nearly 10,000, it is alleged, in 1262; among whom were Dante and Petrarch.

Claudio Duchetti's original engraving of 1562 shows the two leaning towers which are as much a symbol of Bologna as the single leaning tower is of Pisa. These two towers, called the *Torre Asinelli* and the *Torre Garisenda* and dating from 1109 and 1110, are remnants of the old walls and once formed the *Porte Ravegnana*. Both are square brick towers, the former 97,53 metres high and 1,22 metres out of perpendicular, the latter (unfinished) 49,68 metres high and 3,05 metres out of perpendicular.

The early history of Bologna remains little known: it was sacked by the Magyars in 902. The first constitution of the commune appears to date from about 1123. From the twelfth to the fourteenth centuries, Bologna was an independent city, frequently at war in support of the Guelph, or papal cause, against the Ghibelline, or imperial, factions, and against the neighbouring city states of Romagna and Emilia. The emperor's son, Enzio, was kept prisoner here from 1249 for life. Internal struggles were rife throughout the fourteenth century: the city was sold to Giovanni Visconti of Milan (*q.v.*) and was then governed by the Bentivoglio from 1438, until 1506, when Pope Julius II expelled them, returning Bologna to the papacy under whose control it remained until the Napoleonic period.

PLATE 10

BREMEN

**Brema. Brema urbs
Hanseatici foederis ad
Visurgum flu.** Before
1598.
*Volume V, number 41. 365 ×
480mm.*

Probably after Heinrich von
Rantzau. Bremen, founded
on the right bank of the
Weser, was thought to owe
its name, according to
Martin Luther, to the word
bräm, which meant
"riverbank" and referred to
the narrow ledge on which
the town was built. Bremen
became a bishopric as early
as 787, when St Willehad
established his see here, and
in 848, following the
Norman destruction of
Hamburg (*q.v.*), the
bishopric of Hamburg was
transferred here. In 965,
Otto I granted rights for a
market to be established
here under the control of
Archbishop Adaldag.

Bremen entered the
Hanseatic League in 1283,
but was excluded in 1285
because of disorder in the
town, and was not
readmitted until 1358. Civil
unrest led to exclusion
again in 1427. Readmission
followed in 1433, when the
former aristocratic
constitution of the council,
which had been overturned
in 1304, was reinstated to
restore order. The trade
guilds never regained their
importance, and power
remained in the hands of
patricians. Stability then
allowed Bremen to develop
rapidly in wealth and status.

Clearly shown in this plan
are the *Altstadt*, with its
suburb, and the *Vorstadt*,
spread along the right bank
of the Weser behind the
busy quayside, with the
beginnings of the
Südervorstadt across the
river. In the *Altstadt* may be
seen in some detail the
market square (*Forum*) with
the fifteenth-century
Rathaus (*Curia*) facing, the
twelfth-century cathedral,
der Doem, and
Liebfrauenkirche (*Beate
Mariae*) nearby. At the
northern end of the town
stands the twelfth-century
Romanesque Church of
Sankt Stephan (*Sancti
Stephani*).

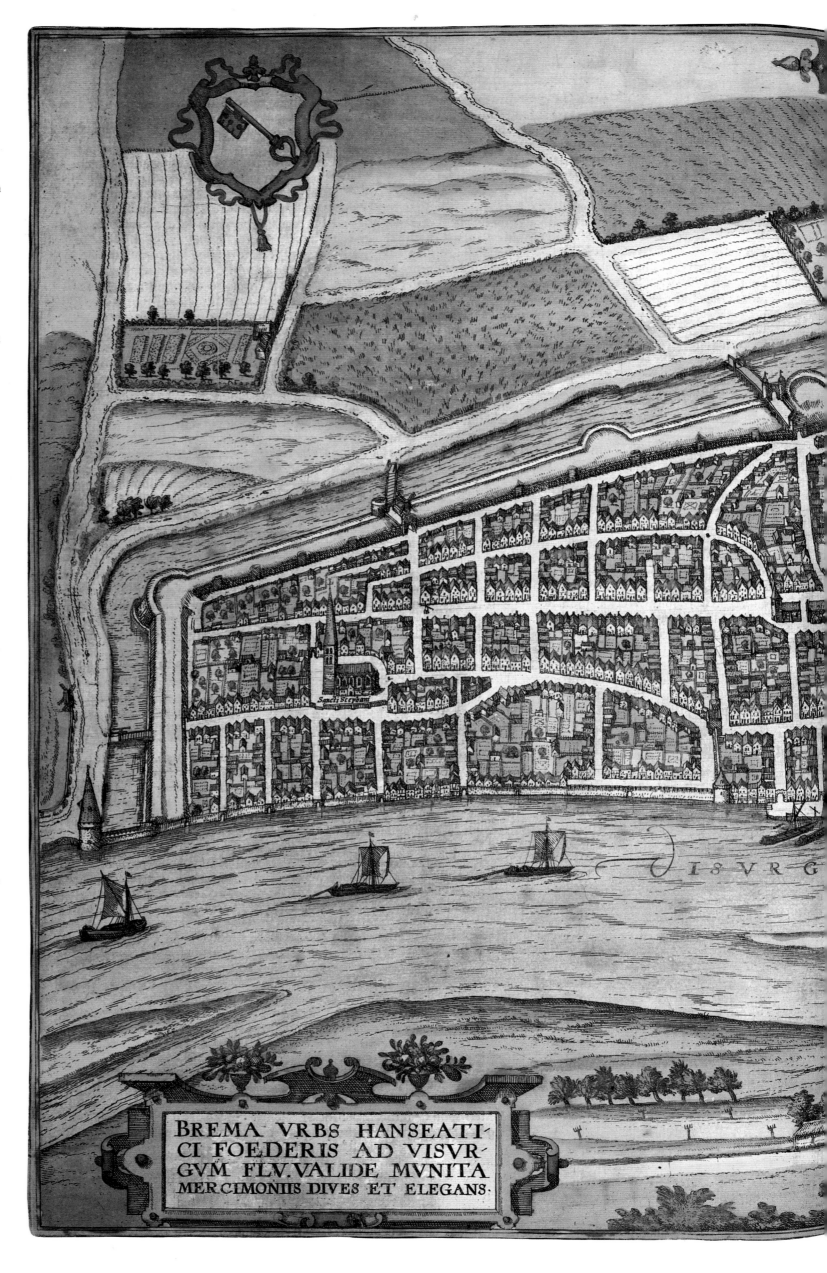

BREMA VRBS HANSEATI
CI FOEDERIS AD VISVR
GVM FLV.VALIDE MVNITA
MERCIMONIIS DIVES ET ELEGANS.

REMA.

Beatæ Mariæ

Curia

Forum

dor Doem

Das Oster thor

FLVVIVS

Waſſer kunſt

Die Weſer

Fluu:

Propugnaculum Pontis

27

PLATE 11

BRISTOL

Brightstowe.
Brightstowe, vulgo
quondam venta,
florentissimum Angliae
Emporium. 1581.
Volume III, number 2. 340 ×
_440mm._

After William Smith, 1568.
Bristol is one of the best
examples of a town which
has, historically, owned its
status entirely to trade. It
was never a shire town or
the site of a great religious
house, and it owes little to
its position as the head of a
feudal lordship or as a
military outpost. Bristol
marked the western limit of
the Saxon invasion of
England, and seems to have
begun as a trading
settlement for the early
wool trade with Ireland
around the year 1000. A
charter granted by Henry II
in 1172 exempted the city's
burgesses from certain tolls
and confirmed existing
liberties. Another
contemporary charter
granted the city of Dublin
to the men of Bristol as a
colony enjoying the same
liberties.

Bristol's period of greatest
prosperity came during the
century and a half following
the charter of 1373 which
extended the city
boundaries to include
Redcliffe, on the south side
of the Avon (_Ratclyffe_ in the
engraving) and the waters
of the Avon and the Severn
as far as the Steep and Flat
Holms, raising Bristol to
the status of a county. Then
followed the era of William
Canyng (1399–1474), five
times mayor and twice the
city's representative in
Parliament. Canyng
operated an extensive cloth

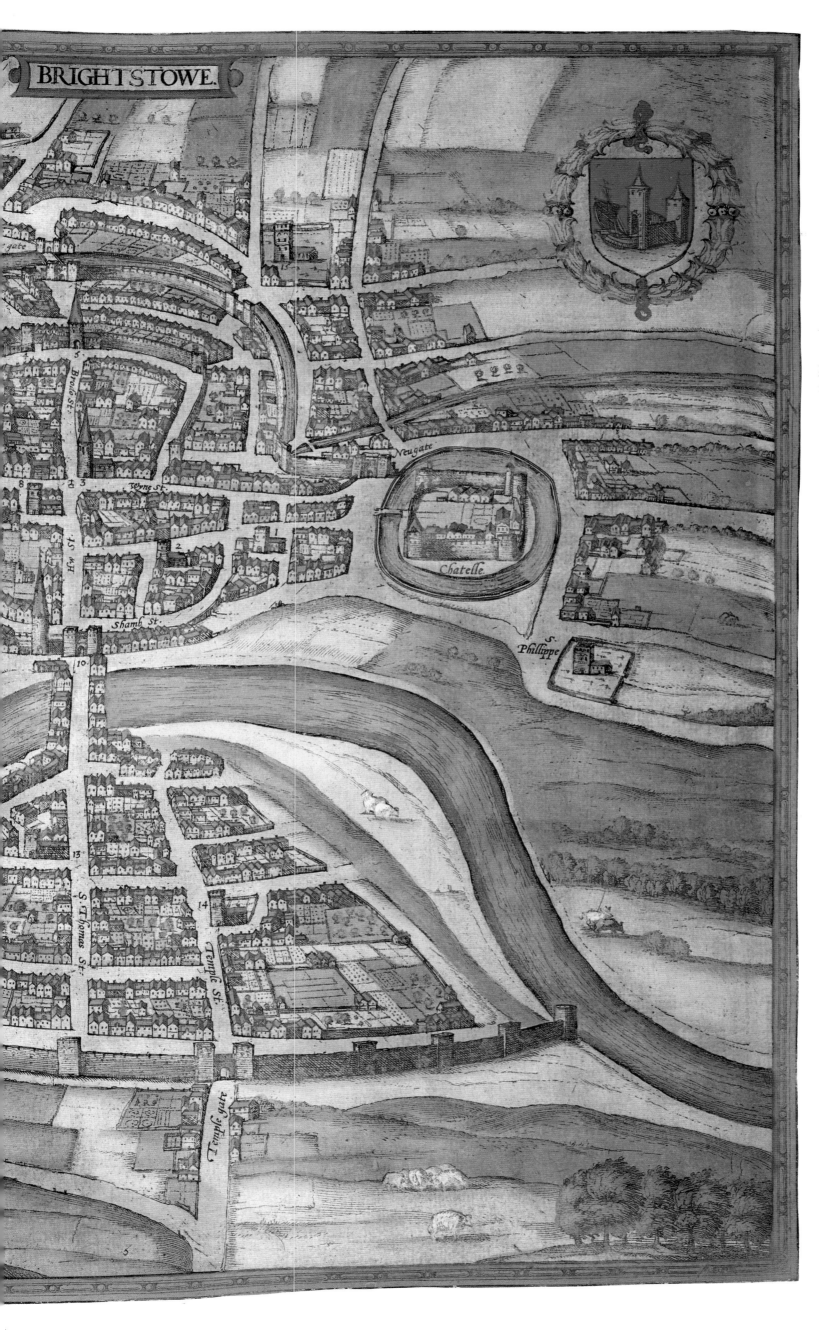

BRIGHTSTOWE.

trade with the Baltic ports and largely rebuilt St Mary Redcliffe from the profits. Bristol merchants exported cloth to France, Spain and the Levant. The celebrated Society of Merchant Venturers was founded in 1467; it rapidly gained influence and, by 1500, held the monopoly of Bristol's foreign trade and a lease of all port dues. The Society was incorporated in 1552.

From the earliest times, the great voyages of discovery into the Western oceans involved Bristol, and led to further mercantile activity. In the sixteenth century Bristol traded with Spain, the Canary Islands and the Spanish and Portuguese colonies in the Americas. It also joined in the attempt to colonize Newfoundland and began the trade in African slaves which flourished during the seventeenth century, taking sugar in exchange.

William Smith's survey shows a well-defined nucleus to the north of the Avon, intersected by Broad Street, High Street, Wine Street and Corn Street, with the southern extension of Redcliffe enclosed by walls. Although he was writing in 1739, Alexander Pope, much taken with Bristol, observed of the port: " . . . you come to a key along the old wall with houses on both sides, and in the middle of the street, as far as you can see, hundreds of ships, their masts as thick as can stand by one another, which is the oddest and most surprising sight imaginable . . . ". This must not have been dissimilar to the appearance of Bristol in Smith's time.

29

PLATE 12

BRUXELLES BRUSSEL
(Brussels)

Bruxella, urbs aulicorum frequentia, fontium copia, magnificentia principalis aulae . . . nobilissima. 1572.
Volume I, number 14. 330 × 470mm.

After Lodovico Guicciardini, 1567. This plan shows the city walls rather too rounded and many of the streets are mapped as too wide. Nevertheless, Braun and Hogenberg's plan was copied in this form by many publishers well into the seventeenth century. Much of the topographical detail appears to have been taken from the unpublished manuscript survey made by Jacob van Deventer in the 1550s.

It is thought that the name of the city is derived from *Broeksele*, a village at a ford on the little river Senne. It was first mentioned in the eighth century. Over the next two centuries or so, the trade guilds grew in size

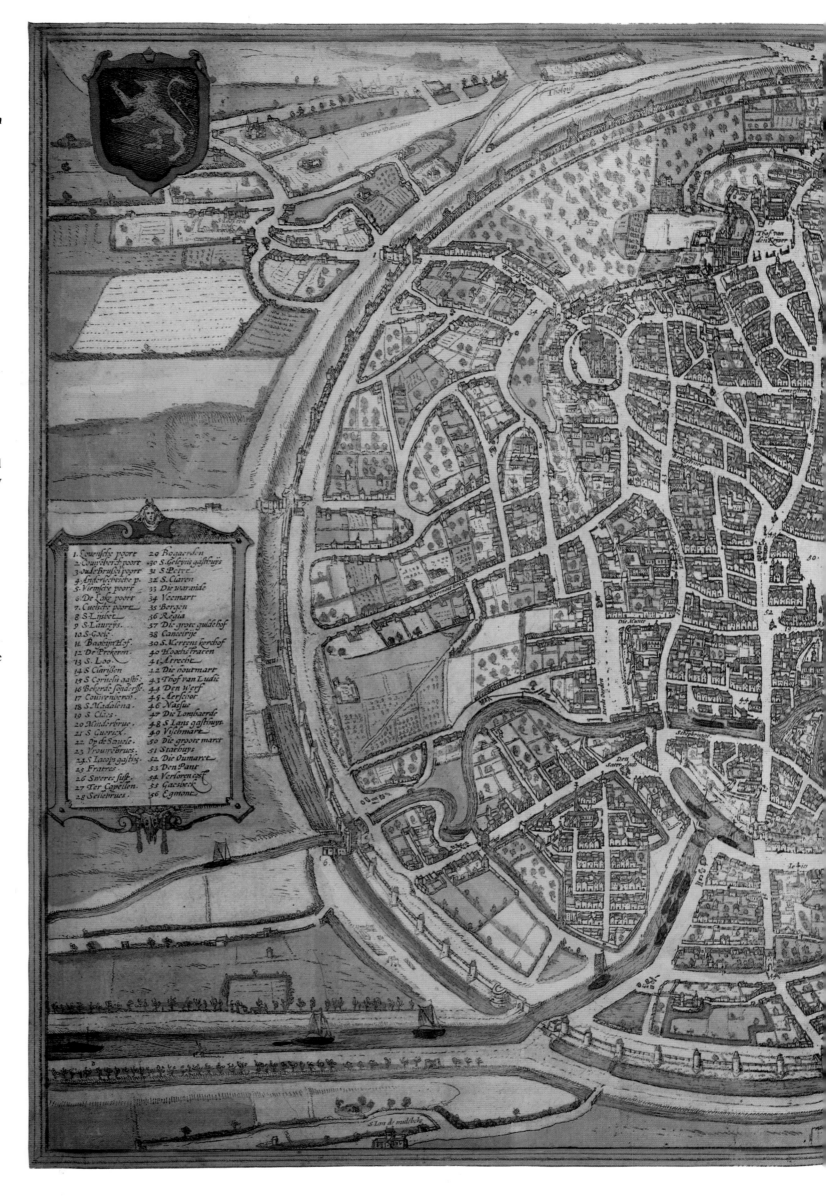

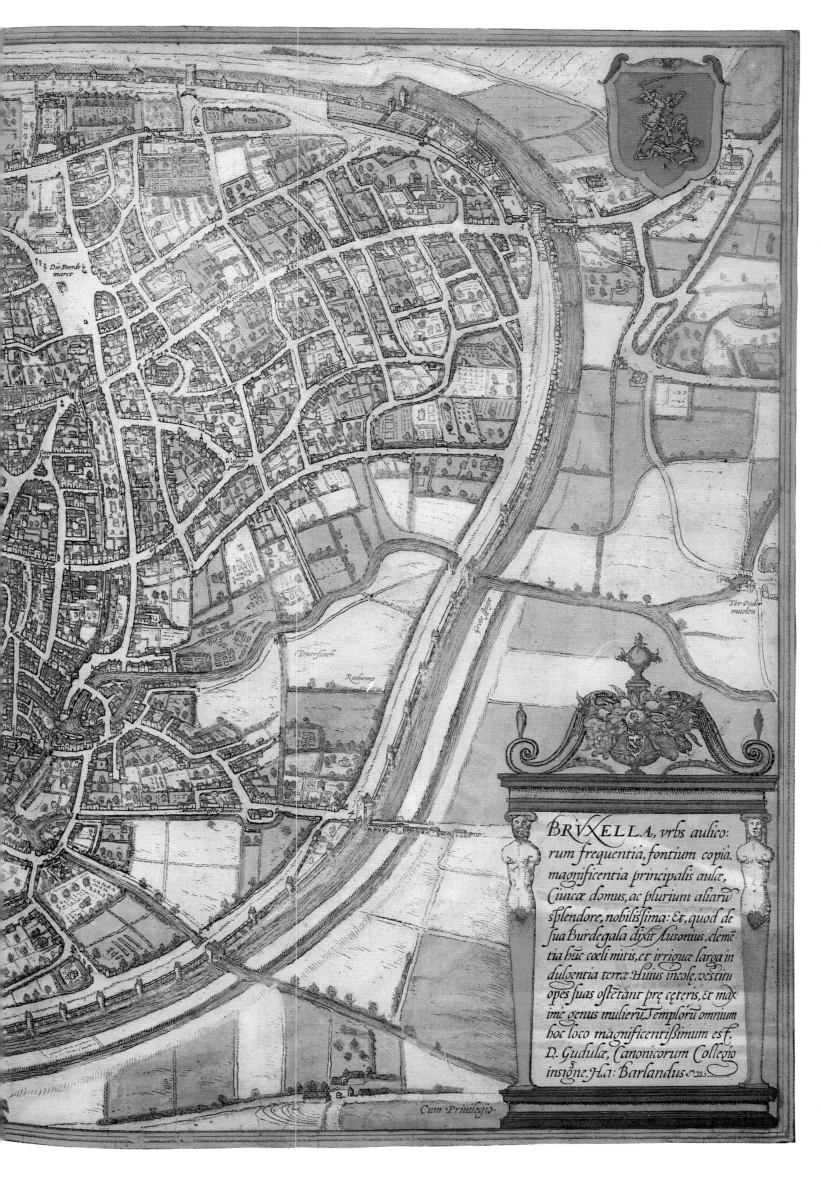

BRVXELLA, vrbs aulico:
rum frequentia, fontium copiâ.
magnificentia principalis aulæ,
Ciuicæ domus, ac plurium aliariu
splendore, nobilissima: Et, quod de
sua Burdegala dixit Ausonius, clemē
tia huc coeli mitis, et irriguæ larga in
dulgentia terræ. Huius incolæ, vestitu
opes suas ostētant præ ceteris, et max
imè genus mulierū. Templorū omnium
hoc loco magnificentissimum est,
D. Gudulæ, Canonicorum Collegio
insigne. Ha: Barlandus.

Cum Priuilegio.

and importance to rival
those of Gent, in the west of
the country. A charter was
granted to the citizens of
Brussels by the Duke of
Brabant in 1312. In 1357 a
larger town wall was built
to enclose both the town
and tracts of open fields; the
enclosure remained
substantially intact until the
time of the Belgian
revolution of 1830–31. By
1383, the Dukes of Brabant
transferred their seat from
Louvain to Brussels, the
city's population is said by
this time to have swollen to
some 50,000 inhabitants.

In 1420 the status of trade
guilds was formalized by
another charter as the Nine
Nations, and the Dukes of
Brabant built their castle
near the site of the modern
Place Royale, seen at
number 17 on the plan.
Other important buildings
are depicted, such as the
Hôtel de Ville at number 51
on the *Grand Place* in the
centre. Also note the small
docks and quays cut along
the banks of the Senne
indicating Brussels' status
as an active merchant city in
the sixteenth century.

31

PLATE 13

BUDAPEST

Buda citerioris Hungariae caput Regni avita sedes, vulgo Ofen . . . 1617. 1617. *Volume VI, number 30. 318 × 478mm.*

After Georg Hoefnagel, 1617. The history of Budapest is that of two separate towns, Buda and Pest, built one opposite the other on the banks of the Danube. Buda, on the right bank, was founded by the Romans in the second century as *Aquincum*. In 376 it was invaded and taken by the Huns. The origins of Pest remain unclear; the name is thought to be derived from the Slavonic word *pestj*, meaning stove or hearth, suggesting that a Slavonic settlement was established on the river-bank. When the Magyars arrived in the tenth century, they preserved both name elements.

Christianity was introduced in the eleventh century. In 1241 Pest was destroyed by the Tatars, after whose departure it was declared a royal free city by Bela IV in 1244 and rebuilt. The following centuries were prosperous for Pest, even though it was overshadowed by Buda, with its huge fortress and royal palace.

The fortress was begun by Bela IV in 1247 and formed the nucleus around which the town of Buda was built. It became the capital of Hungary in 1361. The palace was enlarged by Sigismund and further expanded by Matthias Corvinus between 1458 and 1490. It may be seen as *Arx et Palatium Regium* (letter B in the engraving).

In 1256 Pest was taken and pillaged by the Turks and, from 1541 to 1686, Buda was itself the seat of the local Turkish pasha. In the Turkish period, Pest declined almost completely; by the time the Turks were expelled from Hungary in 1686–87, it was left in virtual ruin. Nevertheless, its commanding position on a trade route was instrumental in the city's recovery; by 1723, it had become the seat and

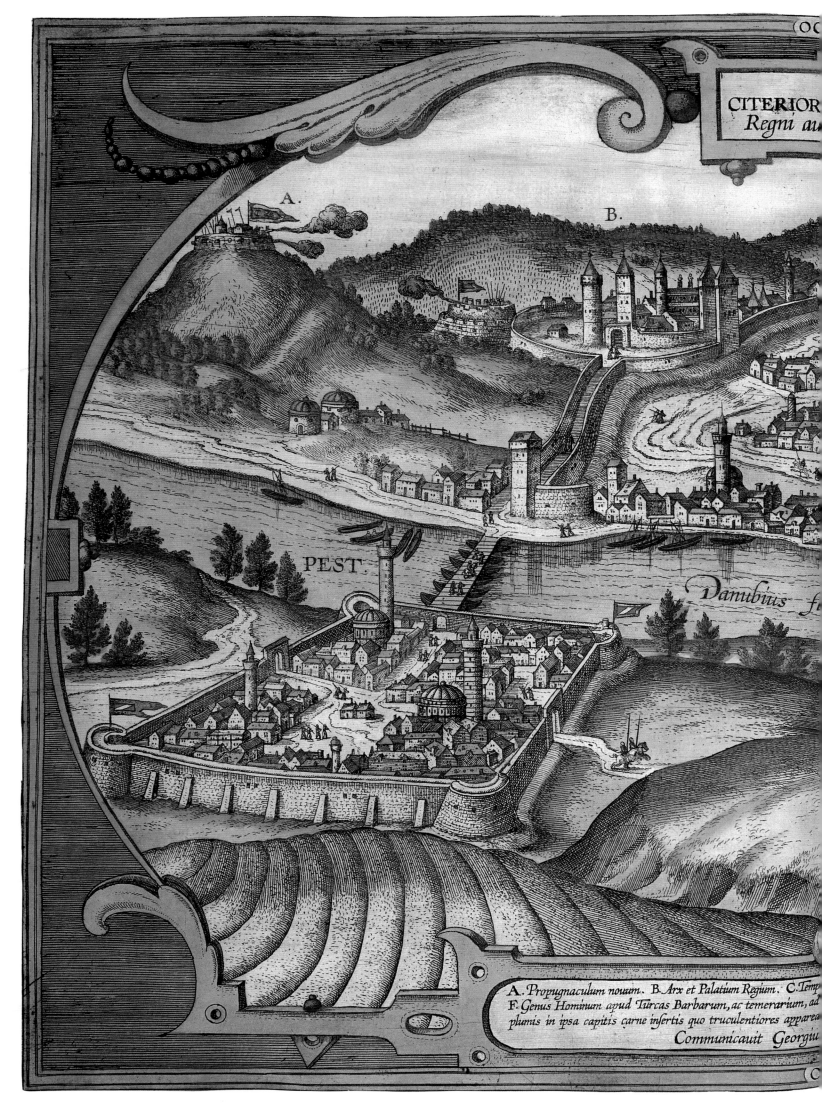

CITERIOR
Regni au

A. *Propugnaculum nouum.* B. *Arx et Palatium Regium.* C. *Temp*
F. *Genus Hominun apud Turcas Barbarum, ac temerarium, ad*
plumis in ipsa capitis carne infertis quo truculentiores apparea
Communicauit Georgiu

Within the engraving:

DENS.

DA
NGARIÆ CAPVT
s. vulgo OFEN.

C.

D.

E

F

Virginis nunc Meskita. D. Colles viniferi. E. Bassa Budensis.
facinus perpetrandum paratum: Dellij vulgo appellantur:
lege plura in descriptionibus Turcicis Ioannis Lewenclauij.
laus Anno 1617.

residence of the Hungarian aristocracy and highest officials.

The *Széchenyi* bridge, designed by the English engineer William Tierney Clark, which links the two towns was not built until 1842. The bridge shown in the engraving is a fine example of a pontoon bridge.

The engraving shows the two towns during the Turkish period, with many of the churches converted into mosques. Letter C, for example, indicates the *Templum olim Divae Virginis nunc Meskita*, and the old church in Pest on *Eskü-ter*, built in the Gothic style in 1500, performs a similar function. Then, as if to emphasize the fact, no doubt to the horror of the Christian reader of the *Civitates*, the only people included in the engraving, in the traditional manner for plates in this series, are shown in Turkish costume.

Describing Budapest, Braun is generous in his praise: "The city has been at all times the metropolis and royal seat of the Crown of Hungary . . . The magnificent royal palace is not only the pride of Hungary, it is almost unique in Europe, especially the castle which glitters both inside and outside with pure gold . . . The principal church was erected by Kings Geysa and Ladislaus in honour of the Mother of God. Opposite the castle is a fairly high mountain, on which the Turks have nowadays constructed fortifications and placed a garrison. The mountain was called St Gerhardtsberg in former times. A church stood upon it which was visited by pilgrims especially at times of plague. Now there is nothing upon it but Mohammedan abominations. On the other bank of the Danube, opposite Ofen, is Pest, also a free city, in a flat and very fertile region with the most beautiful gardens and meadows. It is indeed lamentable that both these beautiful cities with all the surrounding land have fallen into the hands of the Turkish enemy."

33

PLATE 14

CALAIS

Caletum, sive Calesium, vulgo Cales, janua, frenum, et clavis Galliae, Anno M D XCVII. Mense Aprili, in Philippi Hispaniarum Regis potestatem devenit. 1598. *Volume V, number 22. 315 × 395mm.*

After Georg Hoefnagel. Until the end of the tenth century, Calais was a small fishing hamlet in a natural harbour at the mouth of a stream. It was first fortified by Baudouin IV, Count of Flanders, in 997 and improved by Philip Hurepel, Count of Boulogne, in 1224. Following the Battle of Crécy in 1346, Edward III laid siege to the town; the governor, Jean de Vienne, held out for almost a year before famine forced him to surrender. The inhabitants were spared from massacre by the pleas of Eustache de St-Pierre and the six burghers were spared by the intercession of Queen Philippa. From then until 1558, Calais remained in English hands, when François de Guise, with a force of 30,000 men, besieged the English garrison of 800, who managed to hold out for a week.

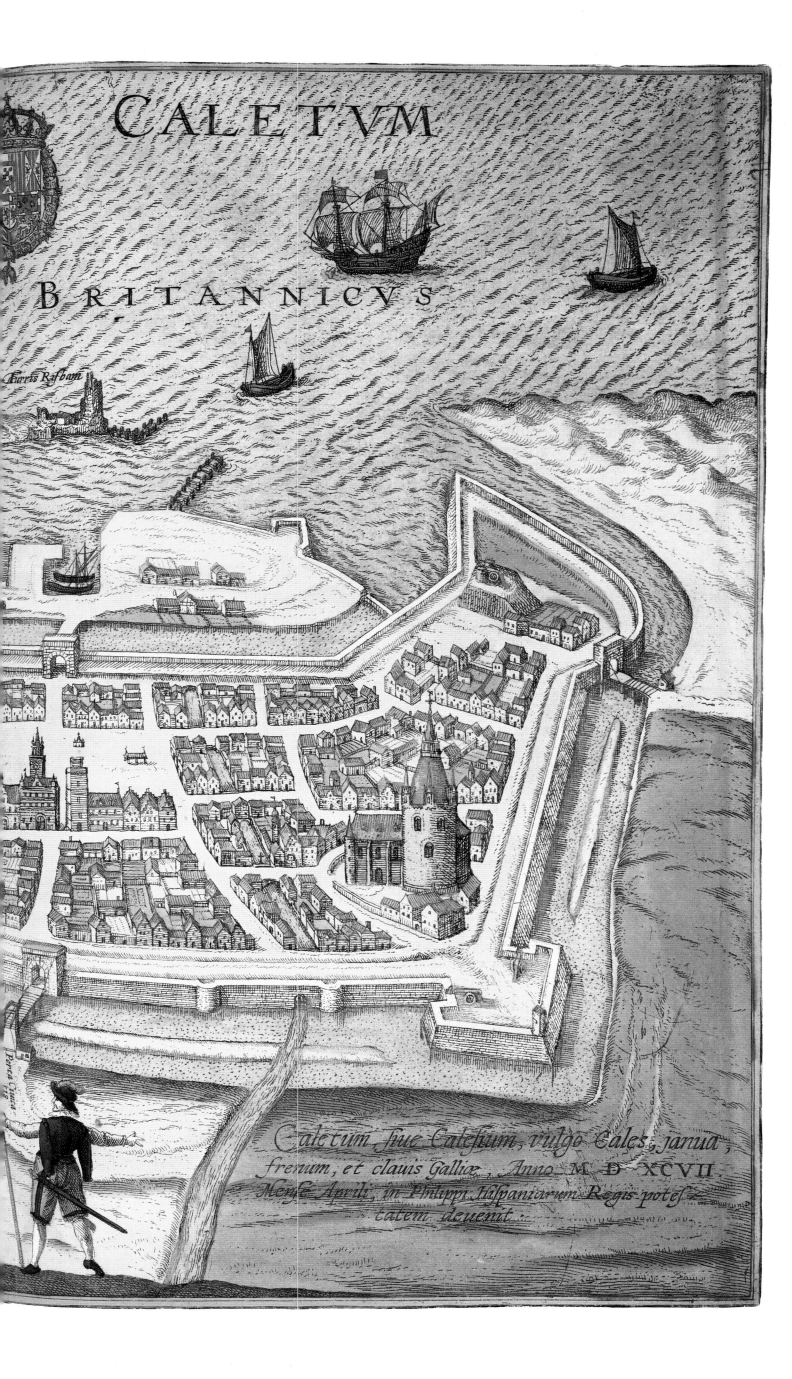

CALETVM

BRITANNICVS

Turris Rsban

Caletum, sue Caletium, vulgo Cales, januâ, frenum, et clauis Galliæ. Anno M D XCVII Mense Aprili, in Philippi Hispaniarum Regis potestatem deuenit.

Apart from a short period from 1595 to 1597, Calais and the *pays reconquis*, as it became known, has remained part of France. The last expulsion, of a Spanish force in April 1597, is that mentioned in a note at the lower right-hand corner of the engraving.

From 1363 to the time of the English explusion in 1558, Calais was a main port in the import of English wool for the Flemish wool trade, especially to Bruges (*q.v.*) The woolstaplers' hall was the building later called the *Hôtel de Guise* (built in the fourteenth century), given to François for his services in the recapture of the town. The large citadel – *Castellum* – on the southwestern side of Calais was built in 1560.

Calais and the surrounding *pays* is now once again joined to England, this time by a submarine link, the Channel Tunnel, running between it and Dover, seen on the English coast at the top of the engraving and reminding the reader of the English connection in the history of the town and indeed this part of northern France.

PLATE 15

CAMBRIDGE

Cantebrigia, opulentissimi Angliae Regni urbs celeberrimi nominis ab Academiae conditore Cantabro, cognomita. 1575. *Volume II, number 1. 330 × 450mm.*

After William Smith, after Richard Lyne, 1574. The name Cambridge seems to have been derived from the eighth-century *Grontabricc*, later rendered as *Grantebrycg* in the *Anglo-Saxon Chronicle* of 875. The name was probably given to an early settlement near the bridge over the Cante, Granta or Cam river. It was a head of river navigation and is referred to as a borough during the time of Henry I. The wharves of the river traffic lay along what are known now as "the backs" of some of the colleges, sloping down to the river.

In the sixteenth century, as now, Cambridge was celebrated for its university, which had its origins in the early religious houses here. The earliest was the Augustinian house of St Giles, founded in 1092, but removed to Barnwell in 1112. In 1224, the Franciscans established themselves at Cambridge, followed by Dominicans, and so on. The monks attracted students so that, by 1231, Cambridge was recognised as a centre of learning in a writ of governance issued by Henry III.

The first college was founded in 1281–84 by Hugh de Balsham, Bishop of Ely. This was *Peterhouse*. The others shown in the plan are: *Clare College* (1326: re-endowed as *Clare Hall* in 1338 by Elizabeth de Clare); *Trinity Hall* (1350: by William Bateman, Bishop of Norwich); *Corpus Christi* (1352: as the "House of the Scholars of Corpus Christi and the Blessed Virgin Mary"); *Pembroke College* (1347: by Mary de St Paul, widow of Aylmer de Valence, Earl of Pembroke); and *King's College* (1441: by Henry VI). The magnificent King's College chapel,

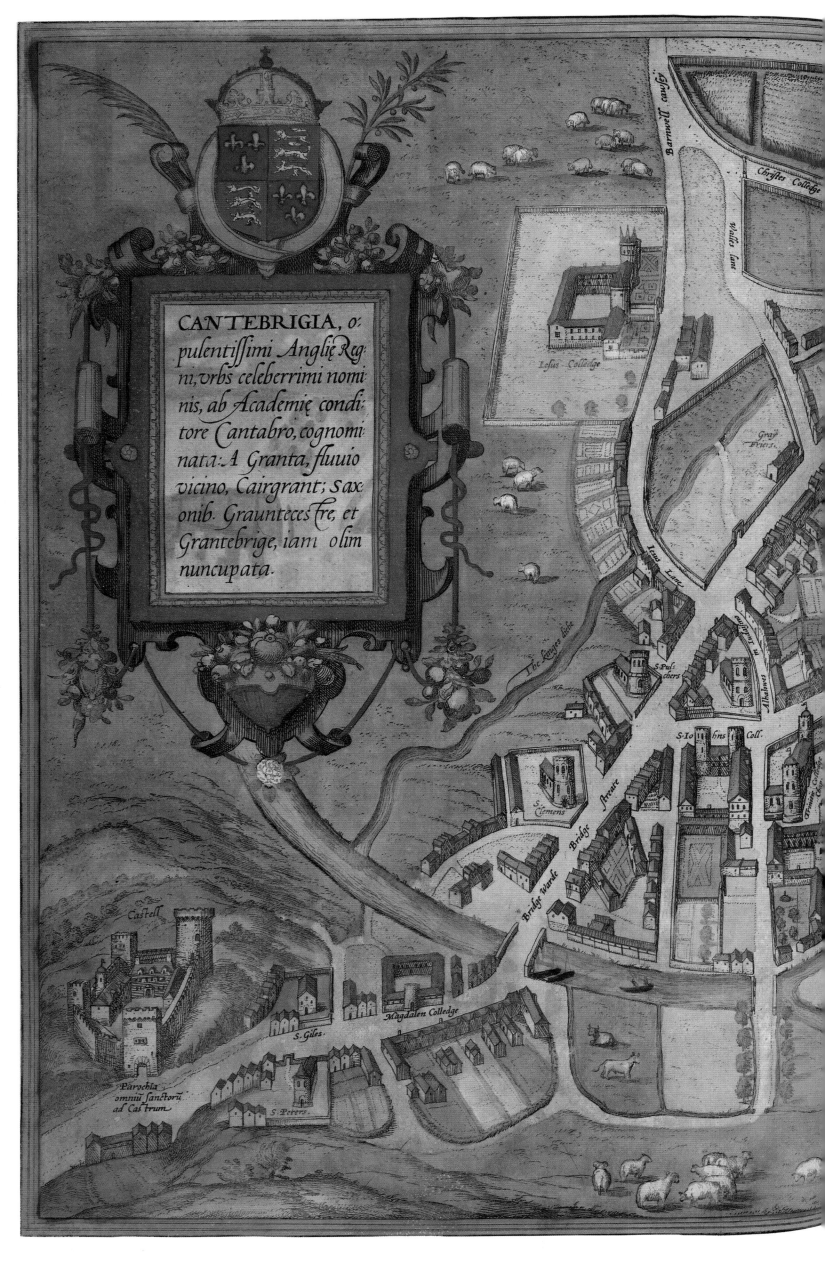

CANTEBRIGIA, o: pulentiſſimi Anglię Reg ni, vrbs celeberrimi nomi nis, ab Academię condi tore Cantabro, cognomi nata: A Granta, fluuio vicino, Cairgrant; Sax onib. Graunteces fre, et Grantebrige, iam olim nuncupata.

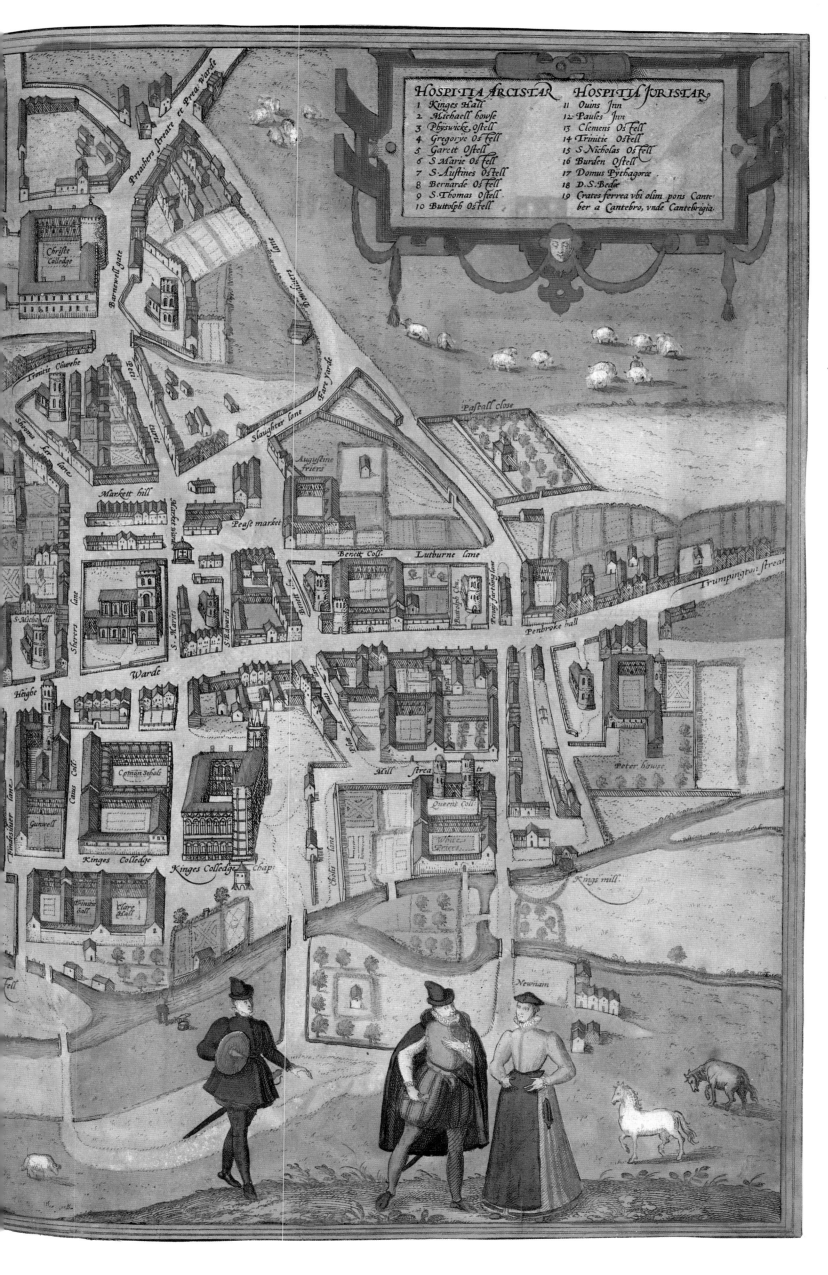

HOSPITIA ARCISTAR
1 Kinges Hall
2 Michaell howse
3 Physwicke, ostell
4 Gregorye Ostell
5 Garett Ostell
6 S Marie Ostell
7 S Austines Ostell
8 Bernarde Ostell
9 S Thomas Ostell
10 Buttolph Ostell

HOSPITIA JURISTAR
11 Ouins Jnn
12 Paules Jnn
13 Clemens Ostell
14 Trinitie Ostell
15 S Nicholas Ostell
16 Burden Ostell
17 Domus Pythagoræ
18 D.S.Bede
19 Crates ferrea vbi olim pons Cante-
   ber a Cantebro, vnde Cantebrigia.

completed by 1515 and one
of the most celebrated
buildings in Europe, is
barely recognisable in the
engraving (right of centre).

Then followed *Queen's
College* (1445: refounded in
1465 by Elisabeth
Woodville, wife of Edward
IV); *St Catherine's College*
(opened in 1473,
incorporated in 1475, by Dr
Robert Woodlark,
chancellor of the
university); *Jesus College*
(1496: by John Alcock,
Bishop of Ely); *Christ's
College* (1505: by Lady
Margaret Beaufort); *St
John's College* (1511: also by
Lady Margaret Beaufort);
Magdalene College (1428: as
a house for student monks
from Crowland, refounded
in 1542); *Trinity College*
(1546: by Henry VIII);
Gonville and Caius College
(originally in 1348 by
Edmund Gonville,
refounded in 1557 by John
Caius).

On Bridge Street,
diagonally left of centre, is
seen the church of the Holy
Sepulchre (*S. Pulchers*), one
of the four ancient circular
churches of England; it is
associated with the Knights
Templar and is said to date
from 1120–40.

37

PLATE 16

CÓRDOBA
(Cordova)

Corduba. 1617.
*Volume VI, number 5. 332 ×
497mm.*

From an unknown source.
Cordova, on the banks of
the Guadalquivir river,
probably dates from the
time of the Carthaginians.
It was taken by the Romans
under Marceus Marcellus in
152BC, becoming the first
Roman *colonia* in Iberia. It
was a leading settlement of
Hispania Ulterior and
acquired the title *patricia* on
account of the large
numbers of nobles among
its colonists. It ranked as the
largest city in Spain during
the time of the geographer
Strabo (*c.*63 BC–AD 21).
Its prosperity was based
largely on the *Via Augusta*,
the busy trade route linking
Cordova with northern
Spain, and on the mines,
the rich grazing and the
grain-producing districts in
the area.

Cordova's importance was
maintained during the reign
of the Visigoths, from the
fifth to the early eighth
centuries. Abd' ar-Rahman
I made it the capital of
Moorish Spain after 756. It
reached its zenith during the
tenth century under Abd'
ar-Rahman III, in whose
reign the city is recorded,
somewhat exaggeratedly in
the manner of Moorish
chronicles, as having
contained 200,000 houses,
600 mosques, 900 baths, a
university and many
libraries; it was also said
that Cordova ruled over a
caliphate consisting of eight
cities, 300 towns and 12,000
villages!

After about 1016, Cordova
fell into decline. It was
captured easily by
Ferdinand III of Castille in
1236 and never really
regained its former
greatness in art and
literature. Few cities of
Spain, however, can claim
to have been the birthplace

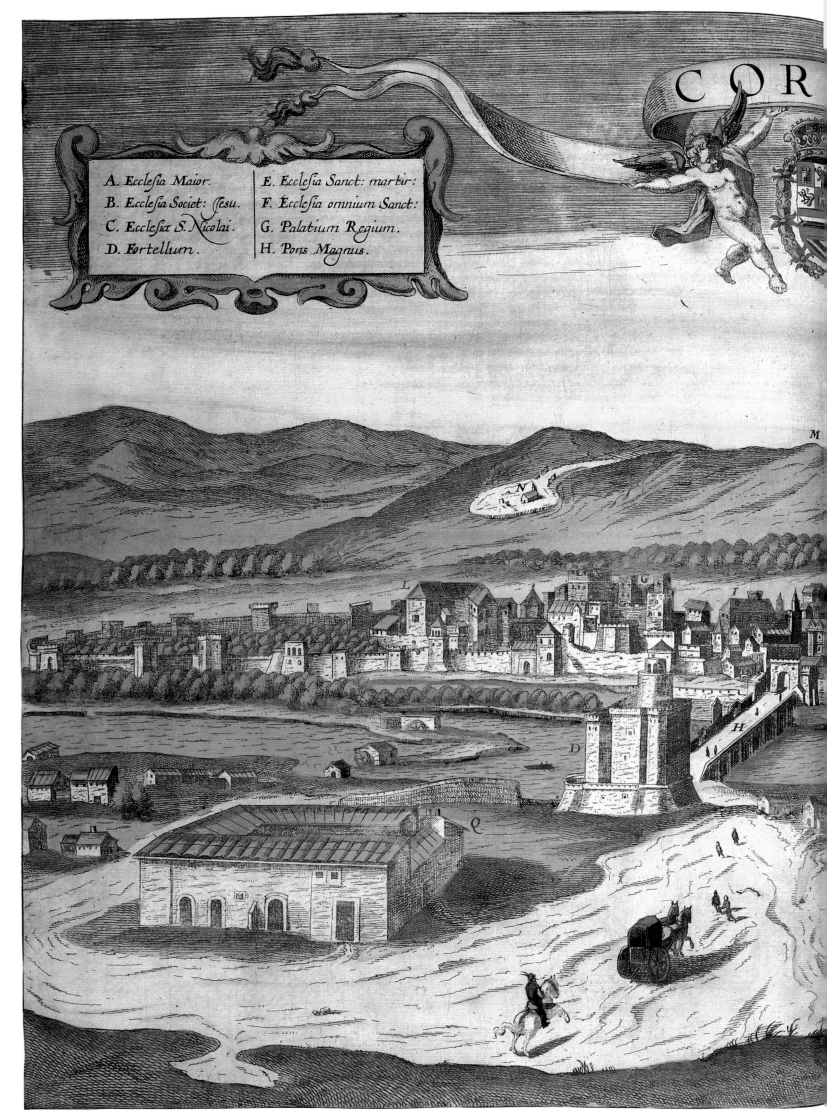

A. *Ecclesia Maior.*
B. *Ecclesia Societ: Jesu.*
C. *Ecclesia S. Nicolai.*
D. *Fortellum.*
E. *Ecclesia Sanct: martir:*
F. *Ecclesia omnium Sanct:*
G. *Palatium Regium.*
H. *Pons Magnus.*

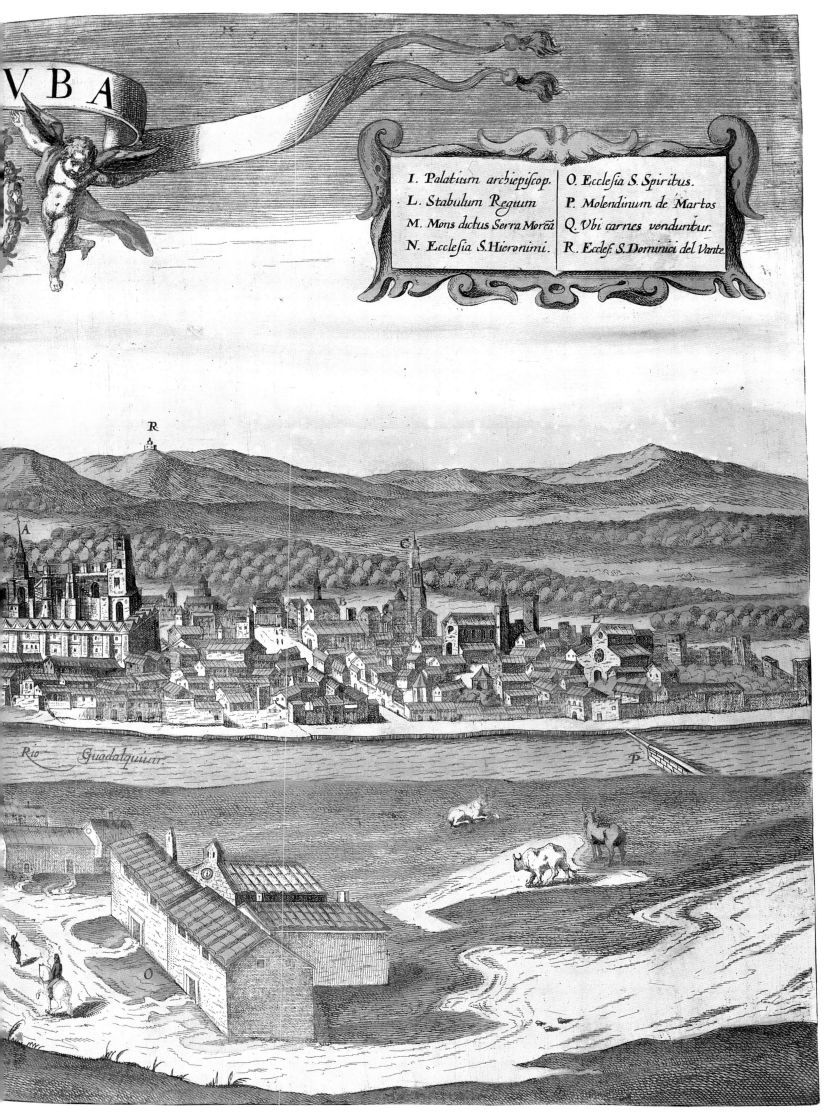

I. *Palatium archiepiscop.*
L. *Stabulum Regium*
M. *Mons dictus Serra Moreã*
N. *Ecclesia S. Hieronimi.*
O. *Ecclesia S. Spiritus.*
P. *Molendinum de Martos*
Q. *Vbi carnes venduntur.*
R. *Ecclef. S. Dominici del Vante.*

of so many early and illustrious figures in the arts, letters and sciences. Among these are Seneca (*c.*3 BC–AD 65); Lucan (39–65); the philosophers Averroes (1126–98) and Maimonides (*c.*1411–56); Juan de Mená (*c.*1411–56); Lorenzo de Sepúlveda (*d.*1574); Luís de Gongola y Argote (1561–1627); the painter Pablo de Céspedes (1538–1608); and the captain and naval commander Gonzalo Fernández de Córdoba, who conquered Naples (*q.v.*) in 1495–98, who was born at Montilla, nearby.

Many buildings may be recognised from this anonymous view. The *Alcázar* (at letter G: *Palatium Regium*), amid the gardens laid out by Caliph Abd' ar-Rahman I (756–788), culminated in the great structure developed by the vizier of Caliph Hisham II (976–1009) into the largest sacred building of Islam after the Qaaba at Mecca. Following the final expulsion of the Moors, the building was altered, clumsily, by Hernán Ruíz; this caused Charles V (1500–58) to remark that he had "built here what could have been built as well anywhere else" and that he had "destroyed what was unique in the World". During the Moorish period, Cordova was celebrated for its silversmiths, said to have come from Damascus. A kind of leather named after the city was also exported, from which the word *cordwainer* is derived.

PLATE 17

DORDRECHT

Dordracum vulgo Dortt.
1575.
*Volume II, number 24. 310 ×
495mm.*

After an unidentified
source. Founded in 1018 by
Dirk III of Holland,
Dordrecht is one of the
oldest, if not the very
oldest, towns of the old
graafschap, or county, of
Holland. Founded on a
dyke, Dordrecht was for
centuries isolated on the
island of the same name,
surrounded by the
Merwede, Dortse Kil,
Oude Maas and Noord
rivers and under constant
threat of siege, inundation,
civil unrest, fire and foreign
control or competition.

The original settlement was
strategically placed to
control the mouths of the
Maas and Rijn rivers, and,
naturally enough, a toll was
demanded here. As early as
1206, alongside
Vlaardingen, Leiden (*q.v.*)
and Haarlem, Dordrecht
was one of the four most
important towns in the
county, and possessed a
charter of urban privileges.

By the close of the
thirteenth century, the
town had become a market
for German wines and
timber, and for the salt
trade of Zierikzee,
Zevenbergen and Tholen to
the southwest. In 1299, it
became a staple town, so
that all goods passing on the
Lek and Merwede had to be
offered for sale in
Dordrecht. The town
exercised some regional
control over the
Zuidhollandse Waard
created *c.*1213. The volume
of trade continued to
increase throughout the
fourteenth century. Indeed,
on more than one occasion,
during the years of
Dordrecht's greatest power
and influence, the Hanseatic
League removed its *kontor*
there from Bruges as in
1388 and 1392.

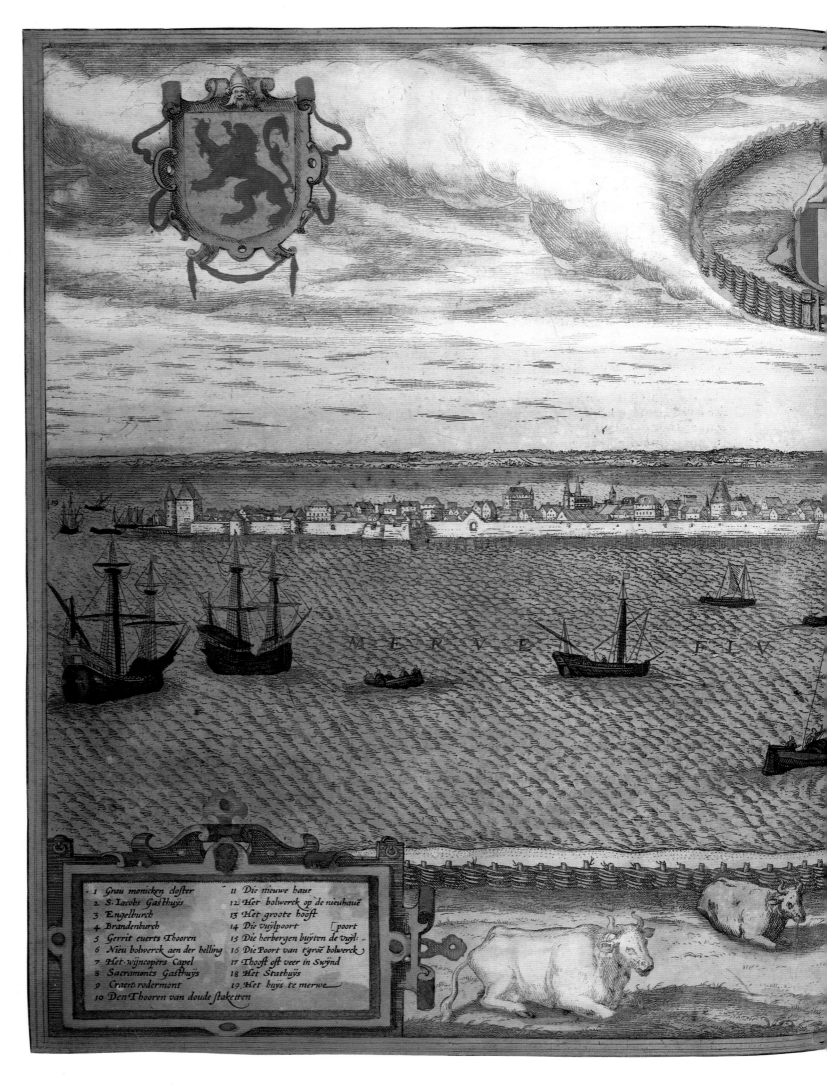

1 Grau monicken closter
2 S. Iacobs Gasthuys
3 Engelburch
4 Brandenburch
5 Gerrit euerts Thooren
6 Nieu bolwerck aen der helling
7 Het wijncopers Capel
8 Sacraments Gasthuys
9 Graens rodermont
10 Den Thooren van doude stakcetten
11 Die nieuwe haue
12 Het bolwerck op de nieuhaue
13 Het groote hooft
14 Die Vuylpoort [poort
15 Die herbergen buyten de vuyl
16 Die Poort van t'groë bolwerck
17 Thooft oft veer in Swynd
18 Het Stathuys
19 Het huys te merwe

DORDRACUM vulgo Dort.

Me Mosa, & Walis, cum Linga, Meruaque cingunt,
Æternam Bataue virginis, ecce, fidem.

The town showed great adaptability under changing circumstances. Originally oriented towards trade and traffic along its waterways, Dordrecht later also served as the market for the agricultural produce of the Zuidhollandse Waard. When that agricultural land was destroyed during the diastrous *St Elisabethvloed* of 18–19 November 1421, when over 10,000 people drowned and at least twenty villages were submerged, Dordrecht became isolated and turned towards the water once again for its trade.

In the fifteenth century, the city enjoyed extensive commerce in wine, wood, iron, copper, slate, chalk, millstones, coal, wood, grain, spices, salt and wool. Dordrecht also served as a base for insurgents throughout the Eighty Years' War. It was only in 1579 that the city's staple status was removed and conferred upon Rotterdam (*q.v.*). As the sea and the rivers had brought life to Dordrecht, so they also took it away again; as the Merwede silted up, Dordrecht declined, enabling Rotterdam, closer to the North sea, to gain ascendancy as its expense.

Almost the last major role that the city played was as the meeting place of the *Statenvergadering van Holland* in 1572, which co-ordinated the resistance to Spanish oppression in the Netherlands. Later, in 1618–19, the Synod met there.

The engraving shows the town across the Merwede from the northwest. At its peak it stretched for 13,000 metres along its dyke, the *Wijnstraat*, *Groenmarkt* and the *Grootekerksbuurt*, and on the west side of the thirteenth-century *Onze Lieve Vrouwekerk*, as the view clearly shows.

PLATE 18

EDINBURGH

Edenburg. Edenburgum, Scotiae Metropolis. 1581. *Volume III, number 4. 340 × 450mm.*

After Ralph Holinshed, *c*1574. Edinburgh's Gaelic name was *Dunedin*, probably a translation of a Saxon name. It was known to the Britons as *Castelh mynedh agnedh* ("the hill on the plain"), interpreted in the engraving as *Castrum puellarum* ("castle of the maidens"), in mistaken allusion to the supposition that Pictish princesses were lodged there.

The engraving shows the old city, dominated by the castle on the crags. The village running in a straight line along the tail or ridge forming the High Street and Canongate, towards Holyrood. This linear town grew rapidly during the twelfth century.

After 1450, walls enclosed this city of high tenements built along narrow streets and alleys. The plan gives an entirely erroneous view of the widths of streets in the sixteenth century. The walls were enlarged and extended after the defeat of the Scottish forces by the English at Flodden Field in 1513. The streets, or *wynds*, were often so narrow and ill-lit that wheeled traffic could pass only along the wider High Street and Canongate, the citizens having to resort to their feet, or to sedan chairs in the case of gentry ill-disposed to walking. In narrow streets and passages lived rich and poor alike.

Lewis Mumford commented in 1961: "But a change for the worse came about toward the *close* of the Middle Ages, despite sanitary regulations. This was due to the rise of the multi-storey tenement house . . . in towns like Edinburgh. Such dwellings discouraged the use of outdoor facilities: the very distance of the upper floors from the ground tempted people to carelessness and foulness in emptying their chamber pots . . . By the sixteenth century, in well-

Castrum puellarum

EDE

EDENBURGUM,
SCOTIAE
METROPOLIS.

managed towns that had made provisions for street-cleaning, there was a ban on keeping pigs in any part of the town, even in the gardens behind the houses . . . "

In 1581, the original text of the *Civitates* described Edinburgh as " . . . built not of brick but of the local squared stone, so that all the houses may be compared with palaces. In the centre of the city is the castle church with a monastery, called St Giles. When the bishops, dukes, earls, baronets and other high personages of the kingdom are summoned to the parliament they have their own palaces in the city. From the High Street innumerable lanes proceed northwards and southwards, all with lofty houses. The most important is Cow Gate, where the noble . . . families and city councillors have their residences, together with other princely houses and palaces, most handsome to behold. St Giles's Abbey Church is the chief church in the city. In the lane which separates the town of Edinburgh at Cnönch Street [Canongate] from the suburbs, inside the city walls, is the Queen's College . . . "

PLATE 19

ESCORIAL, MADRID

Scenographia totius fabricae S. Laurentii in Escoriali. 1617. *Volume VI, number 4. 365 × 497mm.*

After Petrus Perret, 1587, as published in Abraham Ortelius's *Theatrum* in 1591. The great monastery-palace, *El real monasterio de San Lorenzo del Escorial*, built in 1563–87 fifty or so kilometres from Madrid, is one of the most remarkable buildings in Europe. It comprises a convent, a church, a palace and a mausoleum, and was the most important testimony of the Renaissance in Spain. It is set in a sterile and gloomy wilderness and exposed to cold and biting winds from the Sierras, emphasising the spiritual austerity of the structure, which is built of *berroqueña*, the local grey granite.

The Escorial was commissioned by Philip II (1556–98) to commemorate his victory over the French at St Quentin in 1577. The name Escorial was derived from the nearby hamlet which housed workmen engaged on the building and the monks who were later to live within its walls. The building also contained

AD PHILIPPVM II. HISPANIA
RVM ETC REGEM CATHOLICVM

Michaelis vander Hagen carmen.

Cæsareas moles, atq; alta palatia Regum
Ne posthac Latium, aut Græcia iactet ouans;
Pyramides, et aquæductus, mira et Amphitheatra,
Et Circos veteres Inclyta Roma premat;
Prisca fides sileat vasti Miracula Mundi;
Nam facuint nostra ad secula, prisca nihil;

Vnus enim Hesperiæ Rex Maximus ille Philippus
Miracula exuperans omnia condit opus:
Non opus; at Molem qualem neque tota vetustas
Vidit: et hæc ætas non habitura parem.
Nempe Duces olim parti monumenta triumphi
Victi erexerunt ambitione mala;
Atque trophæa Dijs posuerunt capta profanis,
Aut operis magni in secla perenne decus;
Relligionis Apostolicæ verum vnicus ille
Defensor, voti Rex memor vsque pij,

SCENO
TIVS
RENTI

the mausoleum of Philip's father, Charles V, in a manner designed to symbolise Spanish imperial power and Spanish Catholic piety.

The plans for the building were commissioned from Juan Bautista de Toledo, a Spanish architect who, for most of his career, had worked in Italy and who had assisted Michaelangelo at St Peter's in Rome from 1546 to 1548. De Toledo died in 1567, and the work was continued by his pupil, Juan Herrera.

The first stone was laid in April 1563, and the last on 13 September 1584, the ground area eventually occupying some 36,800 square metres. There are seven towers, fifteen gateways and approximately 12,000 windows and doors. The building was finally completed in 1593. It was here that Philip II, half king, half monk, and ruler of the greatest empire in history, died in 1598.

This view, looking east, was based on a plan drawn by Petrus Perret in 1587 shortly after the completion of the main structure, and which was published in Abraham Ortelius's atlas, *Theatrum orbis terrarum* in Antwerp in 1591.

PLATE 20

FRANKFURT AM MAIN

Civitas Francofordiana ad Moenum. 1552.
Volume I, number 35. 330 × 470mm.

By Conrad Faber after a woodcut by Hans Grave. The "Free Imperial, Electoral, and Trading City" of Frankfurt, seen in this view looking eastwards up the valley of the Main, began as *Frankenford* (or Franks' Ford), probably in about 500. The name itself contains elements of the city's history: the ford of the Franks on the Main who drove the tribe of the Alemanni from the valley in 496.

Frankfurt became a domain of Charlemagne and a residence of Louis the Pious (the later *Saalhof*) in 822, and of Ludwig the German from 850 until his death in 876. There followed a period of decay until, in 1147, Frankfurt was chosen by Henry V as his seat of election. In 1356, the Golden Bull of Charles IV declared Frankfurt the seat of imperial elections, and in 1562 the city superseded Aachen (*q.v.*) as the site of the imperial coronation.

The city's constitution took shape during the thirteenth century, and it was ruled by a royal mayor (*Schultheiss*) from 1219. A body of fourteen jurists (*Schöffen*) was formed to assist in municipal government and this in effect was the first step towards representative government.

The great trade fairs, first mentioned in 1150, assumed particular importance during the thirteenth century and between 1220 and 1270 no fewer than ten churches were built. The great monastery of St Bartholomew (1235–39) was established on the site of the old palatinate chapel of Ludwig the German. In 1405 the city council bought two properties, the *Haus zum Römer* (first

CIVITAS FRA

RDIANA AD M⊙:

Ofenbac

Sachsenhausen

Der Main

Die Affen

Newsch haus

Margarten tor

Nurich tera

FRANCOFORDIÆ, vnica est in Francia orientali ciuitas, aut potius, in extremitate eius, ad
Moenium fluuium sita, nobilißimum totius Germaniæ Emporium, cunctis Vniuersæ Europæ populis cog-
nitißimum, In quo Romanorum Cæsar, ab illustrißimis Imperij Septemuiris eligitur, & gladiatoriæ
artis, designantur magistri. Ex multis indicijs constat, quam chara hæc vrbs Pipino, & Carolo
Quarto fuerit. Quibusdam Helenopolis: Gunthero, Franconfurt dicitur. Eam septem libris ab Entran-
do quodam (Diacono descriptam, se vidiße in Monasterio aliquo, restatur Franciscus Irenicus in
sua Exegesi Germaniæ. Forshuic vrbi lapideo elegantique ponte, haud vulgaris magnificentiæ
oppidum, SAXENHAVSEN, Jd est, Saxonum domus, coniungitur, & ipsum propugnaculis, moe-
nibs. vallo, & foßis, ad defensionem idoneis, egregie circundatum.

---

mentioned in 1322) and
Zum goldenen Schwan, using
their upper floors as a city
hall and ceremonial hall for
great occasions, and the
ground floors for trade
fairs.

The engraving clearly
shows Frankfurt as it was in
the 1560s: the *Altstadt*
enclosed by twelfth-century
walls and a now dry moat;
the *Neustadt* established in
1333 as an outer ring within
the new walls and moat
with the great *Eschenheimer
Tor* round tower built in
1400–28; the *Rententurm* of
1456 on the Main (near the
lower edge of the view);
and the *Kuhhirtenturm* of
about 1490 in the southern
suburb of Sachsenhausen
across the river.
Sachsenhausen was
formerly a commandery of
the Teutonic Order, settled
in 1219 and dominated by
its *Deutschordenskirche*.

Until 1944 the lines of the
old inner walls were
marked by streets such as
the *Große-* and *Kleiner
Hirschgraben* within and the
Holzgraben without, and
the great thoroughfare the
Zeil. The outer walls and
moat, begun in 1343 and
also seen in the engraving,
were demolished, along
with the reinforcements of
1625, early in the nineteenth
century.

Several churches are visible:
the Romanesque
Leonhardkirche near the
merchants' quarter on the
waterfront, the foundation
of the Order of the
Penitents (1228), the
Franciscans (1230), the
Antonites (1236), the
Dominicans (1238), the
Carmelites (1246) and the
Knights of St John (1259).

PLATE 21

GDAŃSK
(Danzig)

Dantzigk. Gedanum, Krantio, in sua Wandalia Gdanum; vulgo sed corruptè Dantiscum Germanicè, Dantzigk.
1575.
Volume II, number 46. 326 × 485mm.

After Adam Wachendorf. *c.*1561. Gdańsk, or Danzig, capital of the old German province of Westpreußen, was founded sometime before 997, when it was mentioned as an important town. As Danzig, the town belonged in turn to Pomerania, Poland, Brandenburg, and Denmark, in 1308 falling to the Teutonic Order under whose rule the city prospered for many years.

Danzig was one of the chief cities of the Hanseatic League, ranking alongside Lübeck, Cologne (*q.v.*) and Magdeburg. In 1454, after the decline of the Teutonic Order, Danzig became a free city in union with Poland at the peace of Thorn (Toruń). It was represented in parliament and at the elections of the Polish kings, and governed a sizeable territory in Prussia, with some thirty villages.

Until within living memory, perhaps no city of Europe had managed to preserve its mediaeval aspect so well: that picturesque quality is seen in Wachendorf's view, looking from the west. (Wachendorf, incidentally, was secretary to the London *kontor* of the Hanseatic League). The view shows the clustered streets around the great stump of the *Pfarrkirch* dedicated to St Mary, a brick church founded in 1343 and finished in 1503, and once one of the largest Protestant churches in Europe. Nearby may be seen the Gothic *Rathaus* on the *Lange*

GEDANVM, Krantio, in sua Wandalia Gdanum; vulgo, sed corruptè, Dantiscum, Germanicè, Dantzigt. opulentissima Prussiæ vrbs, ac nobile Mercatorum Emporium. Cuius topographica icone, Clarissimus vir, ac singularis Doctor, viror. Mecœnas, D. Adamus Wachēdorff, Hanseatici Londinēsis Emporij Secretari⁹ prudens, atq̃, fidelis, digno amplissima hac sua prīa ciuis, suis sumptib. depicta, plurimum Splendoris ac ornamenti, operi nostro perbenignè contulit.

Gasse, begun in 1379, its tall Renaissance tower being added in 1561.

From Danzig vessels sailed to all parts of the Baltic, to the North Sea, to Bristol (*q.v.*) and to London (*q.v.*). The prosperity of the town's merchants may be judged from the appearance of the costumed figures in the foreground of the view, many of which have a distinctly Dutch appearance.

Most of the overseas trade of Danzig was with Holland, Zeeland and Flanders. In 1481, one shipowner recorded 1,000 vessels sailing westwards, a figure easily doubled by grain shipments to Amsterdam during the late sixteenth century.

A report of 1534 by one Maximilian Transilvan, emissary to Hamburg, stated: "The whole profit and increase of the kingdom of Poland and the said town of Danzig lies in this, that the Hollanders come every year once or twice to Danzig with two or three hundred ships, to buy and take off in fourteen days all the grain that they find in the said town of Danzig. For in past twenty-five years all the great lords of Poland and Prussia have discovered therein the means of sending by certain rivers all their grain to Danzig and there to have it sold to those of the said town. And for this reason the kingdom of Poland and the great lords have become mightily rich. For before this time, they knew not what to do with their grain and left their lands uncultivated, and the town of Danzig, which was nothing but a village, is at this time the most powerful and richest city in all the Eastland Sea."

PLATE 22

GENOVA AND FIRENZE
(Genoa and Florence)

Genua [with] ***Florentia.***
1572.
Volume I, number 44. Two subjects, 158 × 480mm, and 156 × 480mm. respectively.

Genoa after G.F. Camocio, 1560; Florence probably after Hieronymus Cock, *c*.1557. Genoa, a city of seafarers, who count among their number Christopher Columbus, must have been a seaport since the earliest days of organised trade in the Mediterranean. Its strategic location in a natural harbour made it ideal for the trans-shipment of goods between the merchants of the Mediterranean and traders from beyond the Alps. It was also important in the carrying trade between northern and western Europe and the Levant during the Crusades.

The nucleus of the old city, immediately west of the *Molo Vecchio*, is shown in the view. Fortifications had existed there from before the tenth century and were extended in the twelfth century. The much larger fortifications seen here enclosing the entire bay in a great arc from the lighthouse, or *lanterna*, were built in about 1320–30; they ran a circuit of some 19 kilometres and enclosed both built-up areas and open land.

An increasing number of patrician families became involved in Genoa's mercantile affairs. From this small group arose a cultured and educated élite, many of whom became officers of the state. A university was founded in 1471 and many of the city's hospitals were among the finest of their kind in Italy.

Florence was founded *c*.200BC on an Etruscan site on the Arno river. Suburbs later developed outside the Roman walls but, by about

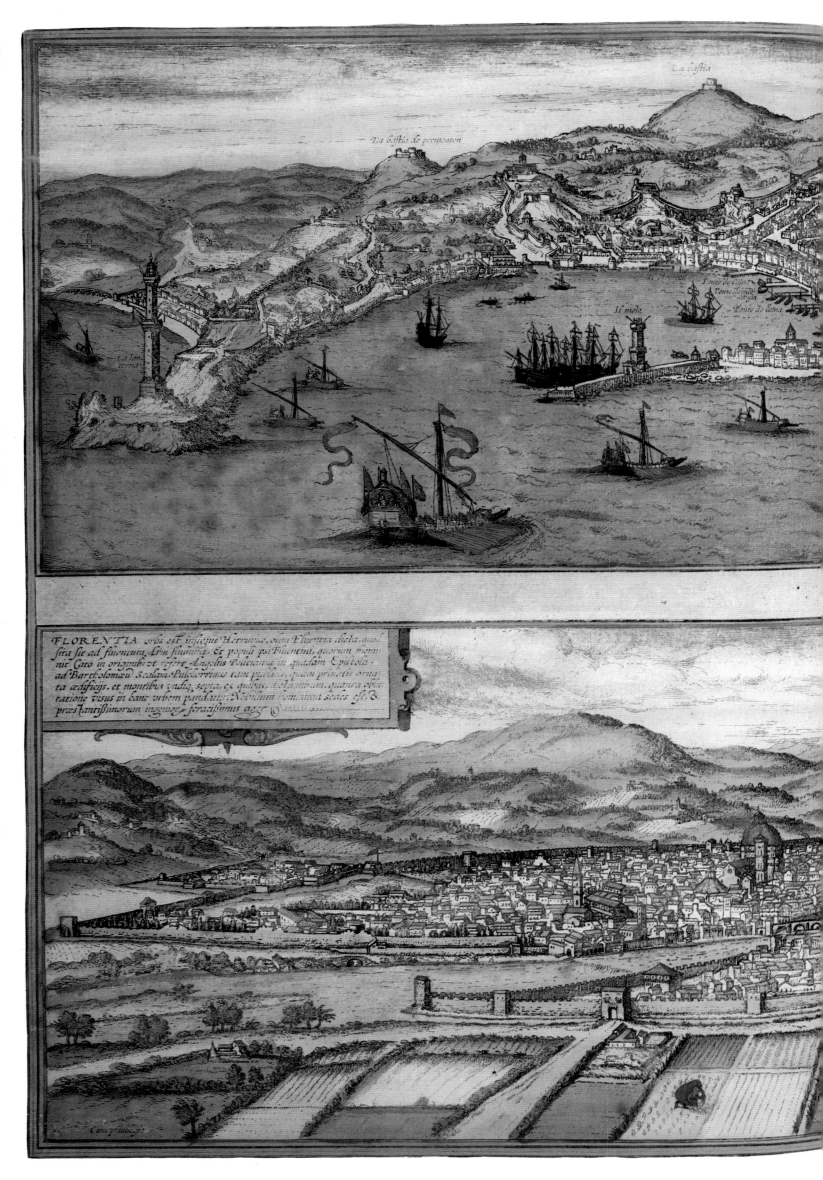

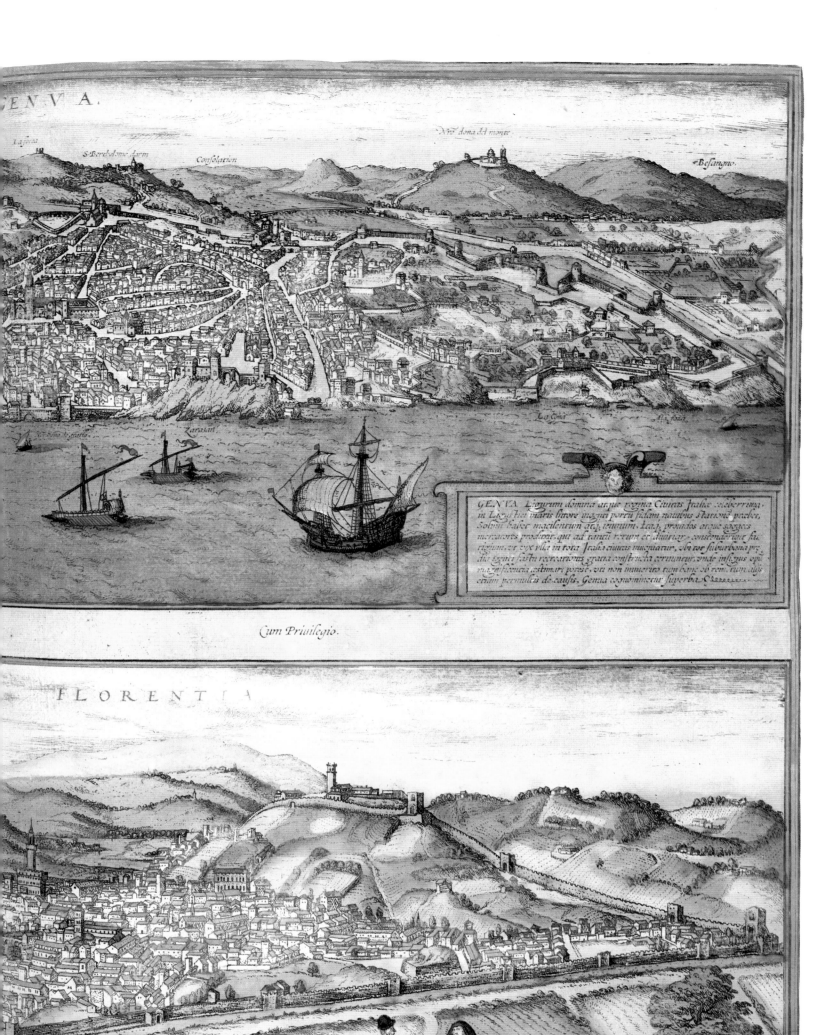

1175, the entire town on both sides of the river was once more enclosed. Continuing expansion made the existing walls inadequate and third circumvallation was begun in 1284; it enclosed an urban area and open land totalling 630 hectares, as seen in the engraving.

Florence is, of course, renowned as the birthplace of the Renaissance and the seat of its greatest flowering. Urban design, where it was not subject to military requirements, was governed by functional and aesthetic considerations. By its lay-out, the magnificent façades of its streets and buildings, and its monumental perspectives, the city was intended to impress. This objective were achieved, notably in the number of outstanding buildings that have survived the ravages of war and pure neglect. Among the most notable are: *Il Duomo* (*Santa Maria del Fiore*), begun in 1298, completed by Brunelleschi and consecrated in 1436, which dominates the centre of the panorama; the nearby *Campanile*, built by Giotto and begun in 1332; and the many noble palaces, including the *Palazzo Vecchio* and *Palazzo Pitti*, to name but two.

Like many great cities, Florence is situated on a river; as well as the periodical danger of disastrous floods, this has brought its own challenges. Many of those who controlled the government of the city lived in the *Palazzo Pitti*, on the left bank, to the right of centre in the engraving. To ease his journey to the part of the city on the right bank, Cosimo I de' Medici commissioned Giorgio Vasari, in the mid-sixteenth century, to build an enclosed gallery from the *Palazzo Pitti*, across the *Ponte Vecchio* and along the *Lungo Arno* to the *Palazzo Vecchio*, the seat of Florentine government.

PLATE 23

GRANADA

Granata. *1563.*
Volume 1, number 4. 325 ×
505mm.

After Georg Hoefnagel.
Granada, a flourishing
town in Roman times, fell
to the Vandals, with the rest
of Andalusia, in the fifth
century. Under the caliphs,
however, Granada rapidly
rose to prominence as the
capital of a kingdom which,
by the fall of the Omayyad
dynasty in 1031, ranked
alongside Seville (*q.v.*) as an
independent principality.

Granada, a Moorish city for
almost 800 years, was an
asylum for Moorish
refugees from Seville,
Valencia and Murcia.
Several dynastic families
ruled in succession.
Granada was for a time
united with Almería and
Málaga under Abu
Abdullah Mohammed Ibn
al-Ahmar, founder of the
Nasrid dynasty (1238–
1492).

The Nasrid dynasty ruled in
an unbroken line of twenty-
five sovereigns who
maintained power either by
force or by paying tribute
to stronger neighbours.
The Nasrid encouragement
of eommerce, especially of
the silk trade with Italy,
made Granada the
wealthiest city in Spain.
The dynasty also patronised
art, literature and science
and attracted many learned
Muslim scholars, such as
the historian Ibu Khaldun,
and the geographer Ibn
Batuta. They created a
brilliant civilisation, of
which the *Alhambra* (Red
Fortress) is the supreme
monument. It was begun in
1250 as the last bastion of
Spanish Islam.

Aside from the *Alhambra*,
the principal Moorish
buildings remaining here
are the thirteenth-century
*Cuarto Real de Santo
Domingo*, the fourteenth-
century *Alcázar de Genil*
and, of the same period, the
former university building,
the *Casa del Cabildo*. The
Spanish university was
founded in 1531 by Charles
V. The cathedral, which
commemorates the
Reconquista or Expulsion of

the Moors, in 1492, was begun in 1529 but was not completed until 1703. It contains the tombs of Ferdinand and Isabella, the first rulers of a united Spain (1452–1516). The last of the Moors were driven out of Spain on 2 January 1492.

Granada comprises three main districts: *Antequerela*, *Albaicín* and Granada proper. The first was founded by Moorish refugees from Antequera in 1410; Albaicín (Arabic *Rabad al' Bayazin*, or Falconers' quarter) lies adjacent, its name associated with the Moors of Baeza who had fled here in 1246. Granada proper is to the north of Antequerela and west of Albaicín.

The origin of the city's name is uncertain but is thought to derive from *granada*, or pomegranate, grown widely in the region. The Moors called it *Karnattah al-Yahud*, which can be taken as meaning "hill of strangers".

PLATE 24

HAMBURG

Hamburgum. 1588.
Volume IV, number 36. 368 × 470mm.

Probably after David Frese and Heinrich von Rantzau, before 1588. Hamburg probably originated as a small fortress erected by Charlemagne in 808, on a rise between the Elbe and the Alster as a defence against the marauding Slavs. It was called *Hammaburg* after the surrounding forest, or *Hamme.* The church that was established there in 811 became a centre for the evangelisation of northern Europe, with Hamburg missionaries introducing Christianity into Jylland, in Denmark, and into Sweden and Norway. Hamburg later became an archbishopric, St Ansgar, the apostle of the north, being the first metropolitan.

The original settlement lay around the *Domplatz* to the right of centre in the engraving, with the *St Petri* adjacent across the *Speers ort.* Growth in this early settlement was in the direction of the *Adolfsplatz* (named after Adolf II, Count of Holstein), to the west of the *Markt* in the centre of the view. Several decades later, on what was then marshy ground in the bend of the Alster centred on the *St Nicolai* and the *Hopfenmarkt,* the *Neustadt* was established; this was a merchants' community and the fortress of the markgrave.

The imperial charter granted to Hamburg in 1189 by Frederick I greatly favoured the growth of the city: it was exempt from tolls, had a separate court and jurisdiction and enjoyed fishing rights in the Elbe from the city quays as far as the sea. Then, in 1216, the episcopal and mercantile towns were combined under the leadership of a markgrave with a single town council and a single law court, forming a liberal system of government adopted by many cities elsewhere in northern Europe, as in Rīga (*q.v.*) The *Rathaus* where

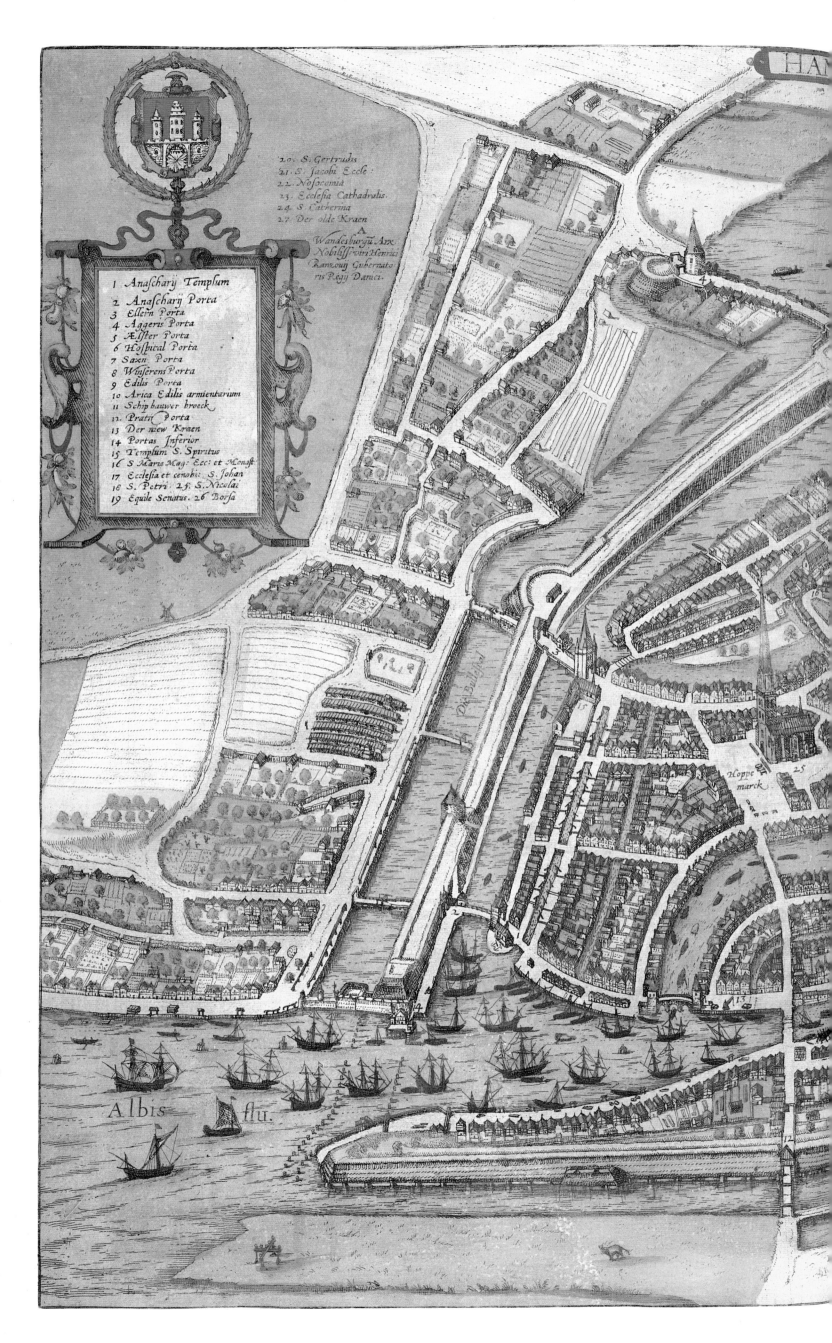

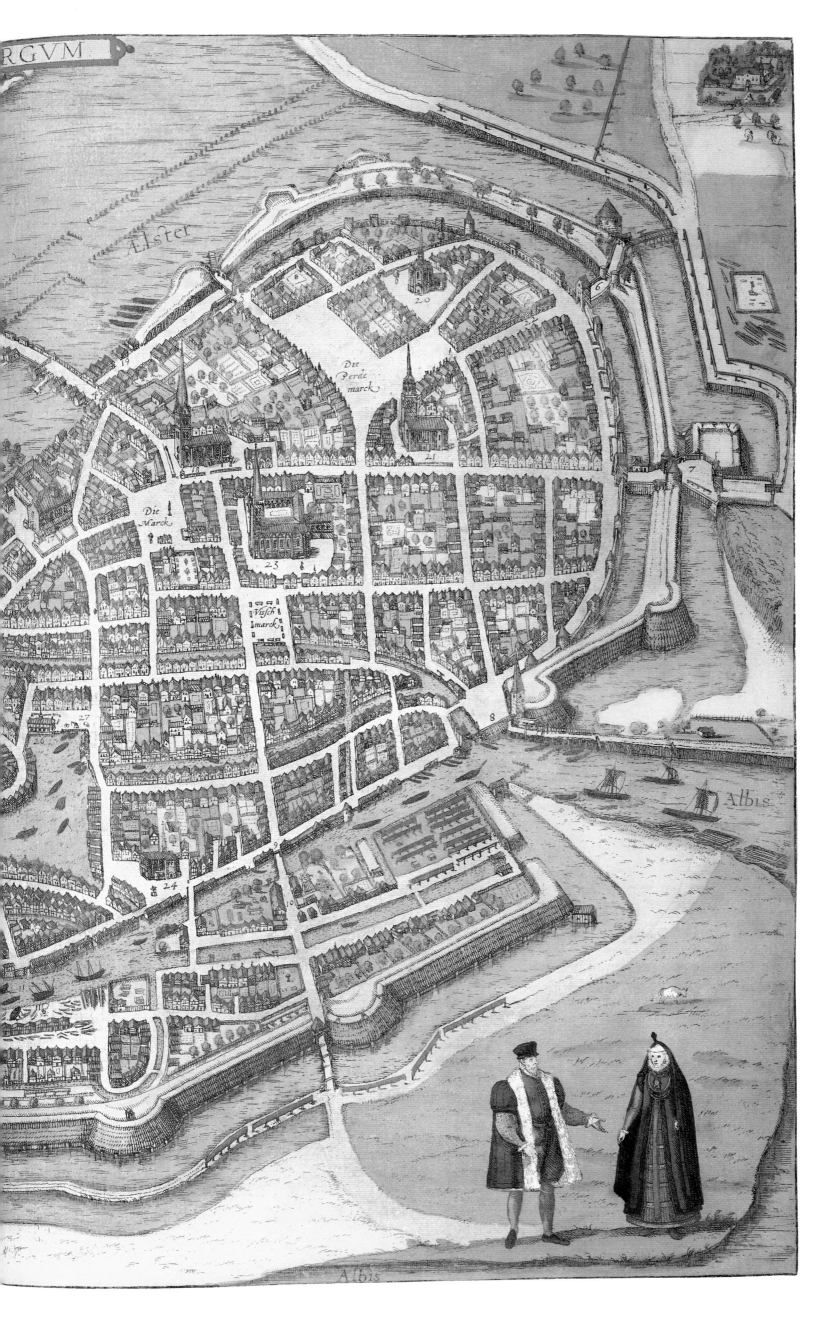

the two communities met, first mentioned in 1190, was established backing onto the Alster. The Alster canal, cut during the latter part of the thirteenth century, protected the urban westward extensions, the *Neuer Wall* fortification line being erected in 1405. The two Alster lakes were created during the thirteenth and fourteenth centuries by damming the river (*q.v.* Amsterdam) to provide waterpower to drive a mill. The outermost canal, *Bleichen Fleth*, followed in the 1450s to form the outer moat of the defences in the west.

The engraving shows the *Altstadt* as it existed before 1600, crowded and cramped, and traversed by narrow canals, or *Fleeten* (a word which has left its own trace in the toponymy of London, *q.v.*), bordered by warehouses, cellars and stores. At one time, the fleets were subject to tides which left them dry at low tide and flooded at high water. After 1600 a *Neustadt* was established to the west of the *Bleichen Fleth* (not of course shown on the engraving) which contained new markets and new residential quarters.

PLATE 25

KALININGRAD, USSR *(Königsberg)* [with] RĪGA, LATVIA.

Die Fürstliche Hauptstatt Königsbergk in Preussen [with] ***Riga die hauptt Statt in Lyfflantt.*** *1581. Volume III, number 43. 190 × 405mm. and 165 × 405mm. respectively.*

Königsberg was established in 1256 near the mouth of the Pregel [Pregolya] river in the Baltic region of Samland, in eastern Prussia, and is at present under USSR administration. Its founders were the knights of the German Teutonic Order and it was named in honour of Ottokar II of Bohemia, who had provided armies for the German crusade into Prussia led by Hermann Balke.

The southern shores of the Baltic, to the east of Pomerania, saw a steady influx of German and Flemish settlers during the twelfth to fourteenth centuries into the rich, fertile plains where towns and trading cities were established in rapid succession. These waves of colonization in many cases displaced and subjugated the original and sparsely settled Slavic tribes; the land was opened up and the potential of the Baltic developed into a highly profitable international trade in timber, amber and grains. Königsberg itself became a member of the Hanseatic League soon after this mercantile organisation was established in 1358. The city also became an important monetary centre, controlling and financing the eastern Baltic shipping trade in western Europe.

The castle, or *Schloss*, was built in 1257 as a stronghold of the Teutonic Order, becoming the seat of the Grand Masters of the Order after the fall of Marienburg in the fifteenth century. The cathedral (*Dom*), built between 1297 and 1302, is seen in the *Altstadt* beyond the island suburb of Kneiphof with its *Neuerdom*.

Statt Königsbergk

Der Se...
Edelnesst
Barbara
Der Sackhauß
Stat.
Sentb.
Stat beff
Das kloster
Der Neu Pregell
E.G Getraid
Der Thum Collegium
Holtz Prück...
Alstetter holtzwiese
Der Kneiphofer holtzwiese

MONS REGIVS; PRVSSIÆ,
SIVE BORVSSIÆ, VRBS
MARITIMA, ELEGANTIS:
SIMA PRINCIPIS SEDES:

Riga die haüptt Statt in Lißflaintt
S. Peter
Das Rathaus.

F.L.V.

RIGA, percommode ad Dunā
amnem sita, Emporium cele:
bre, & Livoniæ Metropolis.

Rīga, capital of Latvia, was founded in 1201 by the German bishop, Albrecht, during the Baltic crusades. It is sited a few kilometres upstream from the mouth of the Daugava river, where there had been a small Viking settlement consisting of a number of storehouses, or *riji*, the word *rija* being Latvian for barn.

In 1207 Rīga became the seat of the principality of Livonia. It was also the seat of Albrecht's archbishopric and, in 1225, it became a free city of the empire. A factory of the Hanseatic League was opened here in 1279, Rīga achieving full membership of the League in 1282.

The city soon had 3,000 inhabitants, many of whom as in Königsberg, were German merchants in the lucrative timber trade. Not only timber, but grain – chiefly wheat and later rye – amber, wax, honey, hides, furs, smoked fish and so on, were the staples of the city's trade, the kind of goods to be seen stacked on the quayside in the engraving.

The status of Rīga in the Hanseatic League was considered second only to that of the great markets to the east at Novgorod, thanks to its strategic location controlling the Daugava river trade from Lithuania and Livonia proper. In 1290 Rīga adopted the then liberal statutes of Hamburg (*q.v.*) approximating to those of a modern city republic, according rights to German merchants and settlers there.

Rīga possessed many fine buildings befitting its status, in particular the tall spire of the *Pētertornī* built in 1491, the castle of the Teutonic Order (*Das Schloss*) seen at the left in the engraving. Despite the upheavals of recent history, much remains today to make Rīga one of the finest cities of the Baltic region.

PLATE 26

KØBENHAVN
(Copenhagen)

**Hafnia. Hafnia
Kopenhagen Urbs
Daniae primaria qua se
terra marique
conspiciendam exhibet.
Anno Salutis M.D.
LXXXVII.** 1588.
*Volume IV, number 28. 326
× 475mm.*

After Heinrich von
Rantzau, 1587.
Copenhagen is first
mentioned as a small fishing
village, in 1043. Thus it
remained until Valdemar I
presented that part of
Sjælland to Axel Hvide,
also known as Absalon,
Bishop of Roskilde. Also in
1043 a castle was built on
Slotholmen, where
Christiansborg now stands.
The settlement that grew
around the castle attracted
many merchants, traders
and factors, becoming
known, so recorded Saxo
Grammaticus in 1200, as
Portus mercatorum translated
from *Kaupmannahöfn*, or
Købmændens havn, or
traders' harbour.

In 1186 Bishop Absalon
granted the castle and
village, with the adjacent
small island of Amager, to
the see of Roskilde. As the
harbour grew in
importance, the Danish
kings were naturally
anxious to regain it as a
stronghold. In 1245, Erik
IV expelled Bishop Niels
Stigson but, on Erik's death
in 1250, Bishop Jakob
Erlandsen regained the
town and, in 1254, granted
the burghers their first
charter of urban privileges,
which were confirmed by
Pope Urban III in 1286. No
mention was made of trade
nor of the guilds. These
were prohibited by a
charter granted by Bishop
Johan Kvag in 1284;
throughout the Middle
Ages, the town was notable
for the absence of a guild
system and the right of any
burgher to pursue a craft.
Although guilds were
established later, they never
were free of strict control
and were periodically
suppressed.

The prosperity of
Copenhagen was reversed
when Lübeck attacked in
1248, followed by Jaromir

HAFNIA vulgo ꝚꝋꝒꝰ꠹ꝲꝲ vrbs Daniæ primaria qua se te

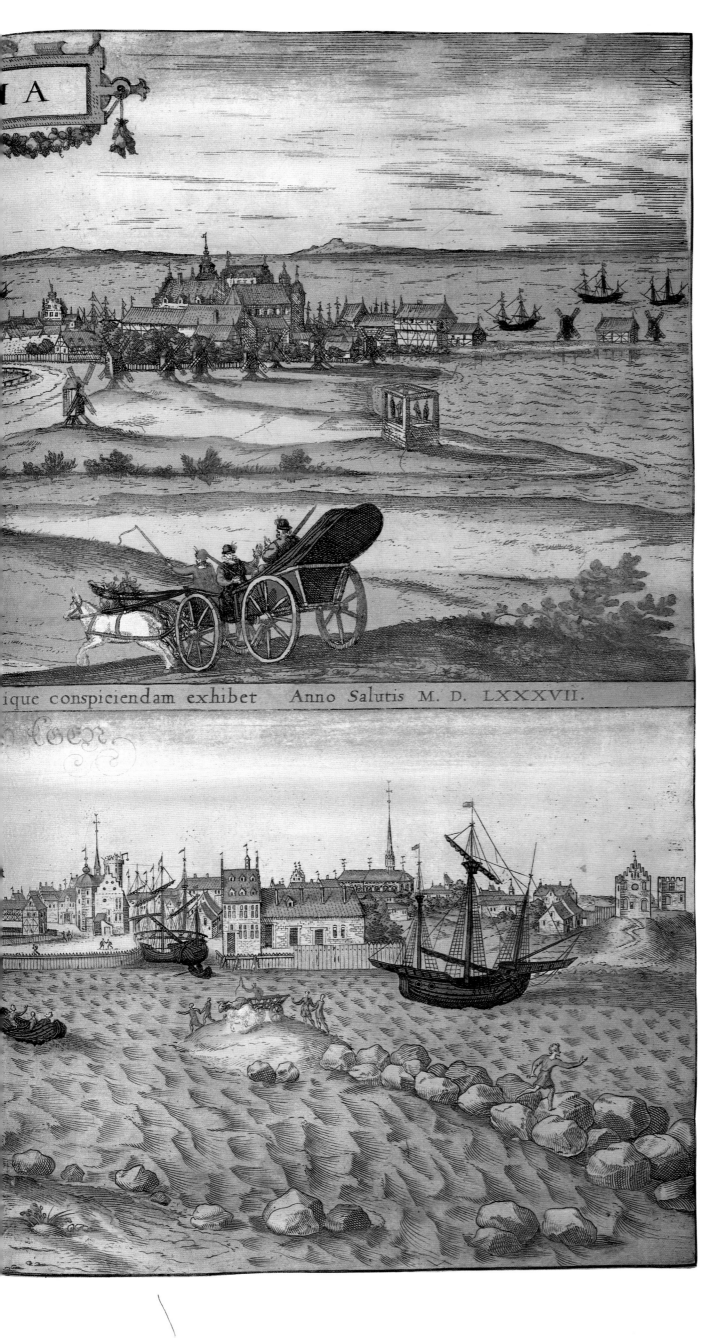

ique conspiciendam exhibet Anno Salutis M. D. LXXXVII.

of Rügen in 1259. The Norwegians were repelled in 1306. The Hanseatic League, established in the fifteenth century, attempted to establish a *hof* (or 'warehouse') here. Many attempts were made to secure Copanhagen from the see of Roskilde, but it was not until 1443 that the town became the royal seat and capital of Denmark, an event marked by the granting of full municipal rights to the community. In 1523–24, Copenhagen defended Christian II against Frederick I who had captured the city and, strengthened its defences with a wall and sea ramparts begun on the Amager shore: so effective were these that the town survived a year-long siege before yielding to Christian III in 1536.

By the middle of the sixteenth century, Copenhagen's inhabitants numbered some 10,000, making it the largest city in Scandinavia at the time. The engraving shows two views of the city: the upper looking from the road to Roskilde to the west of the city and the lower from the Amager side, showing Copenhagen before the extensive building undertaken by Christian IV (1588–1658) and his successors. Fires were a common problem. Christian II (1481–1559) had urged the adoption of a building code prescribing the use of stone and half-timbering. Heinrich von Rantzau's views show how Copenhagen was still concentrated around *Slotholmen* in the late sixteenth century. Prominent are the *Vor Frue Kirke*, founded in the twelfth century, the *Petri Kirke* (since 1585 the church for the German merchants), the *St Nikolaj Kirke* and the old castle on *Slotholmen* itself.

PLATE 27

KÖLN
(Cologne)

Colonia Agrippina. 1571.
*Volume I, number 38. 330 ×
475mm.*

After Arnold Mercator
(1571). Cologne was
established as a *colonia* in
AD50 by Claudius, and
named after Agrippina, his
wife. The plan clearly
shows the phases in the
city's growth, from the
near–rectangular form of
the Roman *colonia*, to the
arc of the town walls built
in 1200. The *colonia* itself
was a small settlement on
the left bank of the Rhine.

The town's first expansion
from its Roman nucleus
was the *Rheinvorstadt*
between it and the river
frontage, established in 980.
In 1106 three suburban
vorstädte followed, and in
1180 the line of the
mediaeval wall was
established. This structure
was completed by 1210
and, enclosing an area of
some 560 hectares, it
formed the outer limits of
the city until 1882, when
the walls were demolished.
Large areas reserved for
agriculture and market
gardens may clearly be seen
in the plan, especially on the
right–hand side of the
southern part.

Cologne's greatness rested
on its trade. Wines and
herrings were the main
commodities. The city's
weavers were also widely
renowned, and brought in
great revenue from the
export of their cloth. The
goldsmiths and armourers
of Cologne were also
famous throughout
Europe. When Cologne
joined the Hanseatic League
in 1201, the city's power
was such that it was the
centre of one third of the
league.

Despite many feuds with
the archbishops, the citizens
of Cologne were staunch
Roman Catholics, and their
legacy is the great number
of churches that stand
within the confines of the
former walls: they included
St Maria im Capitol, the
oldest, dedicated by Pope

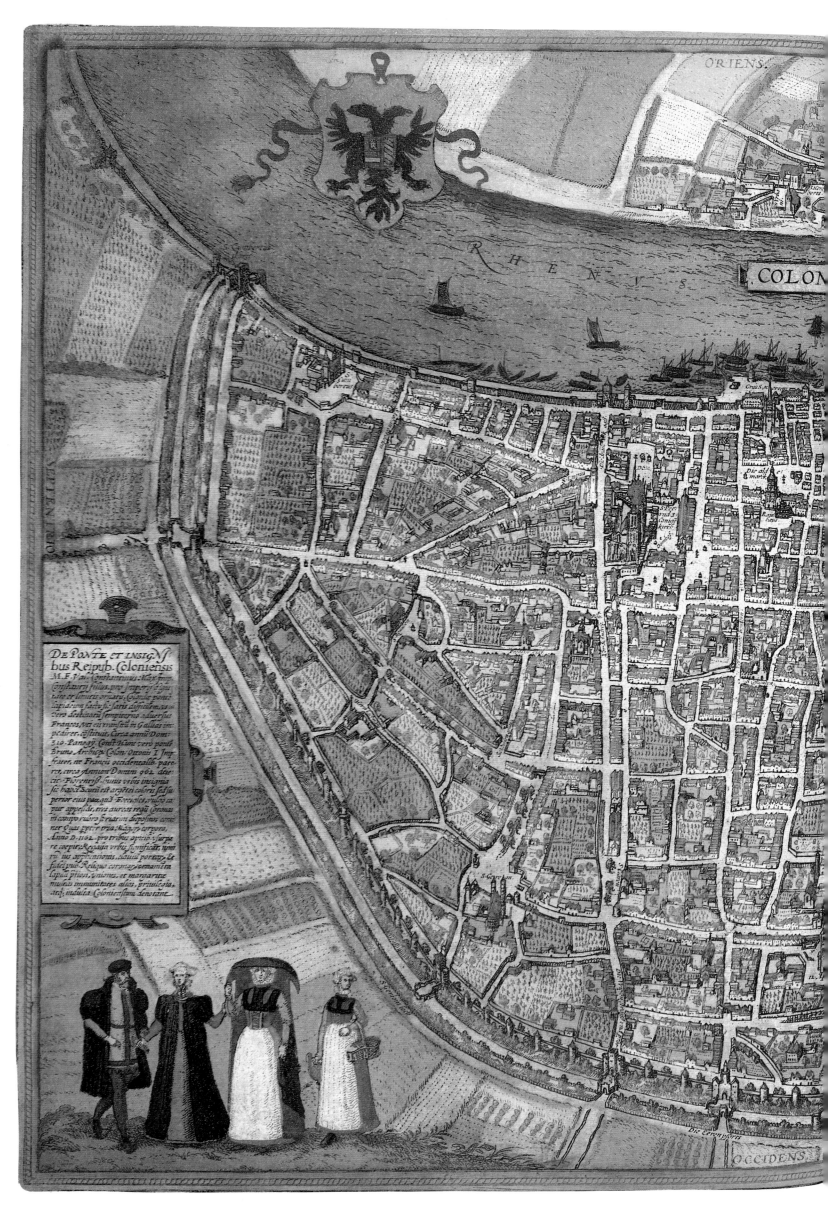

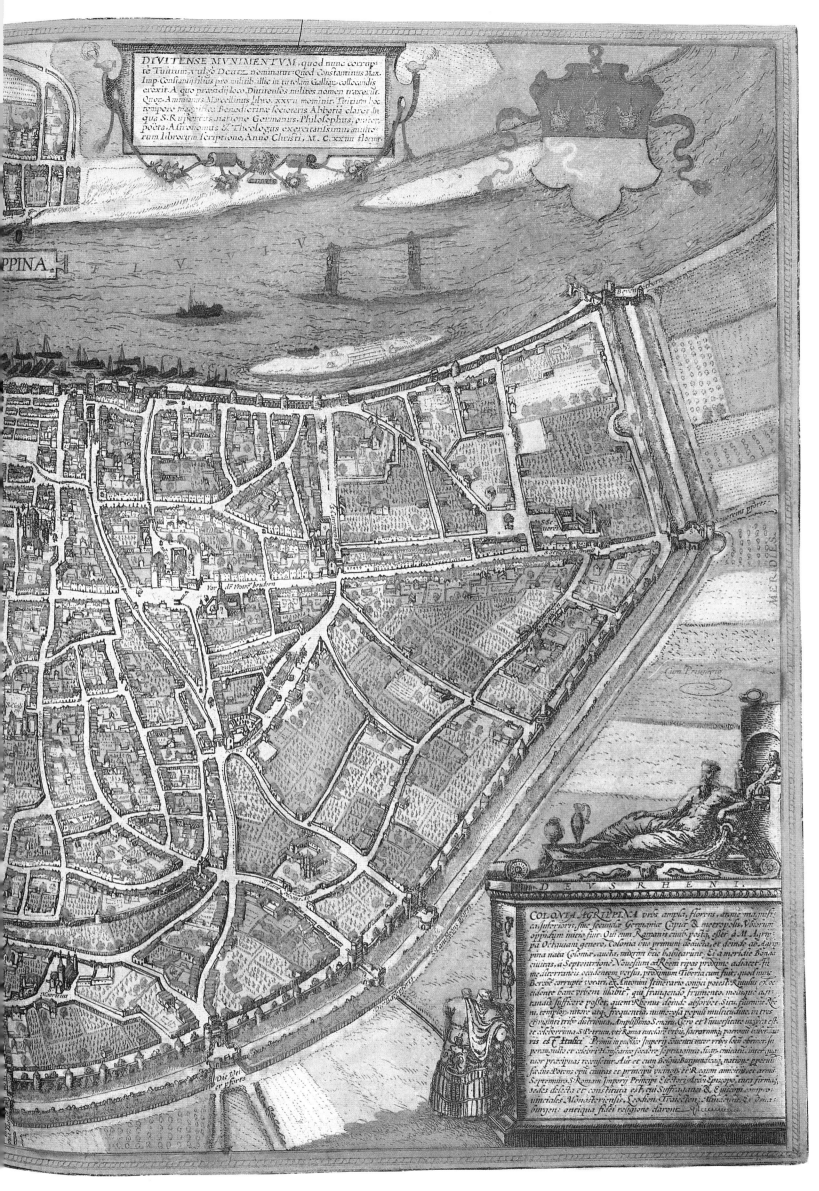

DIVITENSE MVNIMENTVM, quod nunc corrupte Tuitium vulgò Deutez nominatur: Quod Constantinus Max. Imp. Constantinopolis pro uiatib. illic in tutelam Galliæ colligendis erexit. A quo præsidij loco, Diuitenses milites nomen traxecit. Quæ Ammianus Marcellinus libro xxvii meminit. Tuitium hoc tempore magnifica Benedictinæ sectaris Abbatia clarer: In qua S. Ruperti natione Germanus, Philosophus, oriens poëta, Astronomus & Theologus exercitatissimus amulterum librorum scriptione, Anno Christi, M. C. xxiiii floruit.

Leo IX in 1049, the *Dom*, begun by Archbishop Conrad (1238–61) but not finished until 1880, *St Severinus* (1220), *St Andreas* (1414), *Groß St Martin* (tenth to twelfth centuries), and so on. So many churches were built that Cologne was given the soubriquet *heilige Stadt* (or 'holy city').

The university was founded in 1389. During the fifteenth century, a thousand or more students, some from as far afield as Scotland and Scandinavia, were enrolled. The university declined in stature when the influences of the Reformation were kept at bay by the Roman Catholic heirarchy. The final blow came in 1777 with the foundation of the university at Bonn (*q.v.*). Cologne university closed down in 1798 amid revolutionary turmoil.

Similar intolerance almost ruined the city's economy, for the expulsion of the Jews in 1414 and the exclusion of the Protestants from the rights of citizenship hampered mercantile activity. Other contributary causes were the opening up of new trade routes elsewhere, the decline of the trade guilds into corrupt corporations, the war in the Netherlands, the Thirty Years' War and the Wars of Spanish and Austrian Succession. By 1794, when the French occupied the city, Cologne's inhabitants numbered only 40,000, and only 6,000 of them possessed civic rights.

Notable secular buildings in Cologne existing at the time of Arnold Mercator's plan were the *Gürzenich*, built in 1441–47 for official festivities, and the *Rathaus* (seen here as *Raidhaus*), dating from 1407–14 and built on the foundations of a Roman stronghold. This building contained the *Hansa Saal* which was said to have been where the first general meeting of the Hanseatic League took place on 19 November 1367.

PLATE 28

LEIDEN

Leijda, Batavorum Lugdunum, vulgo Leyden, Concinna aedificiorum et incolarum frequentia pulcherrimum nitidissimum opp. ab Hispanis obsidione cinctum, ab Auriacis autem commeatus invectione liberatum Anno parte salutis M D LXXIII. 1575.
Volume V, number 25. 340 × 465mm.

Probably after Jan van Lieferinck, 1574. Leiden, like its old rival Dordrecht (*q.v.*), is an ancient town. The town incorporates three essentially Dutch features: the *burcht, dijkstad*; and *waterstad*, built at the confluence of the rivers Oude Rijn, Nieuwe Rijn and Mare.

The *burcht* was established as a fortified mound on the triangle of land between the branches of the Rijn at some time during the tenth and eleventh centuries. The town that subsequently developed was one of the earliest centres of the *grafschap*, or county, of Holland, obtaining a charter possibly as early as 1186. Here was temporary refuge in times of attack or flood. The *burcht* was fortified and strengthened in the twelfth century.

From early times, Leiden was a favourite residence of the counts, Willem II (1228) and Floris V (1256) being born here. It rapidly assumed a crucial role in the control of trade and traffic between the towns and villages along the *strandwal* behind the coast. By about 1300, Leiden had spread south of the river, with the Gothic *St Pieterskerk* and the *Gravensteen* residence built nearby. In 1266 a wall was begun along the city's western margin – or *Rapenburg* of 1204 and in 1294 another extension was built between the rivers

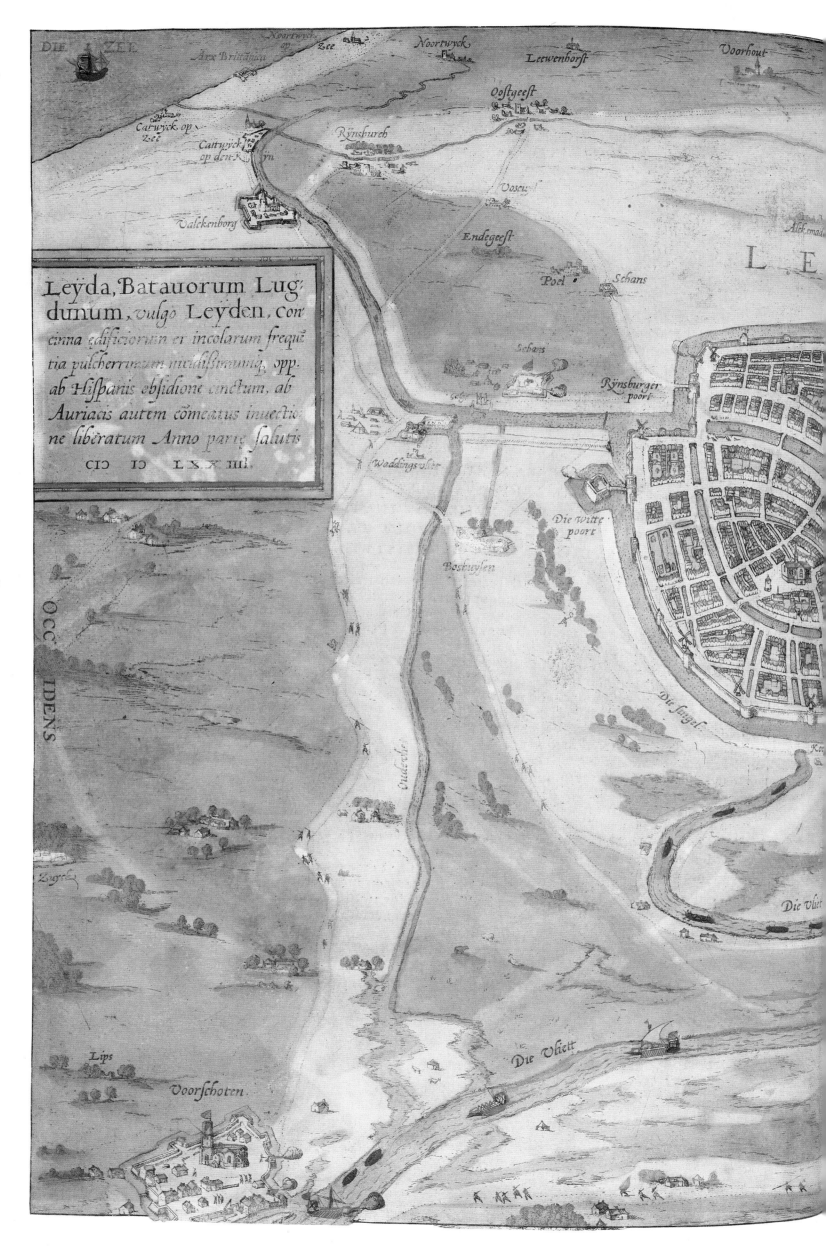

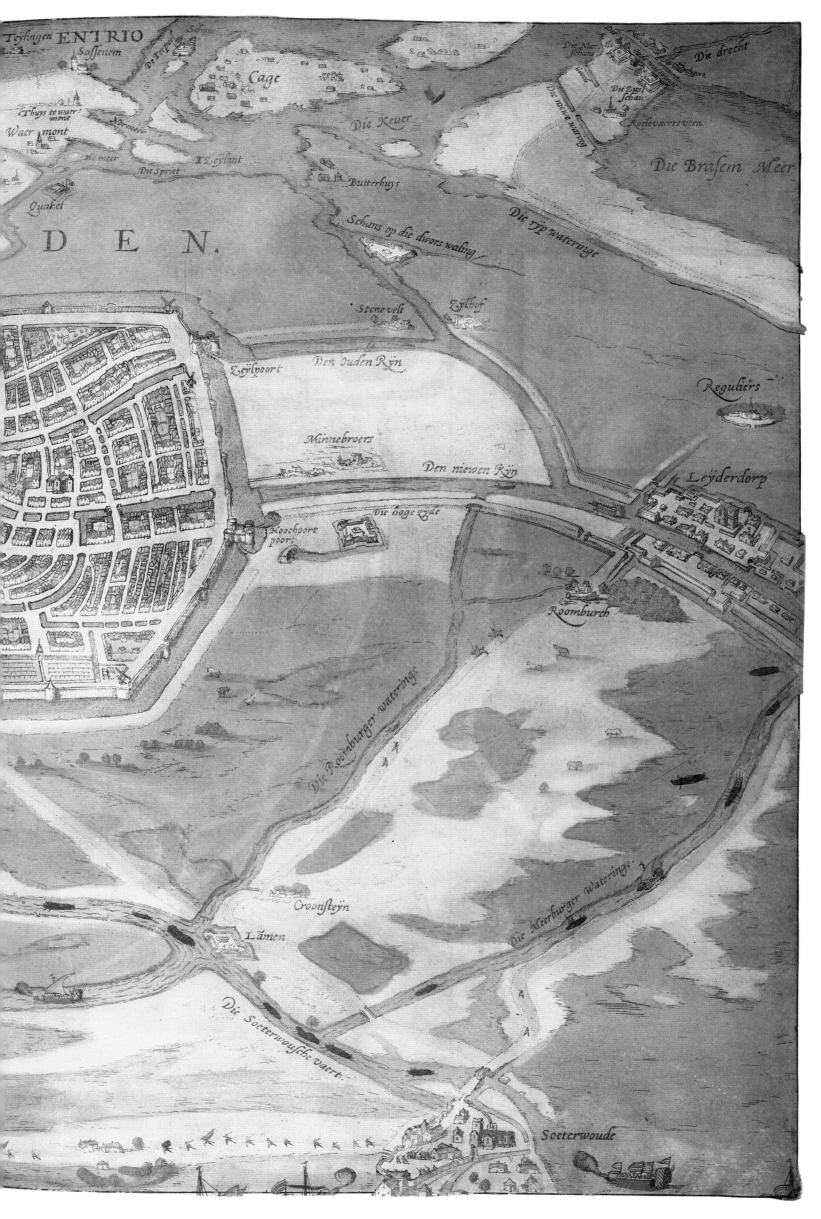

south and east of the *burcht*. This was the *waterstad*, with the reclaimed land marked by four parallel *grachten* connecting the two branches of the Rijn.

In the fourteenth century rapid growth took place. Leiden's industries and annual fairs became famous. The woollen industry prospered from the arrival of refugee weavers from Ieper, in Flanders, who possessed new skills. They settled in the *Oude Singelbuurt*.

Specialist drapers, often former wool merchants, organised sections of the trade and expansion brought new workers into Leiden. They in turn had to be housed, north of the Oude Rijn, near the *Vrouwenkerk*. A fourth extension was begun beyond the *Rapenburg* in 1389. By the early fifteenth century, Leiden contained one hundred draperies and had become one of the richest towns in Holland. However, it never quite equalled the wool trade of Bruges (*q.v.*), nor yet achieved the annual exports of England. Even so, Leiden was the greatest cloth manufacturing town in the area of the present-day Netherlands. By 1541 it counted some 15,000 inhabitants, and was also the largest town in Holland. It was, however, soon to be superseded by Amsterdam (*q.v.*).

The plan shows the great *Pieterskerk*, whose 120-metre spire collapsed in a storm in 1512. The famous university, also visible here, was established in 1575 by William the Silent and Janus Dousa, champions of Dutch liberty, in recognition of the fierce resistance that Leiden put up against the Spaniards, as is acknowledged in the title to this plan. As befits a university town, the seat of learning enjoys a setting of repose and dignity beside the waters of the *Rapenburg*.

PLATE 29

LEIPZIG

Lipsiae insignis Saxoniae urbis et celeberrimi Emporii vera Effigies. Anno M.D.C.XVII. 1617. *Volume VI, number 17. 268 × 460mm.*

Source unknown. With this engraving, Leipzig, in Saxony, eastern Germany, makes its second appearance in the *Civitates*, having first been illustrated in Volume I in 1572, in which a plate showing both Dresden and Leipzig was published. This new perspective view of Leipzig, dated 1617, shows a town of narrow streets and tall houses along four principal thoroughfares: *Grimmaische-, Peters-, Hain-,* and *Katherinenstraße*, each with its own gate in the perimeter wall and each converging on the *Rathaus* built by Hieronymus Lotter in 1556. Close by is the *Hof*, built in the 1530s and immortalised in Goethe's *Faust*, and the *Pleissenburg* citadel where, in 1519,

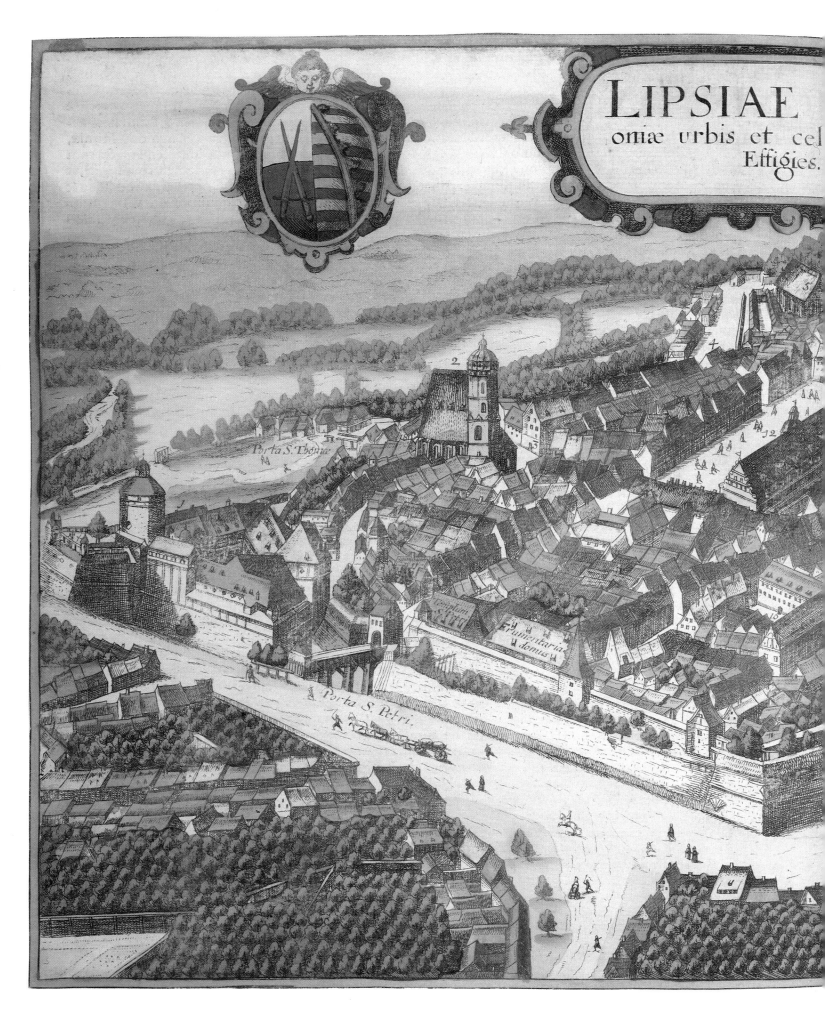

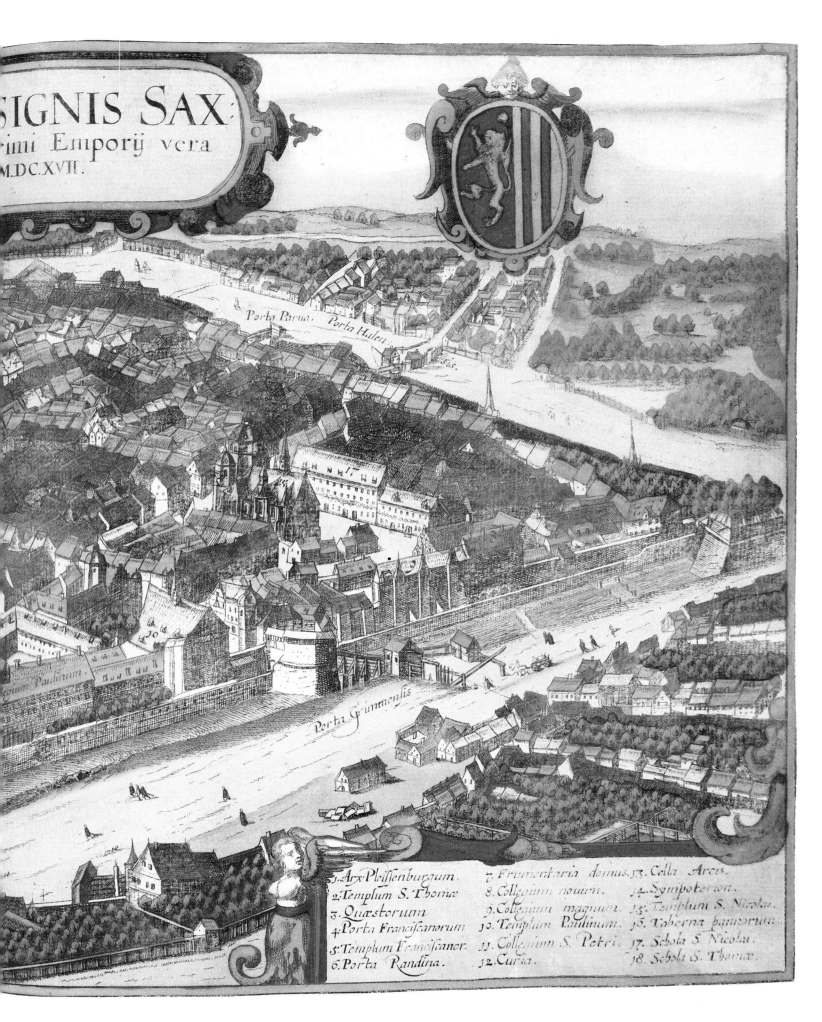

SIGNIS SAX·
rimi Emporij vera
M.DC.XVII.

Porta Parua. Porta Halen

Porta Grunniensis

1. Arx Pleissenburgum.   7. Frumentaria domus. 13. Cella Arcis.
2. Templum S. Thoma.   8. Collegium nouum.   14. Sympoterion.
3. Quæstorum   9. Collegium magnum.   15. Templum S. Nicolai.
4. Porta Franciscanorum 10. Templum Paulinum.   16. Taberna pannorum.
5. Templum Franciscanor. 11. Collegium S. Petri. 17. Schola S. Nicolai.
6. Porta Randina.   12. Curia.   18. Schola S. Thoma.

Martin Lüther held his disputation.

Perhaps the most important feature of the history of Leipzig is the famous commercial fairs, or *messe*, held at Easter and at Michaelmass since about 1170, with a smaller New Year's *messe* established in 1458. These fairs enjoyed imperial protection from 1497, and from 1507 by strict edicts prohibiting the holding of any others within a certain radius of Leipzig itself. Hides, furs, leather, wool, cloths, linen, glass and, later, books, were all brought for sale at these great fairs. Salt was also carried on the east–west trade routes from northern and western Europe into Poland.

Immigrants from the Netherlands were encouraged to settle and trade in Leipzig in the sixteenth century, and a flourishing trade with Hamburg (*q.v.*) and England developed there.

PLATE 30

LISBOA
(Lisbon)

Olissippo quae nunc Lisboa, civitas amplissimae Lusitaniae, ad Tagum, totius Orientis, et multarum Insularum Aphricaeque et Americae emporium nobilissimum. 1598. *Volume V, number 2. 370 × 470mm.*

From an unidentified source. Lisbon owes its name to ancient *Olisipo*, sometimes expressed as *Ulyssipo* after a mythical story of a city founded by Ulysses in Iberia. It was a *colonia* in Roman times, from 205BC to 407BC, and from then until 585BC it was occupied in turn by Alaric, the Visigoths and the Moors, who arrived in 711. Under the Moors the town was called *Al'Oshbūna* or *Lashbūna*. The Moors remained until 1147, when the first king of Portugal, Alphonso I, captured the town.

The town was also subject to early raids by the Normans, but when Alphonso I incorporated Estremadura and Alemtejo into his kingdom, Lisbon was the last portion to fall to him, only after having endured a siege of several months, during which Alphonso was aided by English and French crusaders *en route* for the Levant. The Muslim armies attacked again in 1184, unsuccessfully. In 1373, much of the town was destroyed by Castilian armies; they returned again in 1384, without result. Lisbon became an archbishopric in 1390 and the seat of government in 1422. During the sixteenth

century, the city attained great wealth and splendour from the establishment of the Portuguese seaborne empire in India, the Far East and Africa. From 1580 to 1640, during the union between Portugal and Spain, Lisbon was a provincial capital. It was also from here that the Armada sailed for England in 1588.

The Lisbon of Roman and Moorish times is essentially that part of the city known as *Alfama* on the south-facing slopes of the castle hill or *Castello de São Jorge*, a Moorish citadel later converted into a fortress and barracks. Tradition had it that the *Sé Patriarchal*, a cathedral founded in 1150 by Alphonso I, was originally a mosque; it was damaged in the earthquake of 1334 and rebuilt in 1380. Other buildings visible in the engraving are the twelfth-century church of *São Vicente de Fóra*, which, as the name implies, was originally without the city. The thirteenth-century chapel of *Nossa Senhora do Monte* and the sixteenth-century church of *Nossa Senhora da Graça* is also to be seen. The walls, erected by Fernando in 1375, may be seen flanking the older part of the city down to the water front by the present-day *Praça*. The engraving shows Lisbon as the centrepiece of a vast overseas empire, indicated by the busy activity on the river; this was recognised by Pope Alexander VI when in 1502 he confirmed upon Manoel I (1495–1521) the title "Lord of the conquest, navigation, and commerce of India, Ethiopia, Arabia and Persia".

PLATE 31

LONDON

Londinum, feracissimi Angliae Regni metropolis. 1572.
Volume I, number A. 335 × 485mm.

The first plan in the entire *Civitates* series, London is described in the original text as "a very ancient town, situated in the most fertile and healthy part of the whole of England, in the county of Middlesex, on the north bank of the Thames . . . indeed large in itself, but it also possesses beautiful suburbs and a magnificient castle, called the Tower. It is adorned with splendid buildings and one hundred and twenty parish churches. A stone bridge leads over the river to the south side. It is very long and built on many arches. At both sides the bridge is flanked with small houses, so that it does not look like a bridge, but a beautiful street . . . There is wonderful wealth and abundance of all things and merchandise, which are conveyed here by the River Thames from the whole world . . . "

This first detailed, single-sheet plan of London is based on a now-lost twenty-sheet plan. Known only from two surviving copper-plate engravings covering the Finsbury and City areas immediately north of London Bridge, believed to have been made sometime between 1547 and 1559.

In its present form, this is the most familiar map of Tudor London, providing a picture of the City, Westminster and Southwark substantially as they were during the 1550s. Clearly, the city walls no longer confined the built-up area: it had a population well in excess of 200,000, and Portsoken, Bishopsgate, Cripplegate, Aldersgate and Farringdon wards now extended

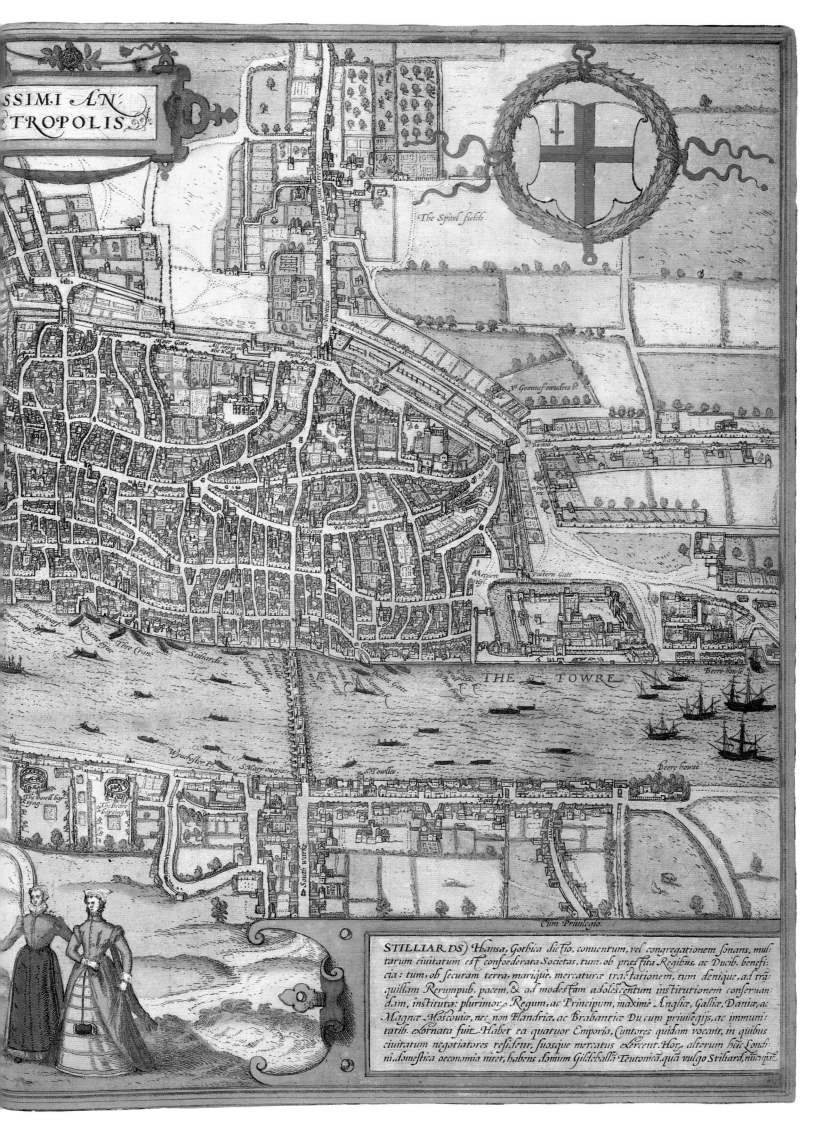

beyond the wall. Houses lined the high roads out of London and through the suburbs. The gardens of the great houses and palaces on the south side of the Strand between the City and Westminster stretch out in the direction of Charing Cross, linking the mercantile City with the royal court at Westminster.

Across the Thames, Southwark had nominally become part of London in 1550, when three royal manors were purchased there. However, its later, somewhat disorderly reputation as the site of theatres and houses of public entertainments was to resist several attempts at control. Immediately west of the Borough may be seen the bull- and bear-baiting rings.

It is interesting to note that, although this plan first appeared in 1572, the topographical detail itself is considerably earlier, since it shows *St Paul's* (at the very centre of the engraving) still with its tall spire, which was destroyed in 1561. The two panels of text which flank the costumed figures in the lower corners of the plan describe the mercantile activity of London, lending some emphasis to the main title which, translated from the latin, means "Capital of the most fruitful Kingdom of England". On the right-hand panel is a description of the semi-fortified *Steelyard* west of London Bridge which, as the *kontor* of the Hanseatic League in London, would have been of particular interest to German readers of the *Civitates*, since the merchants retained their privileges until they were suppressed by Elizabeth I.

PLATE 32

LYON
(Lyons)

Lugdunum. 1572.
Volume I, number 10. 330 × 480mm.

Probably after Balthasar van den Bosch, 1550. Built on a narrow peninsula above the confluence of the Rhône and Saône rivers, Lyons has been occupied since Gallic times, when the Segusians allowed a small Greek colony to be established here in 59BC. They called their settlement *Lugdunum*, after the Gallic name. Then, in 43BC, the Roman Lucius Munatus Plaucus brought a colony to settle at Fourvière. During the Roman period Lyons was the starting-point of the main roads of Gaul – a role still played today on the natural highway between northern and southern France.

After the collapse of the Roman Empire, Lyons became the capital of the Burgundian kingdom in 478. Throughout much of its later history, Lyons was the subject of considerable dispute between imperial, papal and ecclesiastical powers. Pope Clement V was crowned there in 1305 and John XXII elected there in 1316. The Protestants took Lyon in 1562, and it was in the so-called Wars of Religion throughout the latter half of the sixteenth century, during which France was almost torn apart by civil unrest and disorder, that Lyons saw revenge for the St Bartholomew massacre of 24 August 1572.

The engraving shows an apparently tranquil and prosperous town, with bustling quaysides, fertile and abundant gardens and farmlands in the immediate vicinity. Much of the wealth of Lyons was derived from the long-established silk trade that largely owned its existence to royal patronage and to a monopoly granted in 1450

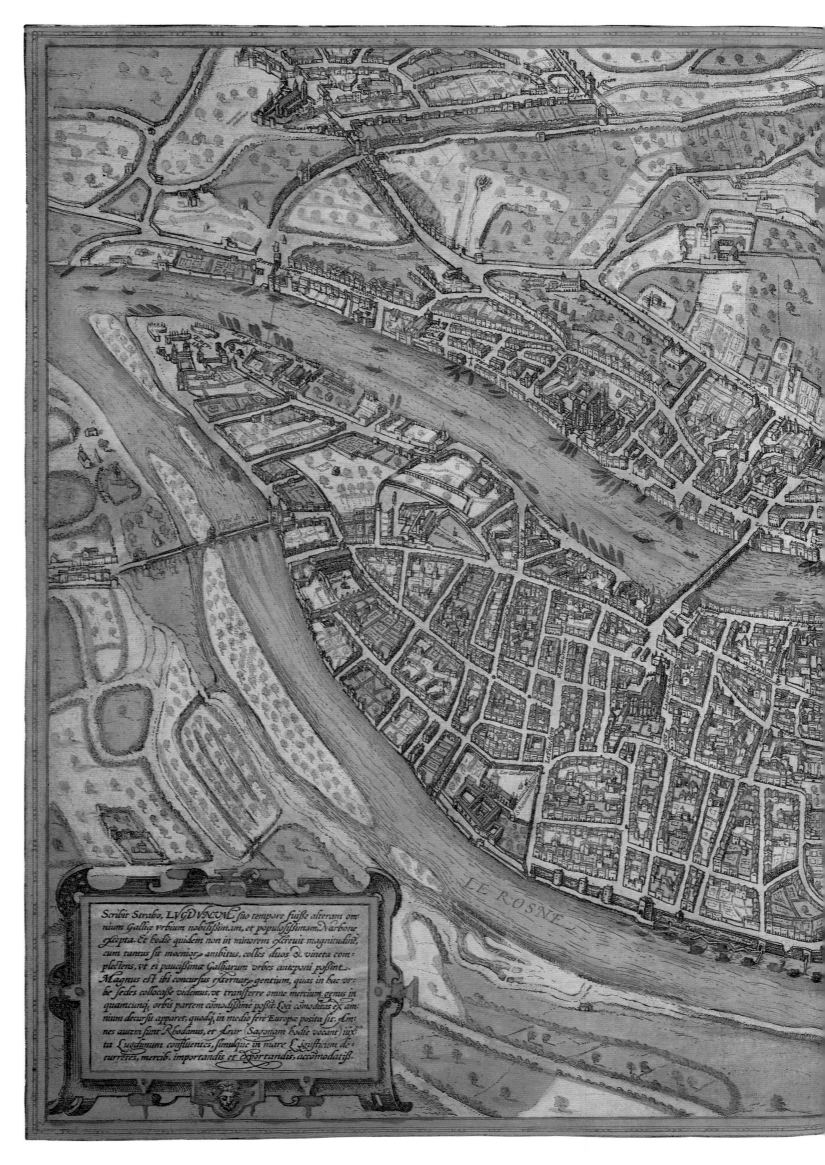

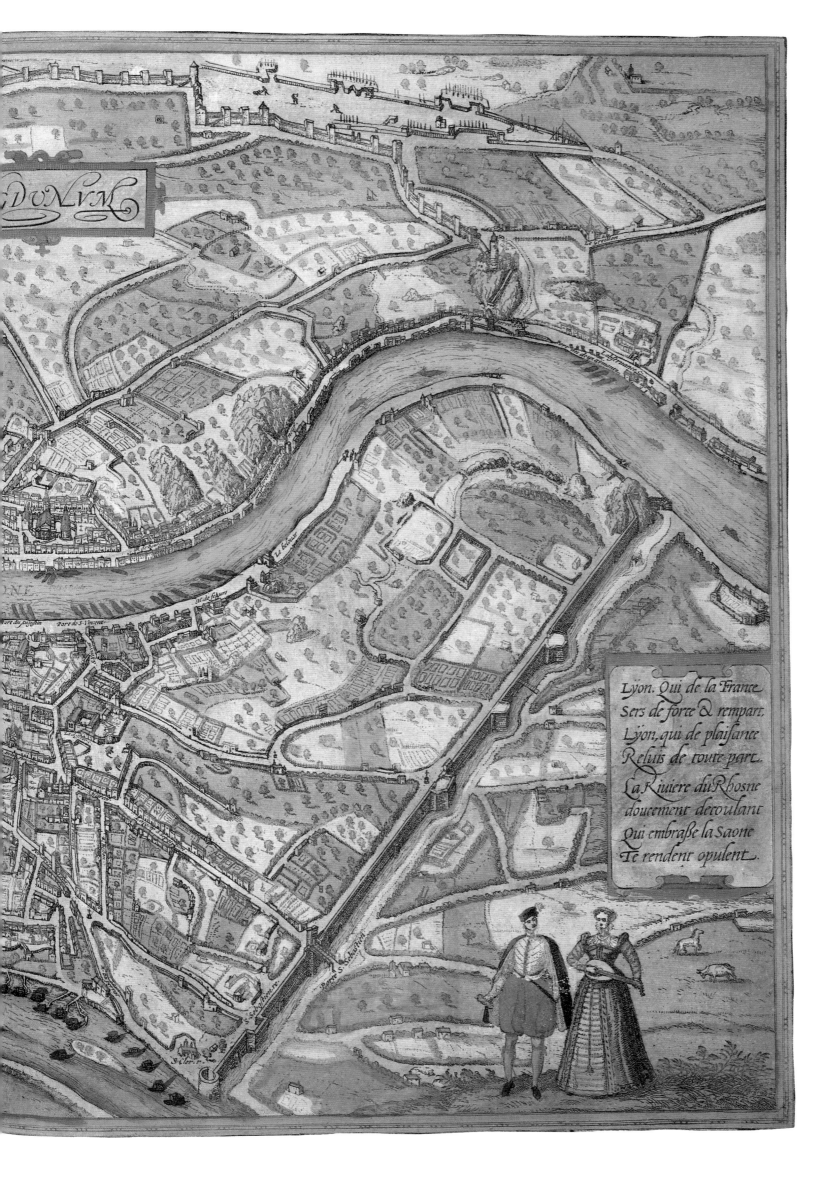

by Charles VII, who had enticed weavers from Lucca, Genoa and Venice to settle there. New fabrics were invented: silks woofed with wool or with gold or silver threads, watered silks, velvets and so on. Upwards of 9,000 looms were in use, rising to 12,000 during the seventeenth century. Printing was also of great importance: Melchior and Gaspar Trechsel, for example, printed folio editions of works such as Ptolemy's *Geographia* there in 1535 and 1541.

The great fairs of Lyons formed an important link between the Hanseatic merchants and the Venetian traders of the Mediterranean shores. Relations with such cities as London (*q.v.*), Antwerp (*q.v.*), Milan (*q.v.*), Venice (*q.v.*), Genoa (*q.v.*), Florence (*q.v.*), Naples (*q.v.*), Seville, Barcelona (*q.v.*) are recorded throughout the sixteenth century.

71

PLATE 33

MARSEILLE
(Marseilles)

Marseille. 1575.
*Volume II, number 12. 320 ×
355mm.*

Probably after Sebastian
Münster, 1575. Marseilles
has the distinction of being
the oldest city in France.
The Greek colony of
Massalia was established by
traders from Phokaia in
Asia Minor in about
600BC, although the
Phoenicians had probably
settled there much earlier.
The great rival of the new
settlement was Carthage,
on the North African coast;
during the Punic Wars,
which ended in the
destruction of Carthage in
146BC, Marseilles took the
side of Rome. During the
Roman period, Marseilles
seems to have held
relatively minor status,
despite Cicero's statement
that without Marseilles'
assistance "Rome never
triumphed over the
Transalpine nations".

Christianity came to
Marseilles at some time
during the third century.
The town was sacked
several times by successive
invaders but, by the tenth
century, it was under the
protection of viscounts. In
the early thirteenth century,
Marseilles became a
republic governed by a
council headed by a *podestat*,
and later by a bishop.

The Crusades brought
prosperity to Marseilles,
though not without
competition from Pisa,
Genoa (*q.v.*) and Venice
(*q.v.*). A period of virtual
independence was ended
when Charles d'Anjou,
Count of Provence,
imposed his authority in
1245 and 1256.
Fortifications were built in
about 1300 and contained
the town for some four
hundred years. The town
was sacked again in 1423 by
Alphonso V of Aragon but
recovered its trade and
commerce soon after,
retaining a certain measure
of independence after the
incorporation of Provence
into France in 1481.

The engraving shows a
harbour defended by fort –
Fort St Jean on the north

A. La loge ou maisõ cõmune de la Ville.
B. Palais ou l'on tient la Cour du Lieutenãt.
C. La grãde Eglise appellee, la Maieur,
    ou est le chef du Lazare.
D. La Cour & cõmanderie de S·Iehan.
E. l'Eglise des accoles, ou Marie Magdel:
    cõmença à prescher la Loy Chrestienne.
    au Roy, & peuple de Marseille, lequel
    elle conuertit, & grand nõbre de peup:
F. Là ou S·Victor fut baptisé. G. l'hospital du S·Esprit
H. Le Monastere des Religieuses de Sion. I. Monast· de S·
    Salueur. K. La chapelle S·Victor aux 4. coings.
L. La place neufue. M. La place de viuaulx.
N. Le grand maseau. O. Le petit maseau
P. La pesquarie. Q. La tour du grand horloge
R. L'acqueduë des fontaines de la Ville
S. Le grand puits. T. La pierre que Raie
V. La tour de. X. Les fourches d'Arenc.

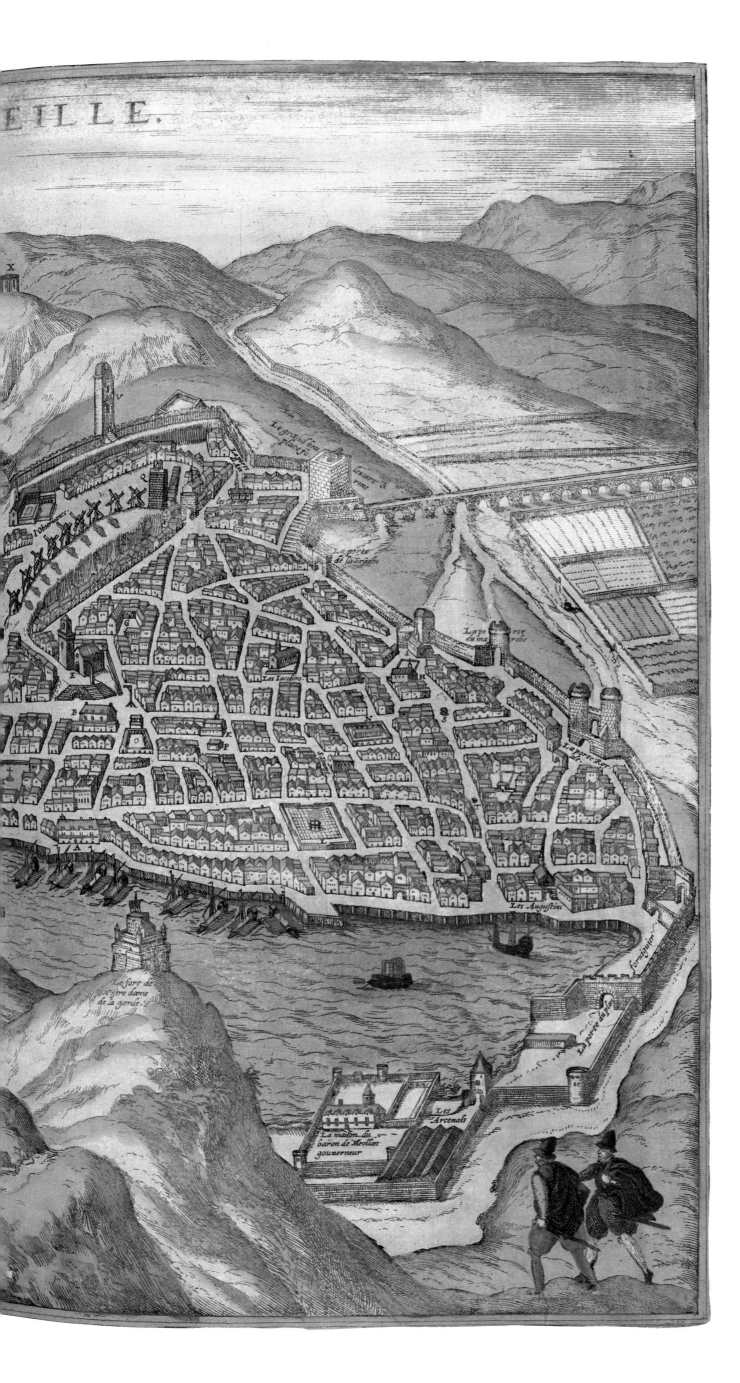

side, and *Fort St Nicolas* on
the south side, with a chain
strung across the harbour
mouth. Little remains of
either the Greek or the
Roman periods, and few
mediaeval buildings have
survived. Most notable is
the twelfth-century
cathedral, *La Major*, (*Ste-
Marie-Majeure*). To the
south, near Fort St Nicolas,
may be seen the thirteenth-
century church of St Victor,
once part of a fourteenth-
century fortress-like abbey;
the eleventh-century crypts
beneath it are said to have
been inhabited by St
Lazaire. The centre of the
old town is marked by the
spire of the ancient church
of *Accoules*. Here also is
*Notre-Dame du Mont
Carmel*, standing on the site
of the citadel of the
Massaliots, built during the
siege of Julius Caesar.

In 1535, an agreement
between France and the
Turks gave Marseille a
foothold in the highly
profitable North African
and Levantine trades, and
prosperity ensued. Situated
at the southern end of the
Rhône valley route via
Lyons (*q.v.*), Marseilles was
well placed to handle trade
in English export cloths.
The French Levantine trade
consisted of raw cotton
from Syria and Asia Minor,
wool from Albania and
Macedonia, silk from the
hosiery manufacturers of
Provence, hides from
North Africa, and olive oil,
grain and coffee. In the
engraving, vessels of a
distinctly Levantine type
may be seen approaching
the harbour, beyond which
may be seen a seine fishing
net in use, a type of vertical
net still in use in the
Mediterranean.

PLATE 34

MILANO
(Milan)

Mediolanum.
Mediolanum Metropolis,
vulgo Milano. 1572.
Volume 1, number 42. 335 ×
480mm.

After Antonio Lafreri,
*c.*1560. Milan, the
Mediolanum of the Celts,
was captured by the
Romans in 222 BC,
remaining in Roman hands
until the fifth century AD.

The Roman city was a
settlement some 549 metres
square. It was not built on a
large river but was,
however, connected to
Lake Como and to the Po,
Adda and other rivers by
streams and canals. From
the Roman period, the city
walls expanded outwards
up until 1200, when it took
nine years to complete new
fortifications. On the death
of Frederick II in 1250 and
the collapse of imperial
power, Milan seemed set to
become the most important
town in Italy. By about
1260, it was certainly the
wealthiest and most
powerful.

The Roman settlement,
barely discernible in the
engraving, was centered
roughly where the *Duomo*,
begun in 1386, now stands.
One of the largest churches
in Europe, it is capable of
holding 40,000 people.

Milan's city centre
remained the *Piazza del
Duomo*, from which streets
can be seen radiating in all
directions. The great castle,
Castel Sforzesco, stands to
the north. It was built by
Francesco Sforza in 1450 on
the site of the earlier castle
of Galeazzo II Visconti that
was demolished in 1477.
The Visconti family, who
controlled Milan from
1287, ruled tyranically over
the city. Their castle thus
protected them as much
against enemies within as
against enemies without.
When they occupied Milan
from 1499 to 1525, the
French had no fear of a
popular uprising and
neither did the Spaniards,

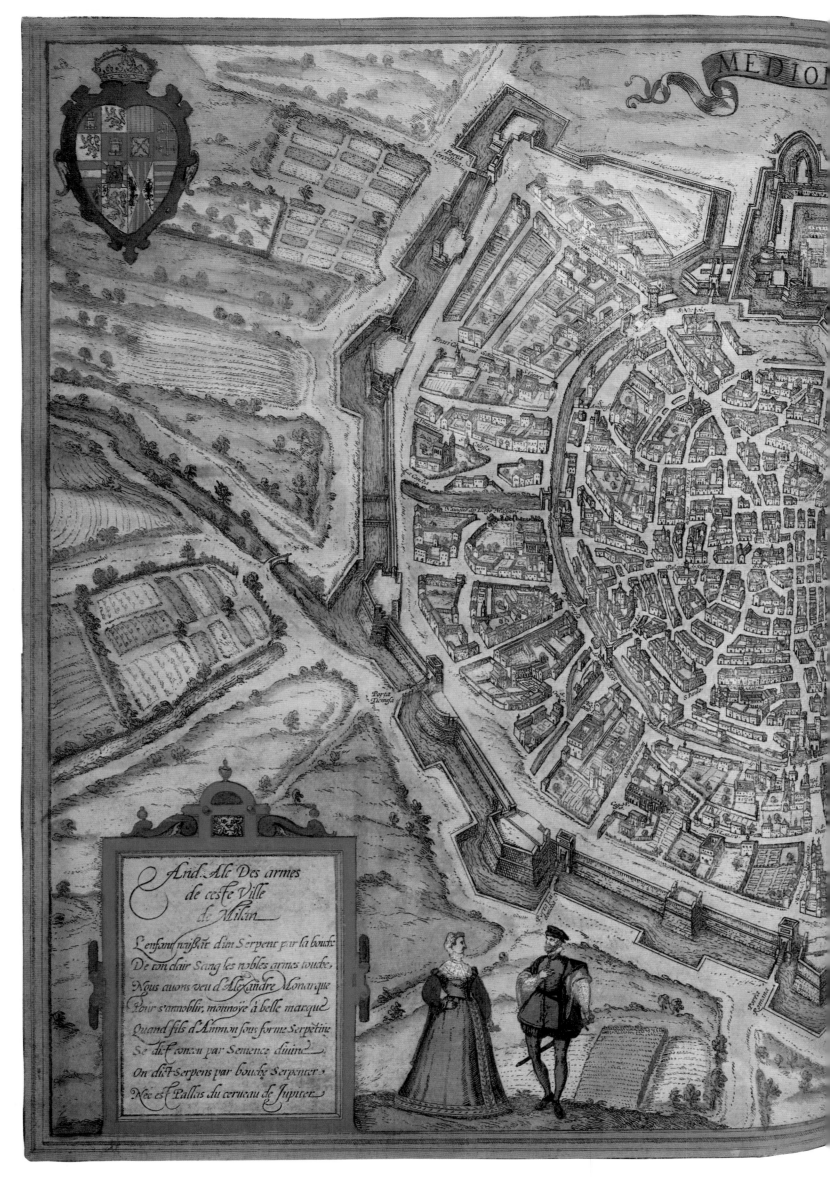

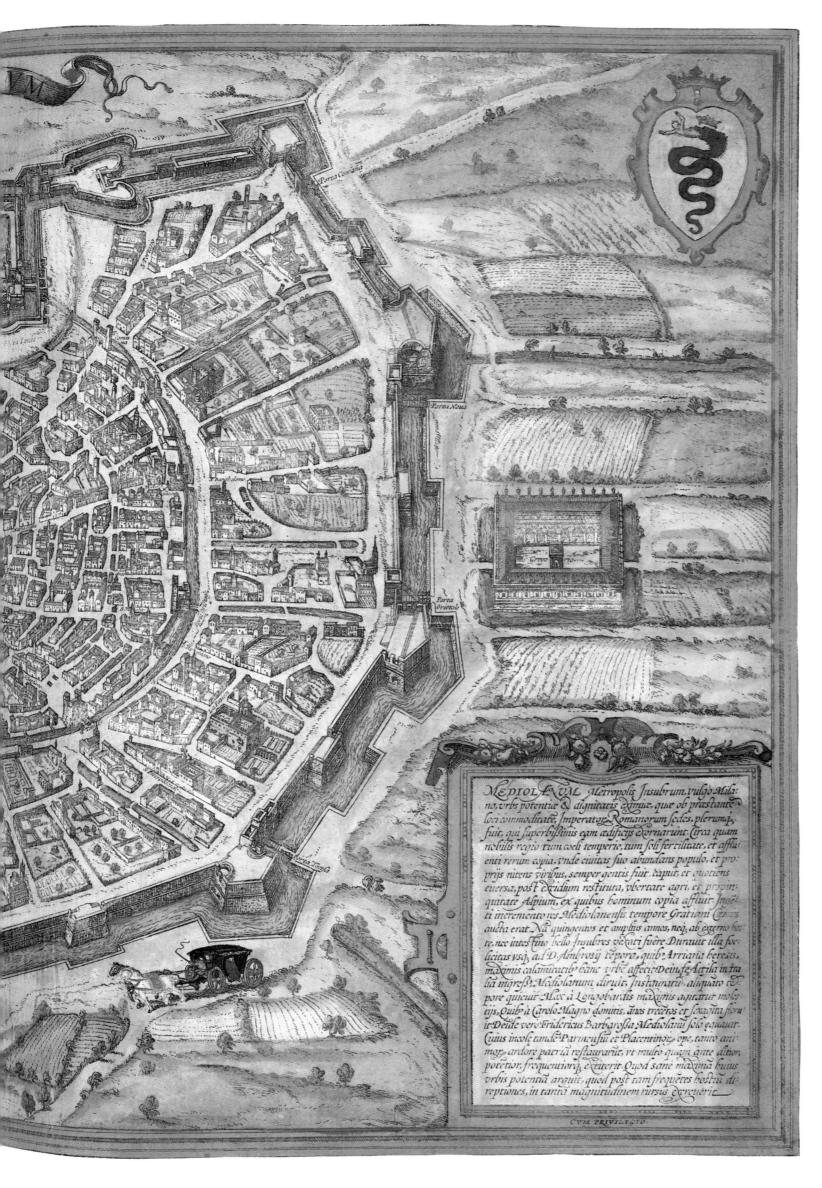

who arrived in 1536 and remained until 1706. Back in the fifteenth century and under the patronage of Ludovico Sforza from 1483 to 1499, Leonardo da Vinci worked on improving Milan, which was beset with pestilence and disease. Under Sforza, the "unsurping ruler of the State . . . It must have been the pestilence decimating Milan in 1484–1485 which gave occasion to the projects submitted by Leonardo . . . for breaking up the city and reconstructing it on sanitary principles". Leonardo's intention was that a hygenic city should be built by grouping its citizens into ten units of 5,000 houses. He sketched a plan in which the circumvallations of *c.*1200 enclosed the proposed city.

Leonardo's own interests in designing healthy town environments may have found greater expression in the *Codex Atlanticus*, in which he evolved a scheme for a beautiful city free of dirt and disease, watered by a beautiful river and canals which would neither flood the countryside nor dry up, and with streets whose width equalled to the average height of the houses, thus allowing lighting and ventilation. Leonardo, however, was centuries ahead of his time and no attempt was made to alter the street plan of Milan until the end of Austrian rule and the unification of Italy in 1870.

PLATE 35

MOSKVA
(Moscow)

**Moscauw. Moscovia,
Urbs regionis eiusde
nominis metropolitica.**
1575.
*Volume II, number 47. 350 ×
495mm.*

After Sigismund von
Herberstein, 1547. This
view is of the old city in and
around the Kremlin. The
nucleus of Moscow was at
the junction of the two
rivers shown here, the
Moskva and the
Neglinnaya, the latter
forming a moat on the
northern and eastern flanks
of the Kremlin.

Moscow was first
mentioned in Russian
annals in 1147. The name
Kremlin first appeared as
kreml' (or high town) in an
account of a fire in the town
in 1331. Until 1367, when
the construction of the
masonry walls began, the
settlement, which was
protected by a wooden
palisade, was called *gorod*
(or fenced-in town).

Outside the moat formed
by the Neglinnaya was a
traders' quarter, protected
by a palisade and later by a
stone wall built in 1534–38.
this led to the area being
called the *Kitai gorod*: it
became the active centre of
commerce and the richest,
but also the most crowded,
part of the town.

As Moscow grew, the
Kremlin became the royal,
religious and secular heart
both of the city and of the
expanding dominions of
Muscovy. For nearly four
hundred years up until the
early eighteenth century,
Moscow was the capital of
Russia, the seat of the
Orthodox faith, the
custodian and guiding
centre of Russian literary
and artistic life, and the
principal commercial
metropolis of the country.

When Tsar Peter I
transferred the seat of his
government from Moscow
to St Petersburg in 1713,
the city lost its status but
became the capital of Russia
once more following the
Revolution of 1917.

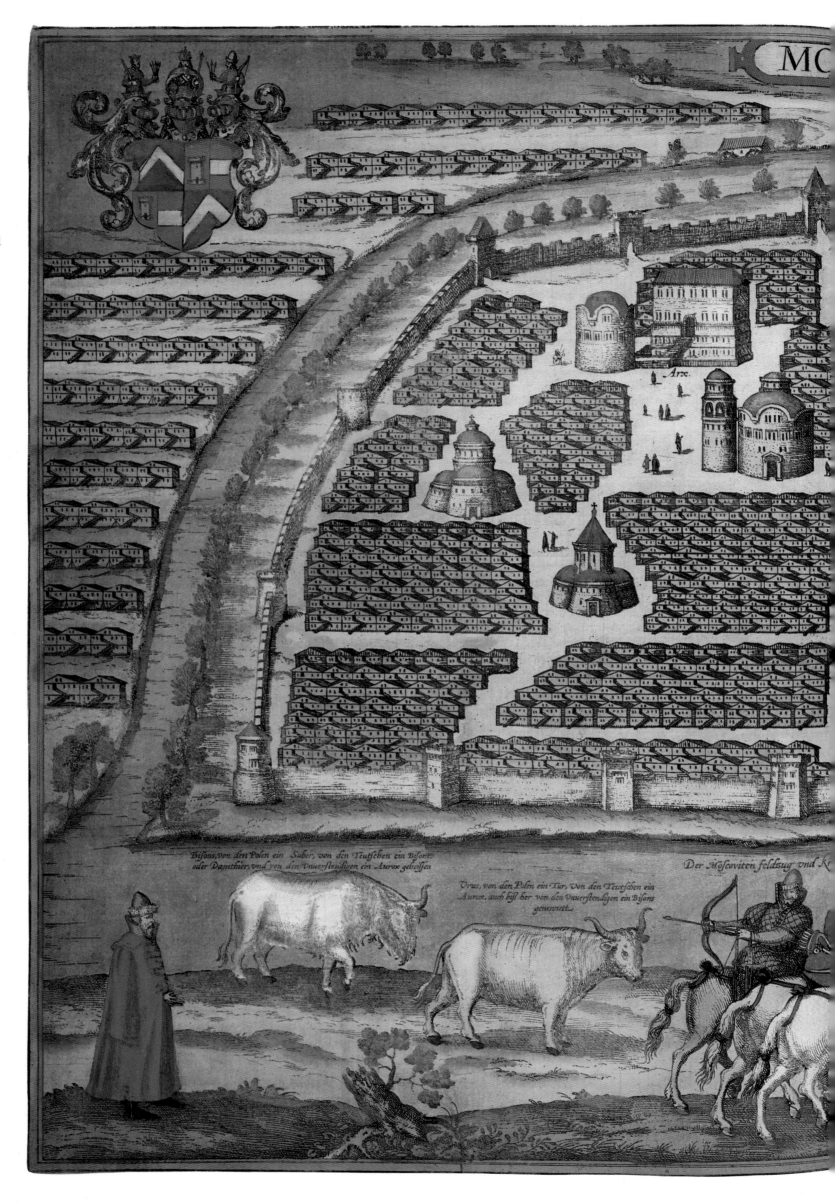

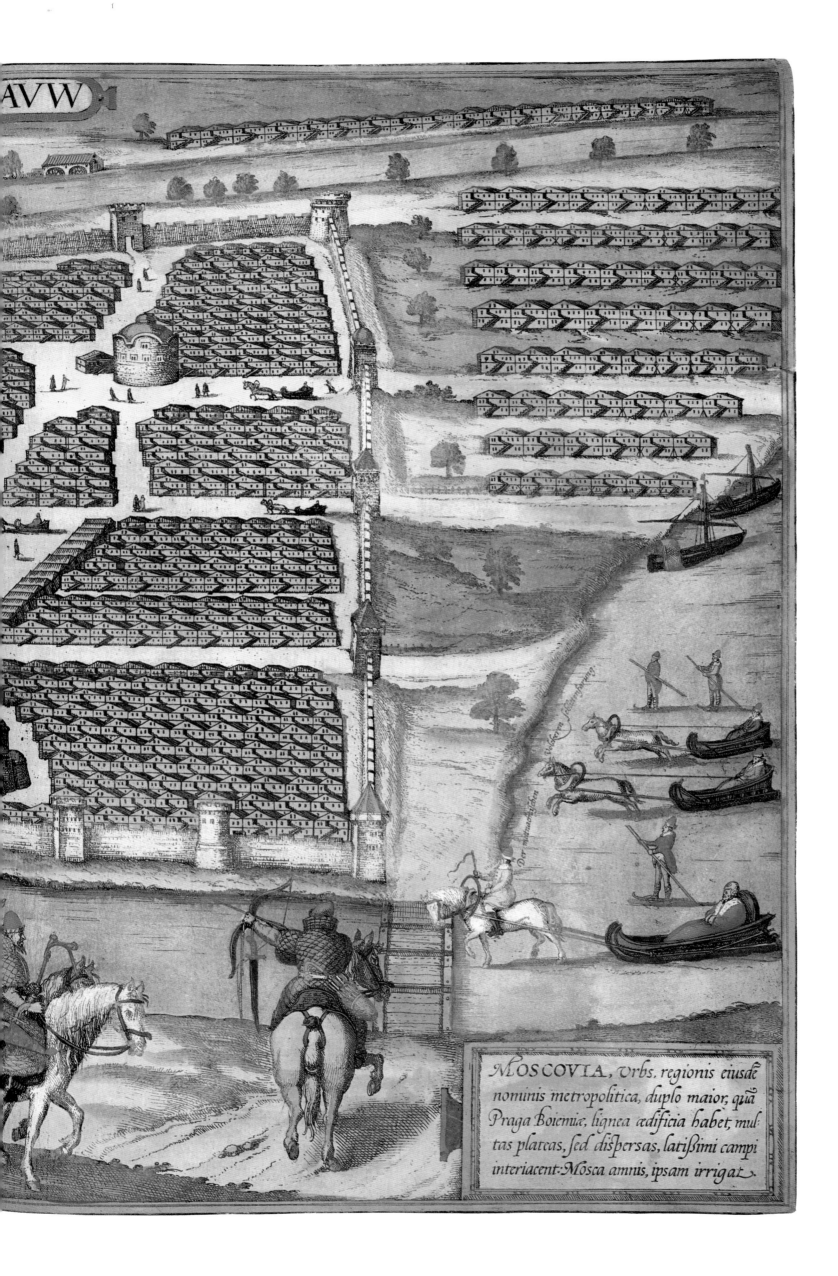

MOSCOVIA, Vrbs. regionis eiusdé
nominis metropolitica, duplo maior, quã
Praga Boiemiæ, lignea ædificia habet, mul-
tas plateas, sed dispersas, latiſſimi campi
interiacent. Mosca amnis, ipsam irrigat.

PLATE 36

MÜNCHEN
(Munich)

Monachium utriusque Bavariae civitas primar . . . Anno dom. M.D. LXXXVI. 1586.
Volume IV, number 43. 282 × 480mm.

After Georg Hoefnagel, 1586. *Forum ad monachos*, so named after the monks on whose land Munich was built, was founded by Henry the Lion (1129–95), Duke of Saxony and Bavaria, in 1158. He sought to profit from the lucrative salt trade (commemorated in the *Salzstraße*) between Austria, southern Germany, Swabia and Switzerland. In 1255 Duke Ludwig of Bavaria made Munich his residence, having fortified and moated the town. A fire almost destroyed the town in 1327, but it was rebuilt at the orders of Emperor Ludwig in the form which Munich retained down to the nineteenth century.

This view shows Munich from a point downstream across the Isar, looking roughly northwest towards the twin towers of the celebrated *Frauenkirche* (1466–92), symbol of Munich in all its modest grandeur. The church was built at the behest of Bishop Konrad of Freising sometime after 1271. At that time probably 5,000 or 6,000 citizens occupied the part of the town bounded by the *Alter Hof*, the *Peterkirche* and the *Frauenkirche*, itself on the lines of the old walls, which date from before 1253. These may be traced on old plans by the *Färbergraben*, *im Rosen Thal*, *Augustiner Gasse* and so on. The marshy river terrace protected the Isar frontage

A. *Waßer Thurn.*
B. *Geißingen.*
C. *Die Aw.*
D. *Alpes noricæ.*
E. *Isara ffu.*
L. *S. Saluator oder newe Goites Acker.*
M. H. *Ferdinandus Lustgartten.*
N. S. *Jacob oder Vrawen Closter zu Auger.*
O. *S Peters Goites Acker vnd Brouderhaus.*
P. *Iser Thor.*
Q. *Heiliger Geist vnd Spital.*
R. *S Peters Pfarkirchen.*
F. *Talkirchn.*
G. *Vnter Sentling.*
H. *Ober Sentling.*
I. *Zimmer Stadel.*
K. *Die Lende.*

MONAC
BAVARIA

IN LAVDĒ CIVITAT: MONACHIĒ: ANÇELMI
STÖCKLII EQVITIS ICOSITETRASTICHON.
Aspice turritis Incinctam mœnibus vrbem,
Aspice Boiarici metropolimque Soli.
Indigitata quidem Monachi de nomine claret,
Pandiculans Monachus Symbolon estq̃ loci
Ædibus eximijs, mundis plateisque, prealtis
Vrbs decus ostentat turribus ampla suum.
Circumit vndiuago ratiger pomœria tractu
ISARA, qui paßim flexus In vrbe fluit.
Islimis manat fabrefactis fontibus vnda
Vrbis et ornata gratia nulla deest.
Sed decus accumulat, noua que modo fabrica surgit
Vt, quæ visa fuit, non videatur ea.

SEN
PRINC
.D. G
COMI
VTRIVSQ BAV
CLEMENTISS:
SVI MONVM:

UTRIVSQVE
TAS PRIMAR

S. *Rats Thurn.*
T. *Schön Thurn.*
V. *S. Augustin.*
X. *Der Landtschaft.*
Y. *Vnser Frawen Pfarrkirch.*
Z. *Alten hoff.*
AA. *Alten Hoff kirchen.*
1. *Newe Stalling.*
2. *Konst Camer.*
3. *S. Francisc. oder barfüßer.*
4. *Vnser Frawen Gottes acker*
5. *Libere∫ vnd Antiquarei.*
6. *Jager Puchl.*
7. *Newevest.*   9. *Vnter bläich.*
8. *Hoffgartten.* 10. *Schloß dachaw.*

SIMO
DOMINO
ELMO
RHENI
DVCI DŌTO SVO
MILLIMI OBSEQVII
HOEFNAGLIVS D.

Nil tamen exornat mage prestantißima, diuis
Proxime, quàm virtus, DVX GVILIELME tua.
Quin etiam posuere suas hic numina Sedes
Pallas, Atlantiades, Pieriusque chorus.
Relligio, pietasque, fides, Astræa moratur
Hic, venerandorum docta caterna patrum.
Hesperus vt rutilans presulget in æthere stellis,
Sidera consimili nulla nitore micant:
Sic vrbs hæc alias superat splendore, vel ullus
Qua princeps habitat, Teutonis ora, tuus.
Effigiauit eam Solers Hoefnaglius, vnde
Vrbis adaugescit gloria, nomen, honor.
Anno doñi. CIƆ. IƆ. LXXXVI.

of the town. Also seen here is the bridge erected across the Isar and connecting Munich with Salzburg and the Tirol.

New walls were built in the fourteenth century by Ludwig, Emperor from 1328 to 1347, who was preoccupied with the idea of making Munich the capital of the Holy Roman Empire. This his successor, Charles IV, achieved at Prague (*q.v.*), in Bohemia. The only expansion that Munich underwent up until 1789 was the extension of the *Hofgarten* on the northeastern side – seen in the trees in the right of the view. In order to protect the road and buildings betwen the *Rathaus* and the *Marienplatz* and the river bridge, the walls were extended in a projection ending in the *Isartor* guarding the street called *im Thal Maria Petri*. Later in the fifteenth century these fortifications were strengthened by an outer bastion, all of which were removed early in the nineteenth century.

Munich illustrates the way in which many European cities grew when they became so crowded that additional ground was needed to accommodate an expanding population. Until long-range artillery made city walls ineffective, defensive fortifications usually followed a circle or semi-circle as the best way of enclosing a space.

Munich has long been celebrated for its artistic crafts – bronze-founding, glass-staining, silver and goldsmiths' work, wood-carving, and scientific, mathematical and astronomical instrument-making.

PLATE 37

NAPOLI
(Naples)

Haec est nobilis, & florens illa Neapolis, Campaniae civitas. 1572. *Volume I, number 47. 335 × 480mm.*

After Antonio Lafreri, 1566. Throughout its long history, Naples has been renowned for its magnificent setting on the shores of a bay dominated by the brooding Mount Vesuvius, some 13 kilometres distant.

Naples is an old city. According to Livy, *Palaeopolis* (Old Town) was settled in around 600BC by inhabitants of Kyme, the oldest Greek colony in Italy, which was founded around 800BC, some 19 kilometres to the west. In 328BC, Palaeopolis was sacked by the Romans in revenge for its incursions into the settlement of the Campanian allies of Rome and its refusal to surrender.

During the fifth century BC, colonists from Greece itself formed *Neapolis* (or New Town) on a gridiron plan which can still to some extent be traced in the engraving. It may have been influenced by the work of Hippodamus of Miletus, the fifth-century Greek architect who introduced a particular system of town planning involving a series of straight streets intersecting each other at right angles. By 400BC the town was the economic capital of Campania, becoming a Roman *municipium* in 82BC, when it surrendered without resistance – and therefore sacking – to Sulla. In later years, Naples became a kind of resort for wealthy and aristocratic Romans – Lucullus, Piso, Pompey, Caesar and Virgil, among many others.

As in most European cities, society in Naples comprised an upper class of nobles and wealthy merchants; *la milizia*, a hereditary middle class; and *il popolo*, the lower classes, consisting of

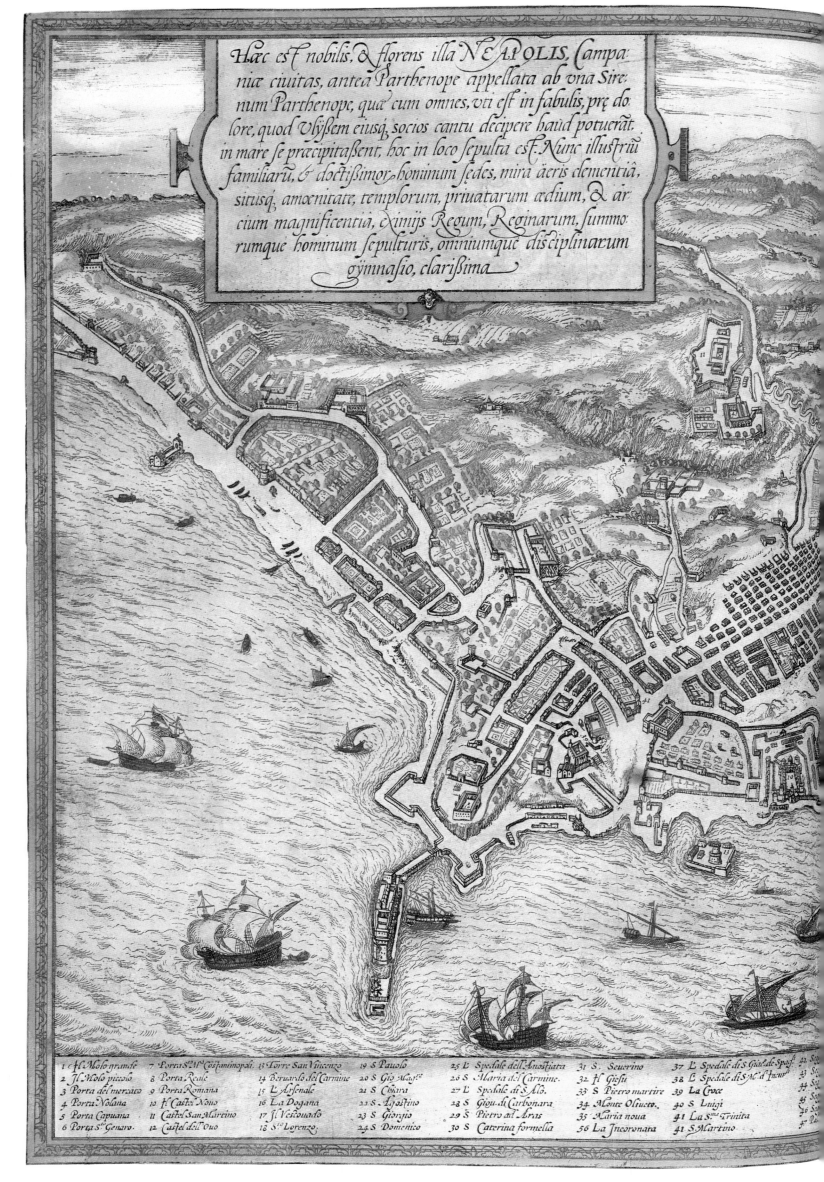

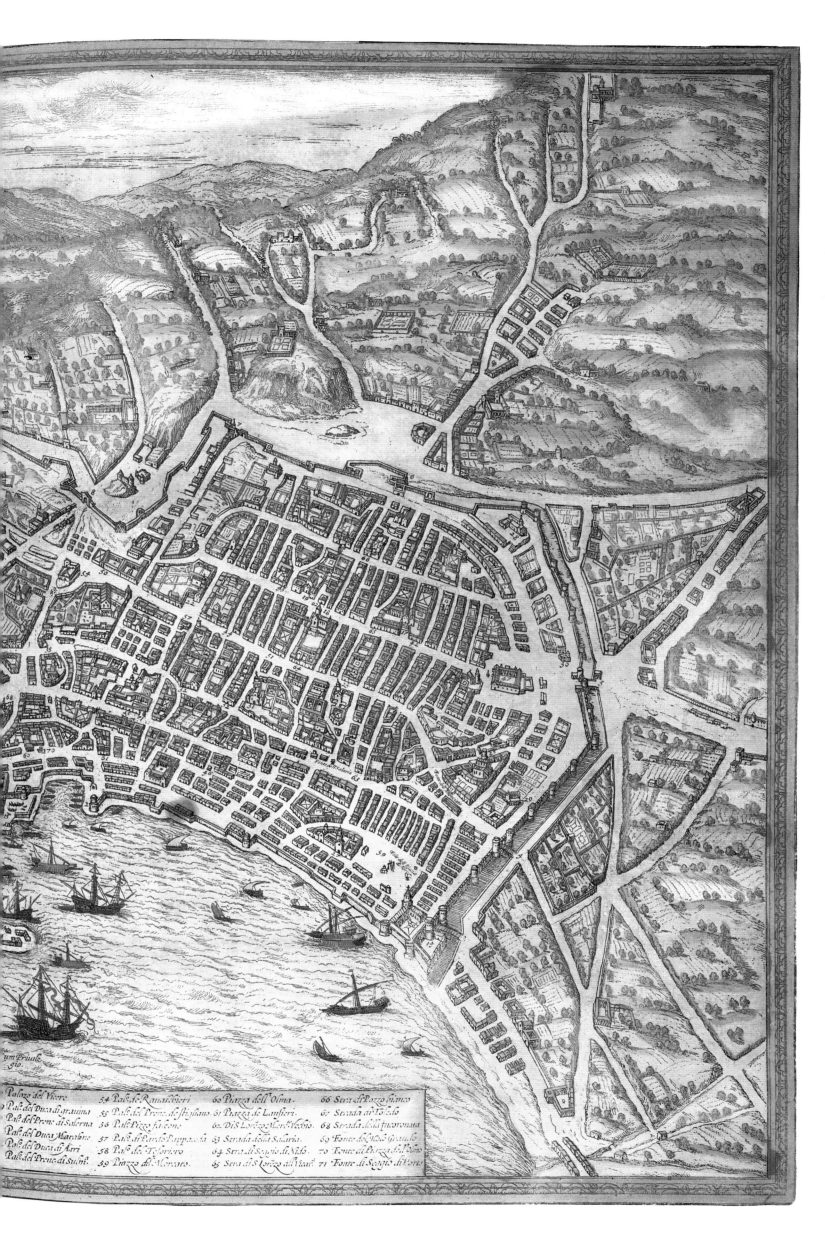

tradespeople, each trade being concentrated in a single street or recognised quarter. Foreign merchants were allocated their own quarters in the city.

In the sixth century, bishops had supreme authority and in the eighth century dukes assumed this role. After the twelfth century, Naples was ruled by various foreign powers. However, although most made a certain contribution to the fabric of the city, little in the way of systematic planning seems to have been undertaken. Under Alfonso II of the Aragonese dynasty, an ambitious plan was undertaken to enlarge the city by extending the gridiron street plan. Other works concerned the elimination of porches, corners and projecting parts, the construction of an aqueduct, the building of fountains and public places at intersections, the erection of a large building for royal administrative functions, and the reconstruction of the fortifications. It is largely this city then, remodelled between 1488 and 1499, that we see in the engraving.

PLATE 38

NEUSS, BONN, BRÜHL and ZONS

Novesium, vulgo Neuss . . . A[nn]o D[omi]ni M.D.L.XXV [with] *Verona, nunc Bonna, communiter Bonn . . . illustre 1573* [with] *Brula, vulari idiomate. Broell. 1573* [with] *Sontina, Zunss . . . 1575.* 1575. *Volume II, number 33. 115 × 465mm, 104 × 470mm, 102 × 225mm and 102 × 228mm respectively.*

Sources unknown. Several plates in the *Civitates* series combine two or more subjects; four towns are shown here – Neuss, Bonn, Brühl and Zons. Of these, the best known today is, of course, Bonn, a handsome provincial city elevated to the rank of national capital.

Bonn, *Castra Bonnensia* to the Romans, is frequently mentioned by Tacitus. It was the site of a fierce battle in AD70 in which the Batavii defeated the Romans; it was restored by Julian in *c*.359, sacked by the Norsemen in 889 and fortified by Archbishop Konrad von Hochstaden of Cologne (*q.v.*) from 1238–61. His successor, Engelbert von Falkenberg (*d*.1274), was expelled from Cologne in 1265 whereupon his seat was established at Bonn. From 1265 to 1794, Bonn was the residence of the electors of Cologne. It was graced by several imposing churches: the *Münster*, dating from the eleventh to thirteenth centuries, and the *Minoritenkirche*, built between 1278 and 1318, to mention but two. Bonn was also the city of Beethoven.

Neuss, *Novaesium* of the Romans, like Bonn, of which Tacitus wrote, is close to the Rhine. Drusus, brother of Tiberius, built a bridge across the river here. His name is preserved in the *Drusustor*, part of which contains Roman masonry. In 1474–75, Charles the

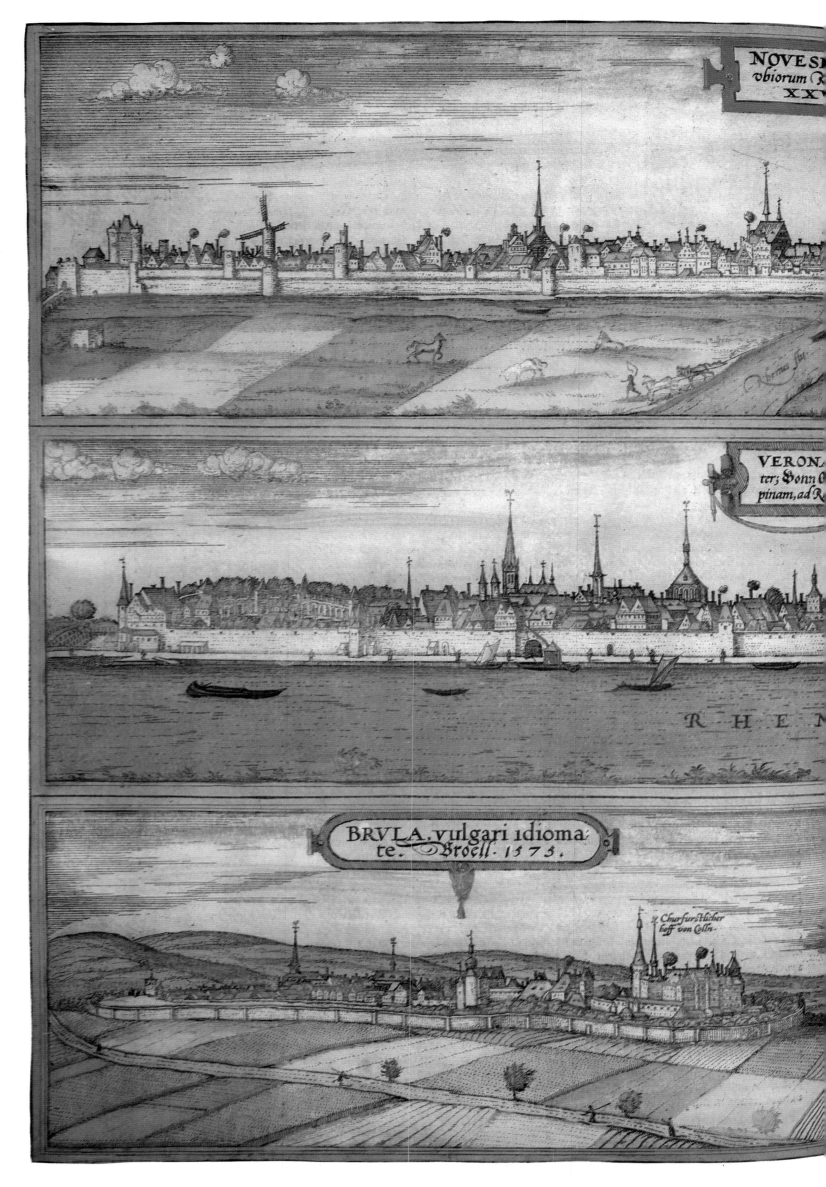

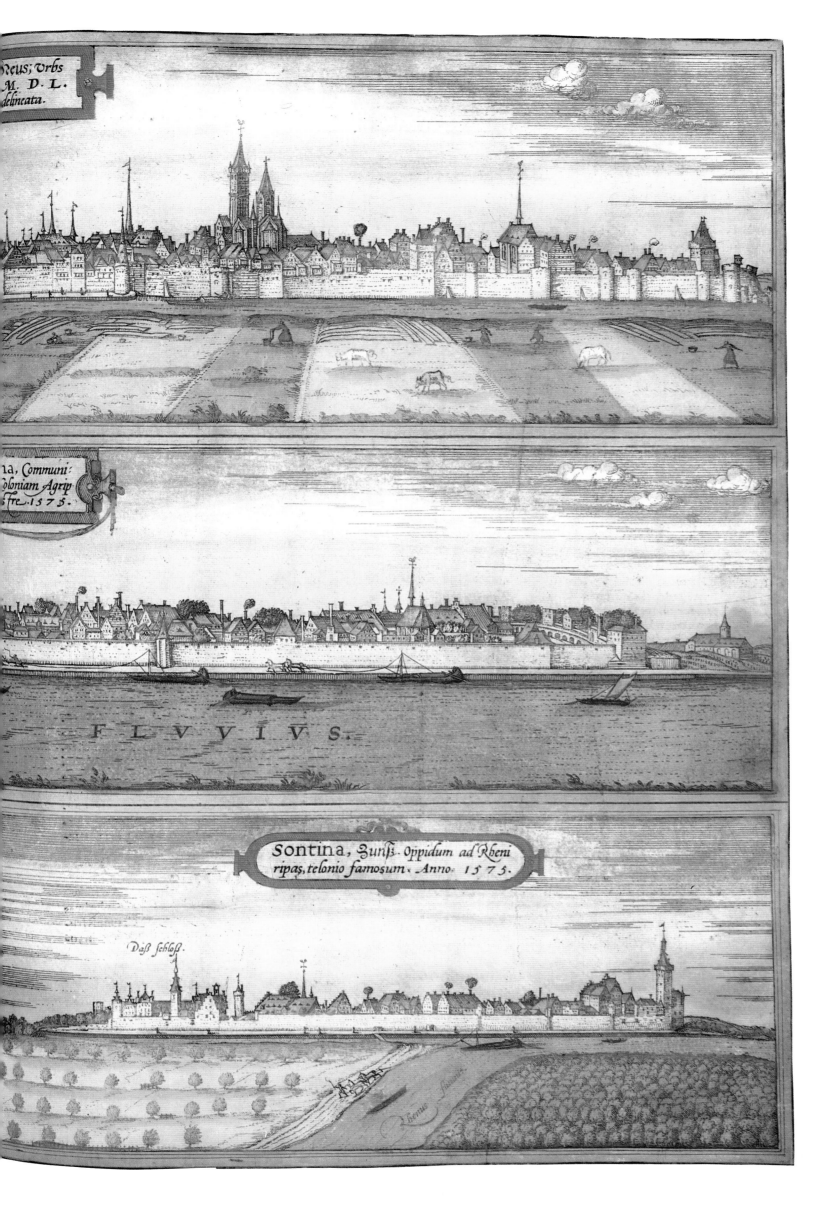

Neuss, Vrbs ... M. D. L. ... delineata.

... la, Communi: ... oloniam Agrip ... fue. 1575.

FLVVIVS.

Sontina, Zuriß. Oppidum ad Rheni ripas, telonio famosum. Anno. 1575.

Daß schloß.

Bold of Burgundy laid siege to the city for the eleven months, during which he lost some 10,000 men. Neuss was captured and sacked by Alexander Farnese in 1584, shortly before this view was published. A prominent feature of the town is the *St Quirinus*.

Brühl was a favourite resort of the electors of Cologne; the fact is recorded by the text (*Churfurstlicher hoff von Colln*) that appears next to the castle that dominates this view of the walled town. In the hinterland may be seen the hills of the Eifel range.

83

PLATE 39

NÜRNBERG
(Nuremberg)

Nurnberg. Norenberga urbis nobilissima . . . Cornelius Chaÿmox . . . promovit. 1575.
Volume II, number 43. 305 × 490mm.

After Cornelius Chaÿmox. This is one of the loveliest of the views and plans in the *Civitates* series, prized almost as much as a costume plate as a topographical view of Nuremberg. The city is viewed here from the southeast. It was first mentioned in 1040 during the time of Henry III, when the town received an imperial grant to establish a market and a mint.

Under the protection of the castle, two royal courts developed which served as the centres around which settlements grew. Around one, in the eleventh and twelfth centuries, was established a community of imperial administrative officers who built the *St Sebaldus*, dedicated in 1274 (seen near the centre of the view). Around the other court arose an early settlement of merchants and craftsmen who chose *St Lorenz* as the patron saint of their church, remodelled in the thirteenth and fourteenth centuries (seen to the left of centre).

As late as the fourteenth century, the Lorenz district was referred to as *civitas*, while the Sebaldus closest to the castle was known as *oppidum*. Each had an aristocratic monastery – *St Aegidius* in the Sebaldus district, and *St Jakobus* in the Lorenz settlement. These were given to the Teutonic Order by Henry VI in 1209, remaining there until 1803, the only Roman Catholic enclave in the Lutheran city. Between the two settlements, the upper and the lower, was a marshy tract through which

Die feßten   Das Lugnis landt   Iner lauffer durn

S. Dießling

Lauffer dor

flowed the Pegnitz. The areas was later graced with mills, houses and bridges, and a hospital endowed by Konrad Gross, the wealthiest merchant and mayor of the town.

Nuremberg was, therefore, two cities in one. The free city had developed in the shadow of a heavily fortified castle, some two hundred metres long, which remained little changed until the Second World War.

The prosperity of the city reached its zenith during the sixteenth century. Like Augsburg (*q.v.*), Nuremberg acted as an intermediary between Italy and northern Europe. Its trade, industry and inventiveness were indeed so greatly renowned that the old proverb "Nürnberg's hand goes through every land" was coined. Its merchant and banking families controlled the economy of Maximilian's empire to such an extent that the city was able to pay for an army of 6,000 troops. At its height, Nuremberg rivalled Cologne (*q.v.*) to the west. As early as 1400 there are thought to have been as many as 20,000 inhabitants.

The great glory of Nuremberg lies in its claim to be the fount of German art, architecture, sculpture, painting and printing. The artists Dürer and Wohlgemuth, for example, lived here and it was here that Hartmann Schedel's *Liber chronicarum*, the greatest illustrated history of the world of its day, was printed by Anton Koberger in 1493. Adam Krafft, Veit Stoss and Peter Vischer, the great triumvirate of sculptors, adorned many buildings with their work. Here also were Wenzel Jamnitzer, famed as a silversmith, and Hans Sachs, the *meistersinger* immortalised by Wagner.

PLATE 40

ODENSE

Civitatis episcopalis Othenarum sive Otthoniae, ut vulgo dicitur, Fioniae, insularum Daniae regni amoenissimae fertilissimaeque metropolis secundem . . . M D LXXXXIII.
1598.
Volume V, number 30. 321 × 470mm.

After Heinrich von Rantzau, 1593. Odense apparently derives its name from Odin, the Norse god. One of the oldest settlements in Denmark, it predates the Vikings, evidence of which may be seen in the circular fortified settlement of *Nonnebakken*, shown as *locus Nundeberrig* in the foreground of the engraving.

Odense was a place of pilgrimage to the shrine of King Knud, who was murdered here, and canonised in 1101. Odense was made a bishopric in 1020; the cathedral (C in the

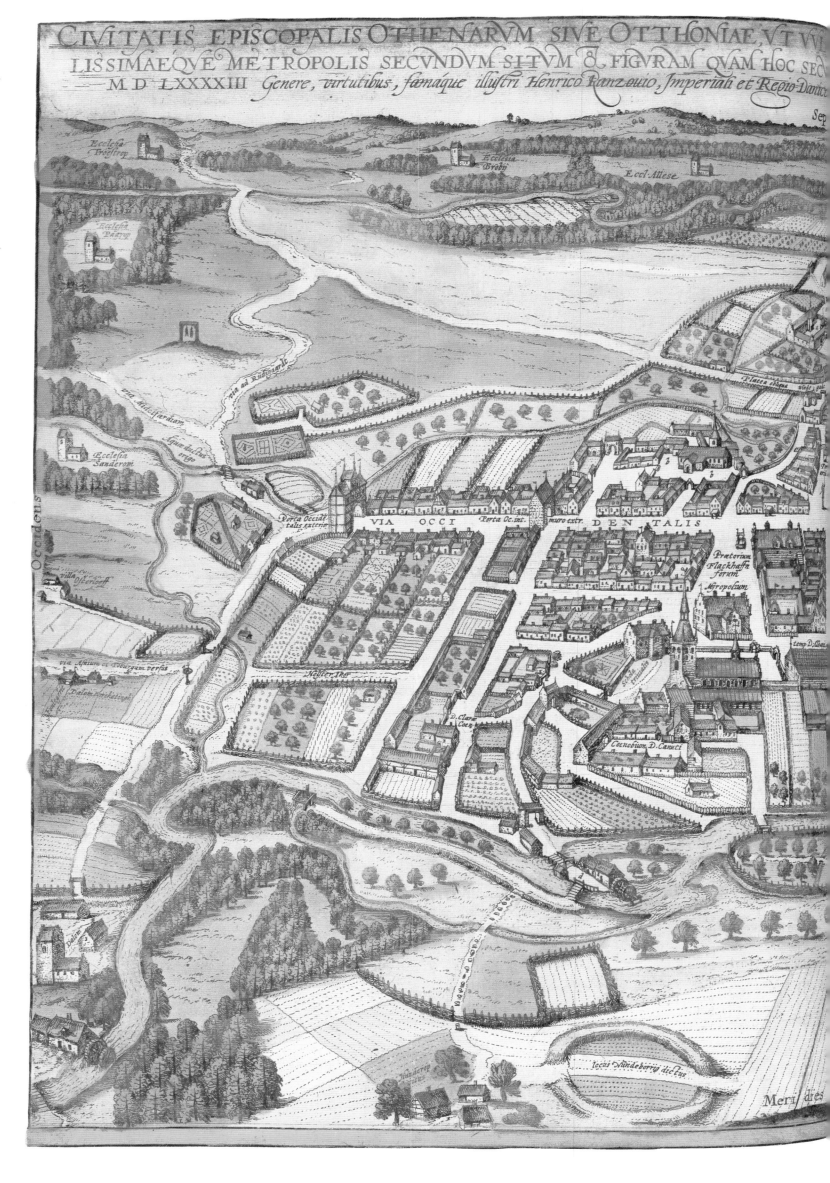

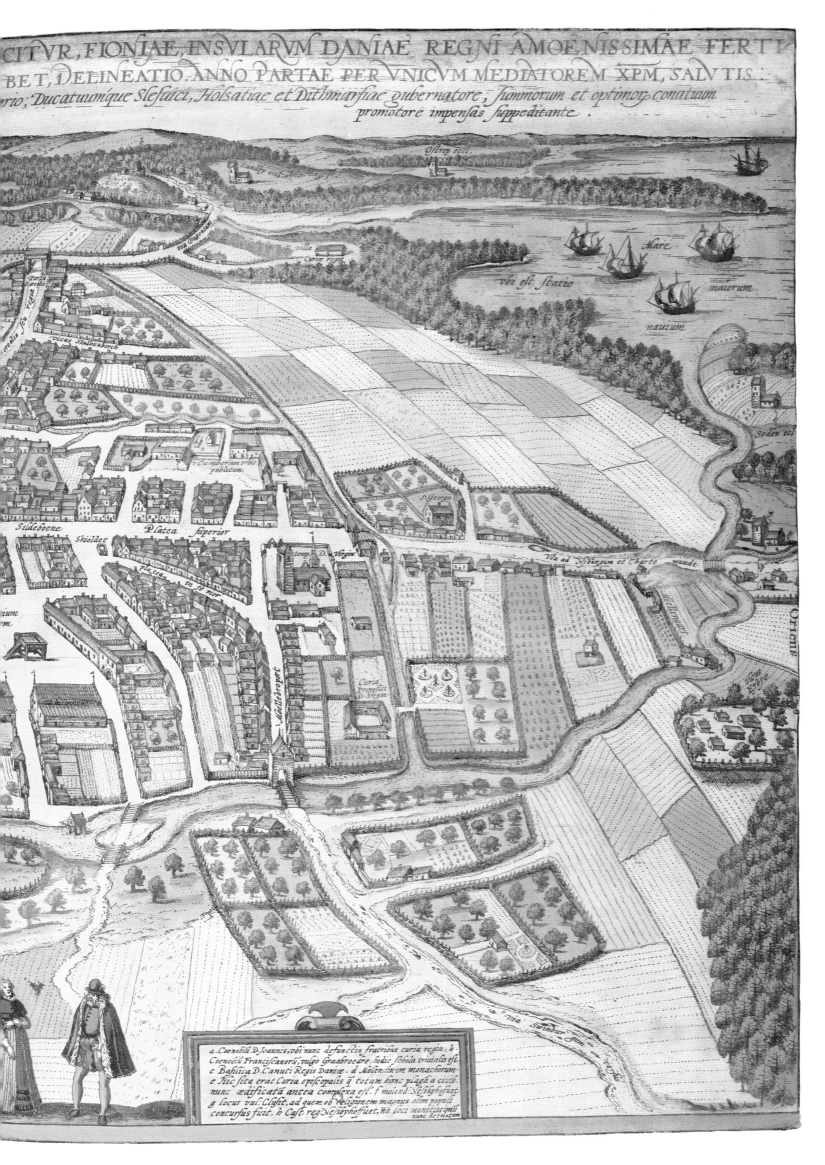

CITVR, FIONIAE, INSVLARVM DANIAE REGNI AMOENISSIMAE FERT[...]
BET, DELINEATIO ANNO PARTAE PER VNICVM MEDIATOREM XPM, SALVTIS [...]
[...]rio; Ducatuumque Slefuici, Holsatiae et Dithmarsiue gubernatore; Summorum et optimor conatuum promotore impensas suppeditante.

engraving) was begun in the thirteenth century and completed during the fifteenth century, and houses Knud's shrine. Near the cathedral is the monastery dedicated to Knud and the *Skt Albanikirke*, now vanished, where Knud met his death.

Also near the cathedral is the old school – *schola trivialis* in the engraving – and a representation of the four main quarters of the inner city: the cathedral and its close; the market square (*Forum Regium sive novum*); the gallows and fishmarket (*Forum Justiarum et piscarium*); and the *Flackhaffn*, with the town hall (*praetorium*).

Other features of Odense depicted here are several of the monks' watermills (D), spanning the Odense Å on the southern side, the royal castle at Næsbyhoved (*Nessbyhoffvet*), abandoned in 1583, and a view of the fjord and several surrounding villages on Fyn island, seen on the horizon.

PLATE 41

ORLÉANS AND BOURGES

Orléans [with] ***Bourges.***
1575.
*Volume II, number 10. Two
subjects on one plate, 175 ×
470mm., and 197 × 470mm.
respectively.*

After Georg Hoefnagel,
from the 1560s. The site of
Orléans, on the north bank
of the Loire between
northern and southern
Gaul, seems to have been a
trading post of some sort
from early times. When
conquered by Rome it was
known as *Cenabum*, but was
renamed *Aurelianum*, in the
imperial province of Gallia
Lugdunensis. Attila
unsuccessfully laid siege to
it in 451 and was driven off
by Aetius. The Saxons,
under Odoacer, also failed
in 471 but, in 498, Orléans
fell to Clovis, who held the
first ecclesiastical council in
France there in 511.

For a century Orléans was
the capital of a separate
kingdom before being
united with Paris in 613.
Fire destroyed much of the
town in 999; it was rebuilt
and became one of the finest
cities of mediaeval France.
Part of the royal domain,
Orléans was the seat of
several kings of France,
some of whom were
crowned there. It also
possessed a royal mint and
was granted a university
charter in 1309. Orléans
was attacked by the
Burgundians and by the
English early in the
fifteenth century, the siege
being raised after Joan of
Arc entered the city in the
spring of 1429. Orléans
later became a centre of
Protestantism in France.
During the so-called Wars
of Religion, Orléans was
besieged by François, Duke
of Guise, who held the
bridgehead on the left bank.

This view, drawn from a
point across the Loire,
shows Orléans as a strongly
fortified city, with walls
and turrets – demolished
between 1563 and 1566 –
still intact, and the *Sainte-
Croix* cathedral (marked as
L'eglise de la S. croije),
which was burned down by
the Huguenots in 1567.

Bourges was built on the

site of the Gallic town of
Avaricum, which was
protected by marshy
ground at the confluence of
the Yèvre and several small
rivers and rivulets. It is
mentioned in Caesar's
Gallic Wars as one of the
most important towns in
Gaul. It was razed to the
ground in 52BC but rose
again to prominence under
Augustus as the capital of
Aquitania Prima. A
bishopric was established in
AD250, Ursinus being the
first bishop.

During the Middle Ages,
Bourges became capital of
the province of Berry and
the residence of Charles VII
during the English
occupation of France in the
fifteenth century. A
university was founded by
Louis XI in 1463, which
long enjoyed an unrivalled
reputation for its faculty of
law.

In this view by Hoefnagel
Bourges is dominated by
the cathedral of St Étienne,
begun in the twelfth
century and completed
during the sixteenth. In
addition, the palace of the
merchant Jacques Cœur (*La
maison Jaques Cœur*) is
indicated; it is possibly the
finest surviving example of
Gothic domestic
architecture in northern
Europe. Cœur was a native
of Bourges, born *c.*1400,
who went to the Levant in
1432, establishing a highly
profitable trade in precious
metals, cloths and the
transport of pilgrims to and
from Jerusalem; he also
negotiated favourable trade
terms with the merchants of
Egypt and Syria on behalf
of Charles VII. Cœur
married into the aristocracy
and saw his son enthroned
as archbishop of Bourges.
The *Palais de Jacques Cœur*
was begun in 1443 as a
residence and place of
business. *A vaillant cœur rien
impossible* was his motto:
"Rich as Jacques Cœur"
went the saying. Cœur
inevitably fell into
disfavour; in 1451 his
possessions were
confiscated and he was
imprisoned, but he escaped
to Rome in 1453. He died
on Chios in 1456, his palace
in the interim having been
converted for use as a town
hall and courthouse.

PLATE 42

OXFORD AND WINDSOR

Oxonium, nobile Angliae oppidum [with] ***Vindesorium celeberrimum Angliae castrum.*** 1575.
Volume II, number 2. 180 × 480mm and 178 × 480mm.

After Georg Hoefnagel, *c*.1560s. As with its great rival, the university town of Cambridge (*q.v.*), relatively little of the early municipal history of Oxford is known. Also like that of Cambridge, the foundation of Oxford's university is alleged to lie in legend. The city's name first appears as *Oxnaford* in 912, in the *Anglo-Saxon Chronicle*, literally meaning a ford for oxen, although the *ox-* element has also been connected with a Celtic word meaning water. As a militery stronghold, Oxford was the chief fort of the Thames valley; it sustained attacks from the Danes, was burned down in 979, 1002 and 1010, and was chosen by King Cnut as the seat of confirmation of Edgar's Law by the Danes and the English in 1020.

The university probably originated in the organised theological lectures given here by Robert Pullen in 1133, although schools were also attached to the great religious houses at Osney and St Frideswide. This view shows Oxford from the north, without many of the "dreaming spires" that were yet to grace the townscape. The colleges extant in the 1560s, when Hoefnagel visited, were: *All Souls* (1433: founded by Henry Chicheley, Archbishop of Canterbury); *Balliol* (*c*.1263: by John de Baliol, later organised by his widow in 1269); and *Brasenose* (1509: by William Smith, Bishop of Lincoln). Here, Robert Burton, author of *Anatomy of Melancholy*, who wrote in praise of the *Civitates*, was an undergraduate in 1593. Then followed *Christ Church* (1546: by Henry VIII as the reformation of an earlier foundation);

Corpus Christi (1516: by Richard Fox, Bishop of Winchester); *Exeter College* (1314: by Walter Stapeldon, Bishop of Exeter); *Lincoln College* (1427: by Richard Flemyng, Bishop of Lincoln); *Magdalen College* (1458: by William of Waynflete); *Merton College* (1274: by grants given by Walter de Merton); *New College* (1379: by William of Wykeham); *Oriel College* (1326: by Edward II); *Queen's College* (1340–41: by Robert de Eglesfield, chaplain to Philippa, Queen-Consort of Edward III); *St John's College* (1555: by Sir Thomas White); *Trinity College* (1555: by Sir Thomas Pope); and *University College* (872: claimed as such, statutes were issued in 1249 in the will of William of Durham and, in 1280, the first statutes of governance were issued).

The view below shows Windsor from the north and easily recognisable today; it has been the residence of English sovereigns at least since the Norman Conquest.

PLATE 43

PADOVA
(Padua)

Patavium nobilissima et litterarum studiis florentissima Italiae civitas. 1617.
Volume VI, number 55. 386 × 486mm.

From an unidentified source. Padua, long claimed to be the oldest city in northern Italy, is said to have been founded by the Trojan, Antenor. Padua quickly became a prosperous and thriving city on the plains west of Venice (*q.v.*), famous for the horses bred there and the quality of its wool. Padua suffered severely during the invasions of Attila the Hun in 452: it then passed to the Goths, Odoacer and Theodoric, and was returned to the Eastern Empire in 568. As in much of northern Italy, there then followed a succession of different rulers: the Lombards and the Franks, bishops, the commune, the despots, followed by the period of Venetian supremacy.

During the period of the commune, in the eleventh century, the citizens of Padua established a constitution comprising a general council and a *credenza*, or executive. War with Venice over navigation rights on the Bacchiglione and Brenta rivers were fought in the twelfth century, a time which saw the emergence of the powerful families of Camposampiero, D'Este and Da Romano, among others; they ruled the city between themselves, beginning with the D'Este in about 1175. The temporary success of the Lombards helped strengthen the town, but the jealousies and petty

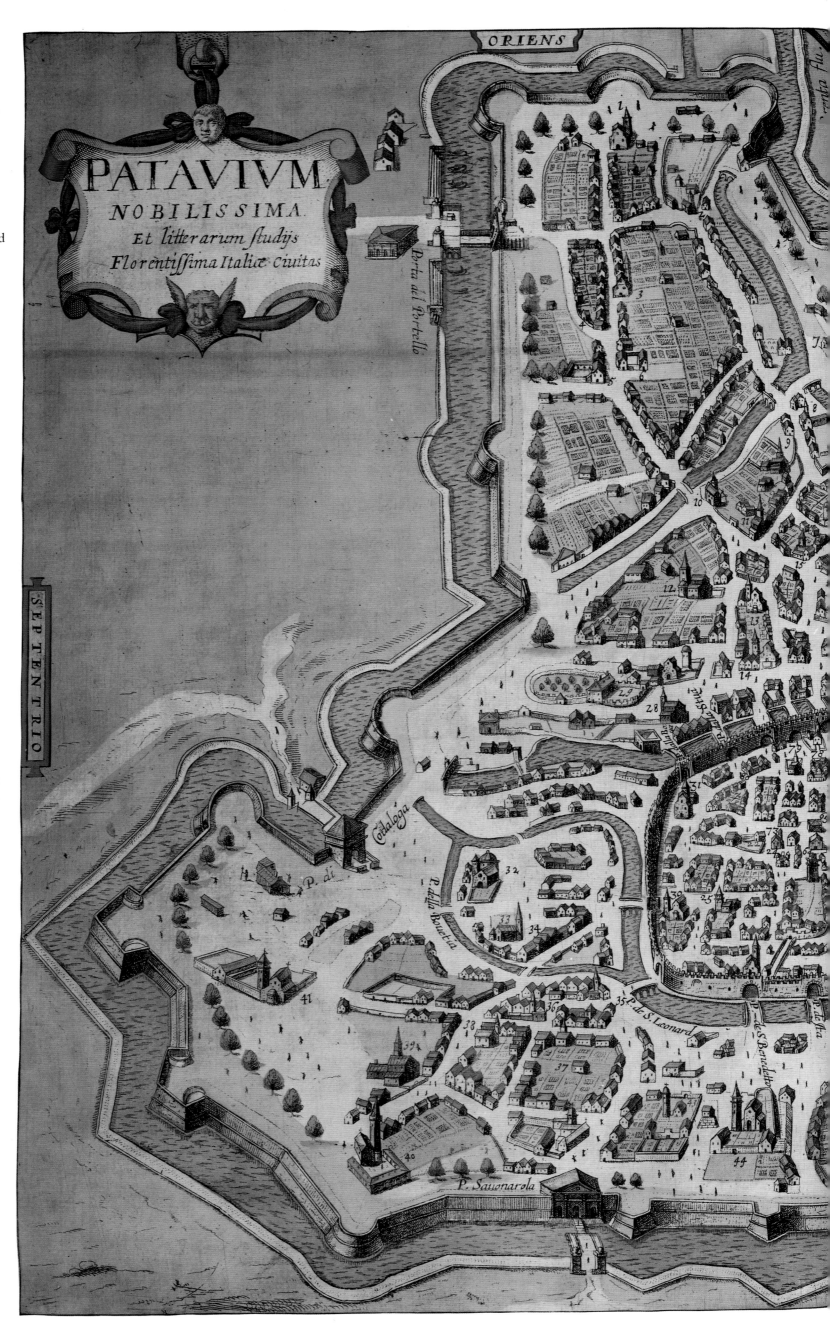

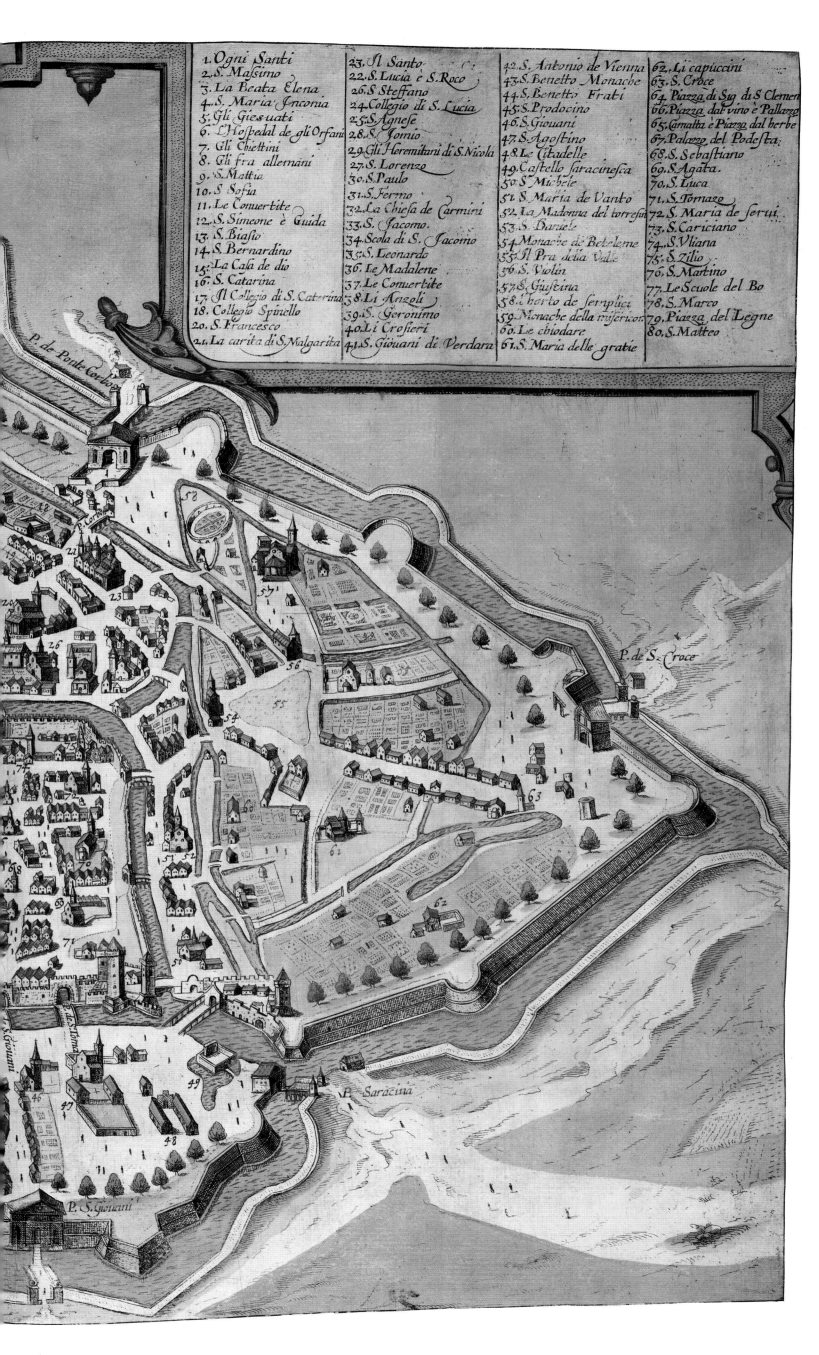

rivalries soon weakened its sense of unity. Frederick II thus imposed his rule on the city and its neighbours with little difficulty. Following the death of Frederick's vicar, Ezzelino da Romano, in 1259, Padua briefly flourished again; a university was founded by Frederick II in 1238, the construction of *Il Santo* began and the city became the overlord of Vicenza. After another period of unrest throughout the fourteenth century, Padua came under Venetian rule in 1405; the city was then governed by two Venetian nobles, a *podestà* for civil affairs and a captain for military affairs, each having a tenure of about sixteen months. Venetian rule ended with the fall of the Serene Republic in 1797.

The engraving shows an ancient city within walls encircled by the moat-like Bacchiglione with its fifteen bridges, and suburbs within the walls erected during the Venetian period. Prominent are the *Palazzo della Ragione*, begun in 1172, completed in 1219 and restored and rebuilt after a fire in 1420; and the palace of the governors, completed in 1532. Churches include *Il Santo*, the thirteenth-century Augustinian *Eremitani*, and the *Madonna dell' Arena*, with its frescoes by Giotto.

Padua occupies a place in the history of art as important as that in the history of learning. The university attracted many great artists of the early Renaissance, Giotto, Fra Filippo Lippi and Donatello among them. Mantegna (1431–1506), another important Renaissance painter, studied under Squarcione (1394–1474), a native of the city.

PLATE 44

PARIS

Lutetia, vulgari nomine Paris, urbs Galliae maxima, Sequanā navigabili flumine irrigatur . . . 1572. *Volume I, number 7. 345 × 475mm.*

After Sebastian Münster, 1569. This great city began as a small settlement on a low, marshy island in the Seine. The *Île de la Cité* seen at the centre of the engraving was where the Gallii Parisii had their settlement, called *Lutetia*, under the protection of the Senones. This small village controlled the convenient crossing-point of a north-south trade route, seen in the engraving as the straight road running from the left (north) to the right (south).

During the Roman period, expansion took place on the left, or south, bank of the river, with a fortified settlement guarded by a citadel on the site of the present-day *Panthéon*. A sizeable Roman town grew, with a forum, theatre and arena and an aqueduct, the extent of which is more or less followed by the turreted wall and moat.

Following the decline of Rome and raids from the north, the inhabitants of *Lutetia Parisiorum* (as the Romans called the town) retreated to the original island site inside fortified banks. Later expansion took place, this time on the right, or north, bank of the river. The first walls can be traced in the rectangular street pattern near the centre of the engraving.

Beyond these, the extent of Paris as observed by Münster in the mid-sixteenth century was bounded by the roughly semi-circular wall built by Philippe Auguste from 1180 to 1210; this enclosed a town which had become the capital of the kingdom of France in 987 under Hugh Capet. Philippe also ordered that the streets of his capital be paved. His walls may be seen as the first line between the densely built-up area and

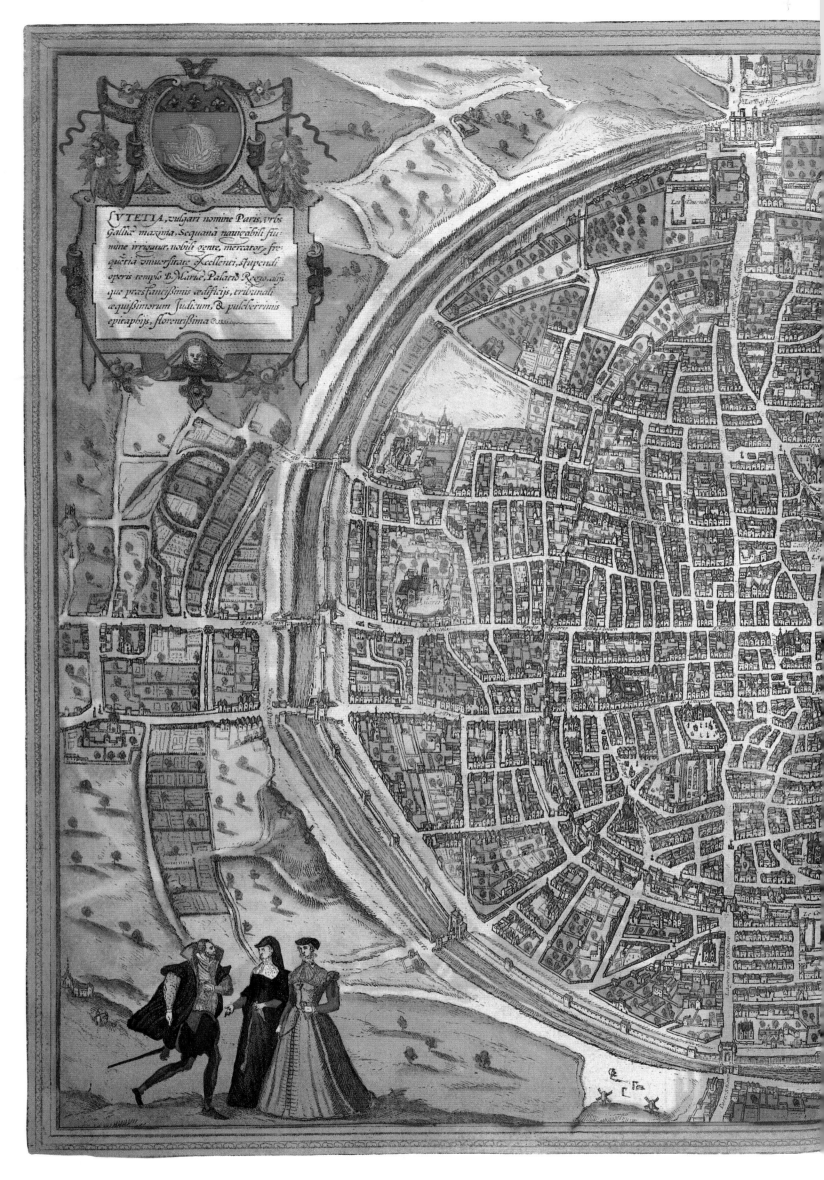

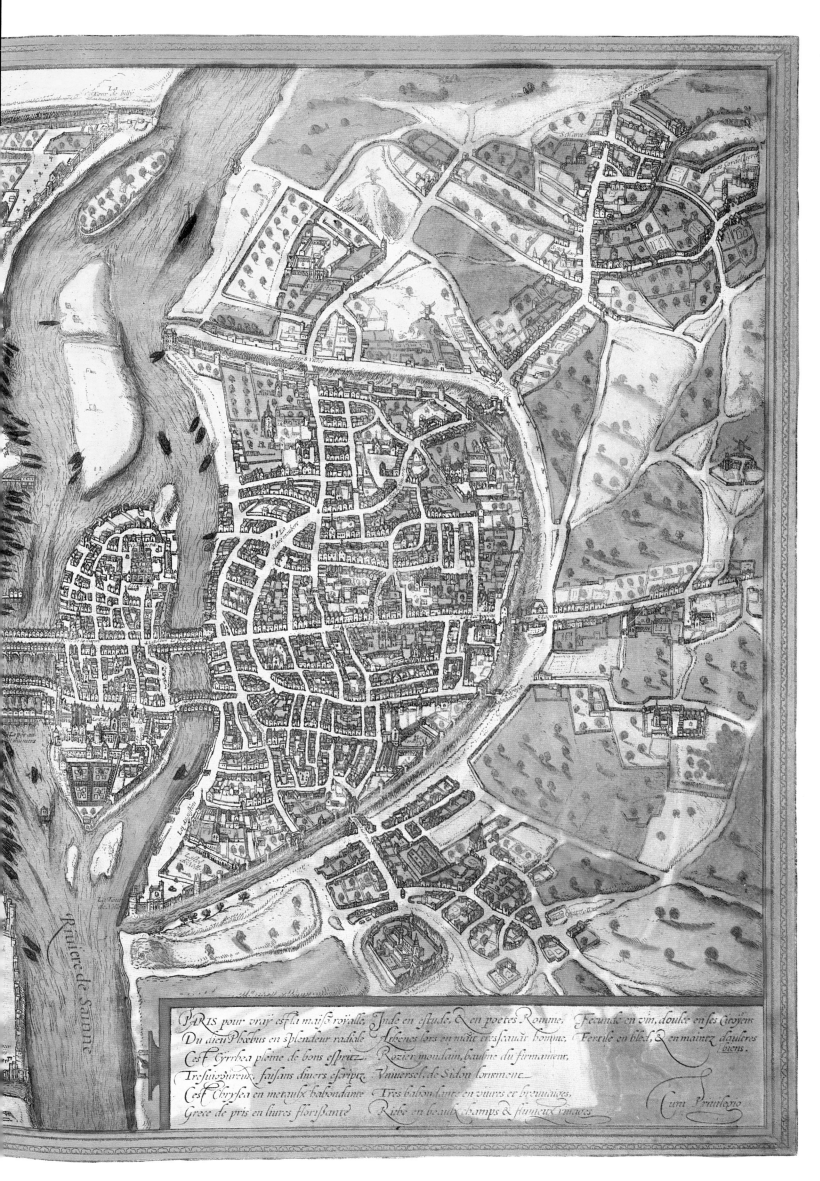

the more open ground bounded by the outer ramparts as raised by Charles V (1337–80) and Charles VI (1368–1422), with the large fort – *La Bastille* – seen at the upper centre of the engraving. These walls enclosed an area of some 440 hectares. During the reign of Henri IV (1553–1610) the first attempts to make Paris an impressive capital and a healthier town for its inhabitants were made, with some success.

Paris became a university city in 1200, the finest of its kind in Christendom, revitalising the former settlement on the left bank. During the thirteenth and fourteenth centuries, the town council met in a small building on Ste-Geneviève on the left bank. During the reign of François I, assemblies were moved to the site of the present *Hôtel de ville*, the *Maison aux Piliers* just visible above the centre.

Mention must be made of that great symbol of Paris, the cathedral of *Notre-Dame* on the Île de la Cité, which may be seen at the eastern end, near the centre of the engraving. It was founded in 1163 and completed in about 1240. The palace of the *Louvre* on the banks of the Seine owes its origin to Philippe Auguste; he built a fortress that was later demolished and developed into the buildings we know today by François I and successive monarchs down to the middle of the nineteenth century.

At the western end of the Île de la Cité may just be seen the citadel, formerly the palace of the Merovingian and Capetan kings, made into a *parlement* of Paris in the twelfth and thirteenth centuries. Here rose the *Palais de Justice* on the site of the buildings seen in this engraving ravaged by fires in the seventeenth and eighteenth centuries. Although we cannot be certain of the population of Paris in the period illustrated here, estimates suggest a total of some 200,000.

PLATE 45

PRAHA (*Prague*) *AND CHEB*

Praga, Bohemiae metropolis accuratissime expressa [with] **Egra. Egra urbs a fluvio, cui adiacet dicta.** 1572. *Volume I, number 29. 185 × 465mm.*

Prague after Johannes Caper and Michael Peterle, 1562; Cheb after Sebastian Münster, *c.*1550. Prague, the ancient capital of Bohemia, the residence of archbishops and imperial governors and now the capital of Czechoslovakia, was the finest example of urban development in the Holy Roman Empire. The old city, on the Vltava river, comprised the *Staré město* (old town), *Nové město* (new town), *Malá strana* (little quarter), *Hradčany* (castle), *Josefské město* (Josef's town, once the Jewish quarter) and *Vyšehrad* (upper castle).

From its earliest beginnings, Prague was destined to be the centre of a country that the diamond-shaped form of its mountains had provided with almost unalterable boundaries for centuries. All roads led from the borders to this hilltop town, or citadel – dominated by the ninth-century *Hradčany* – set above a deep gorge on the Vltava. The river was forded at a secure point at which the *Karlovo most*, or Charles Bridge, replacing an earlier wooden one, was built in 1357. The river was an important highway and the junction that it formed with the bridge and the roads that converged there was protected by a second castle, the *Vyšehrad*, established in the eleventh century.

As Prague expanded in the latter half of the thirteenth century, the *Malá strana*, or civil town, developed, south of the *Hradčany* on the left bank of the river. The *Staré město* settlement on the right bank had developed around the approaches to

the ford. When the bridge was built, it increased in size and gained in importance as a staging post for traders. Socially midway between the Slavic lower class and the imperial aristocracy, with its international connections, a German middle class of craftsmen and merchants put their expertise in town development to good use. A large Jewish community was also important in the eleventh century.

As a legal entity, *Staré město* dates from 1232, its walls and moat dating from 1235. The district forms part of a mediaeval plan centred on the *Staroměstská radnice*, or old town hall, which stood in the middle of a central square, the oldest parts of which date from 1381.

Prague's great period of urban development, as seen in this view, dates from the reign of Charles IV (1346–78). During these years, as the capital of the Holy Roman Empire, Prague was the most important city in central Europe. Charles IV laid out the extension to the south and east of the *Staré město*, planning other developments around three great squares. Two of these remain; they are Charles Square and Wenceslas Square, a widened street. Charles IV founded the city's university in 1348; it played an important part in the history of Bohemia during the Hussite Wars. This, with Wenceslas Square, may be said to be Charles IV's greatest legacy.

Cheb occupies the lower portion of the engraving. The castle was built in the twelfth century and the church of St Nicholas in the thirteenth century.

PLATE 46

ROMA
(Rome)

Roma. *1572.*
Volume I, number 49. 335 ×
490mm.

Probably after G.F.
Camocio, 1569. According
to legend, Rome, the
Eternal City, was founded,
in 753BC. This engraving
of "modern" Rome, viewed
from the west, shows parts
of Ancient Rome with later
building superimposed.
The area is partly enclosed
by the Aurelian Walls of
AD280 as well as by more
recent walls with bastions
constructed to protect the
Vatican and parts of the
west bank of the Tiber.

For about 1,200 years after
the Aurelian Walls,
enclosing an area of some
1,330 hectares, were built,
Rome was effectively in a
state of decline and decay.
There was conflict and
sacking, and a succession of
emperors, barbarian
invaders and popes. The
city's population declined
from about 650,000 in
AD100 to little more than
17,000 in 1377 – hence the
large area of open ground
depicted within the walls in
Camocio's view.

Renaissance Rome
extended from the fifteenth
century down to the
nineteenth century.
Developments were
governed by the site and its
topography. The land
bordering the Tiber was
marshy, malarial and
subject to flooding both
from the river itself and
from streams running
down the valleys between
the seven hills, particularly
the area between the
Capitoline and Palatine
hills. The water supply and
drainage systems of the
ancient city were so
impressive and effective
that parts of the major
sewer, the *Cloaca Maxima*
are still in use today. Aside
from such municipal
organisation, little in the
way of systematic planning
was undertaken: growth
was too rapid, the demands

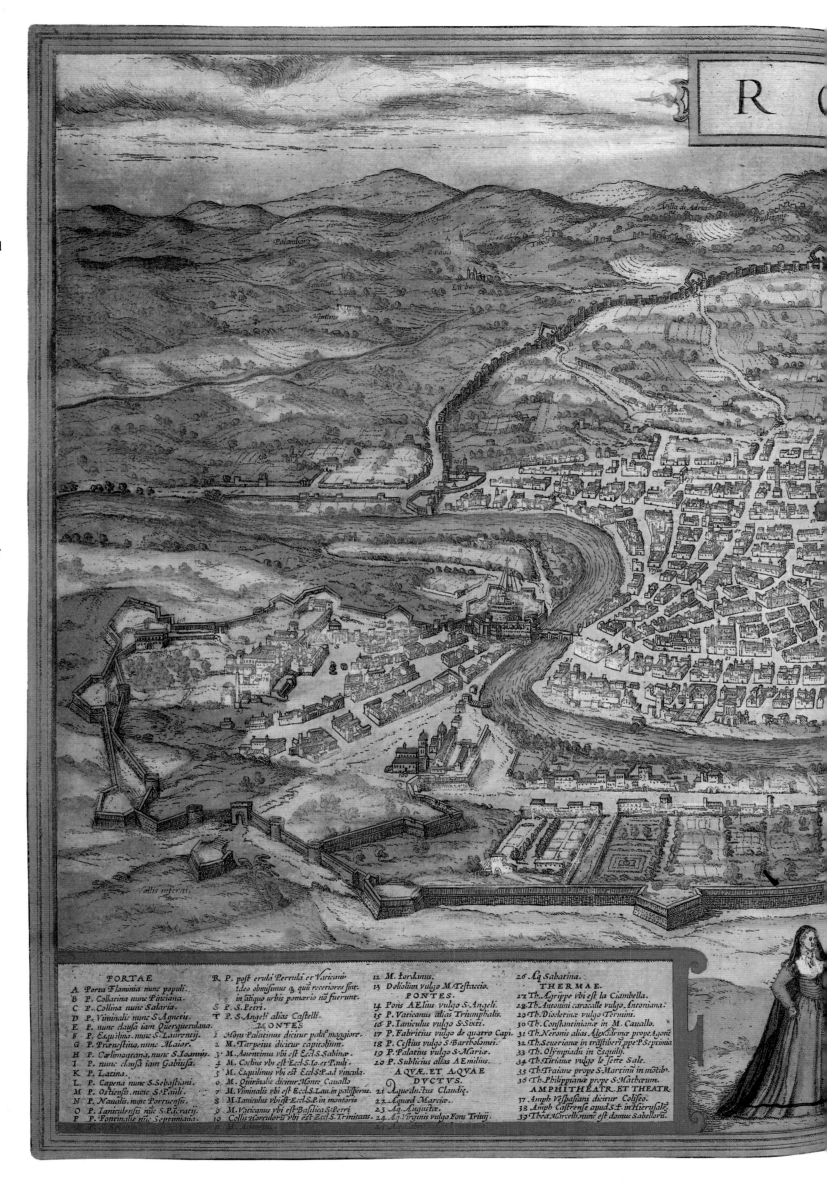

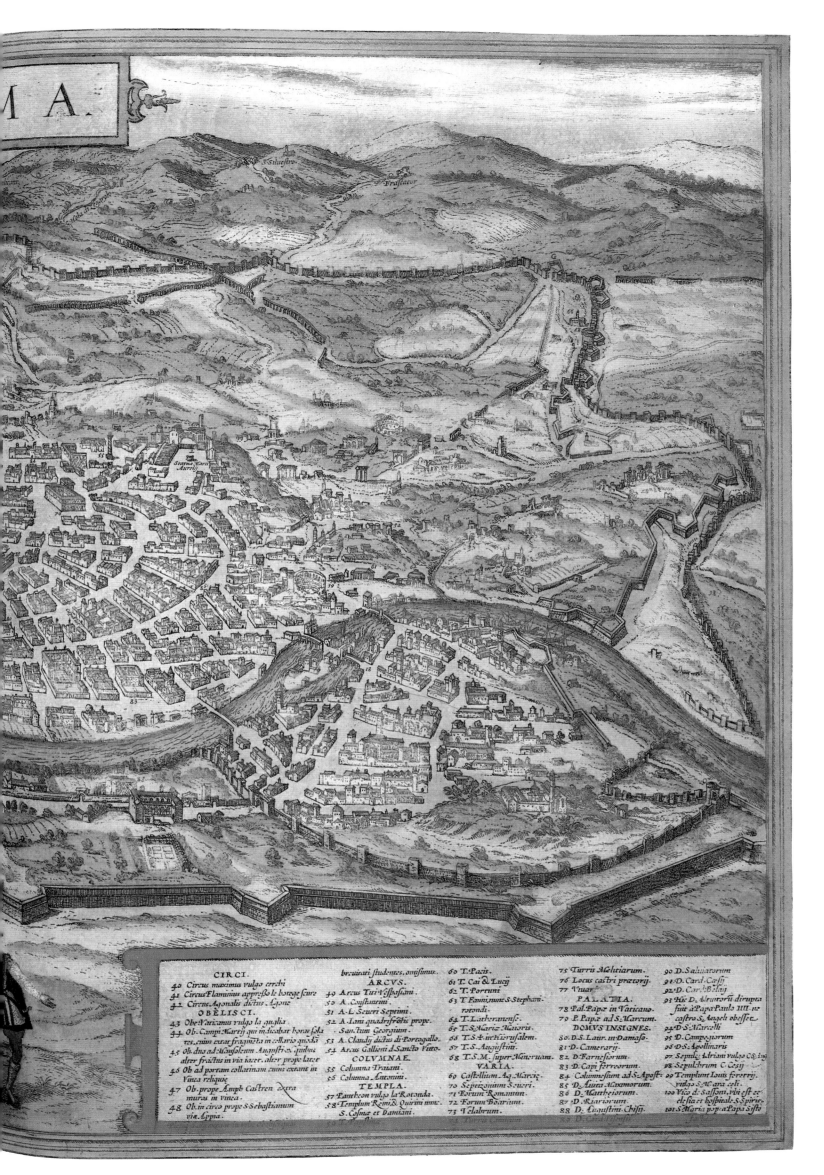

of a great empire too pressing and the ambitions of successive emperors and rulers too conflicting to allow for systematic city planning. A survey made AD132–135 counted eleven baths, nineteen aqueducts, two circuses, two amphitheatres, three theatres, twenty-eight libraries, 1,790 palaces and some 46,602 tenements, and this at a time when Rome had passed its zenith.

More than a millennium later, ambitious projects for reviving the city were put into action, involving not least the popes, during the Renaissance. Highly detailed urban planning resulted in the new basilica of St Peter, begun in 1506 (barely in evidence in the engraving), the *Piazza del Popolo* and *Piazza Navona*, and so on. The most prominent structures visible in this view are the *Castell Sant' Angelo*, with a bridge connecting the Vatican with the east bank of the Tiber, and the *Pantheon*, the large building with the blue-grey dome in the centre of the engraving. The *Colosseum* stands in open land well to the right of centre.

During the fifteenth and sixteenth centuries, the popes achieved an urban plan for the entire city; it consisted of a series of straight avenues linking the seven great pilgrimage churches and creating vistas that both expressed the glory of the Church and facilitated movement around the city itself. The earliest hints of some of these avenues are visible in the engraving: they include the trident form of the streets from the *Piazza del Popolo*, left of centre, to the northern gates built by Leo X and Clement VII; the beginnings of the *Strada Felice* running from the *Sta Maria Maggiore* and the *Sta Croce in Gerusalemme* by the gates at the right-hand edge; and the *Strada di Porta Pia* stretching away from the Diocletian Baths just above the centre.

99

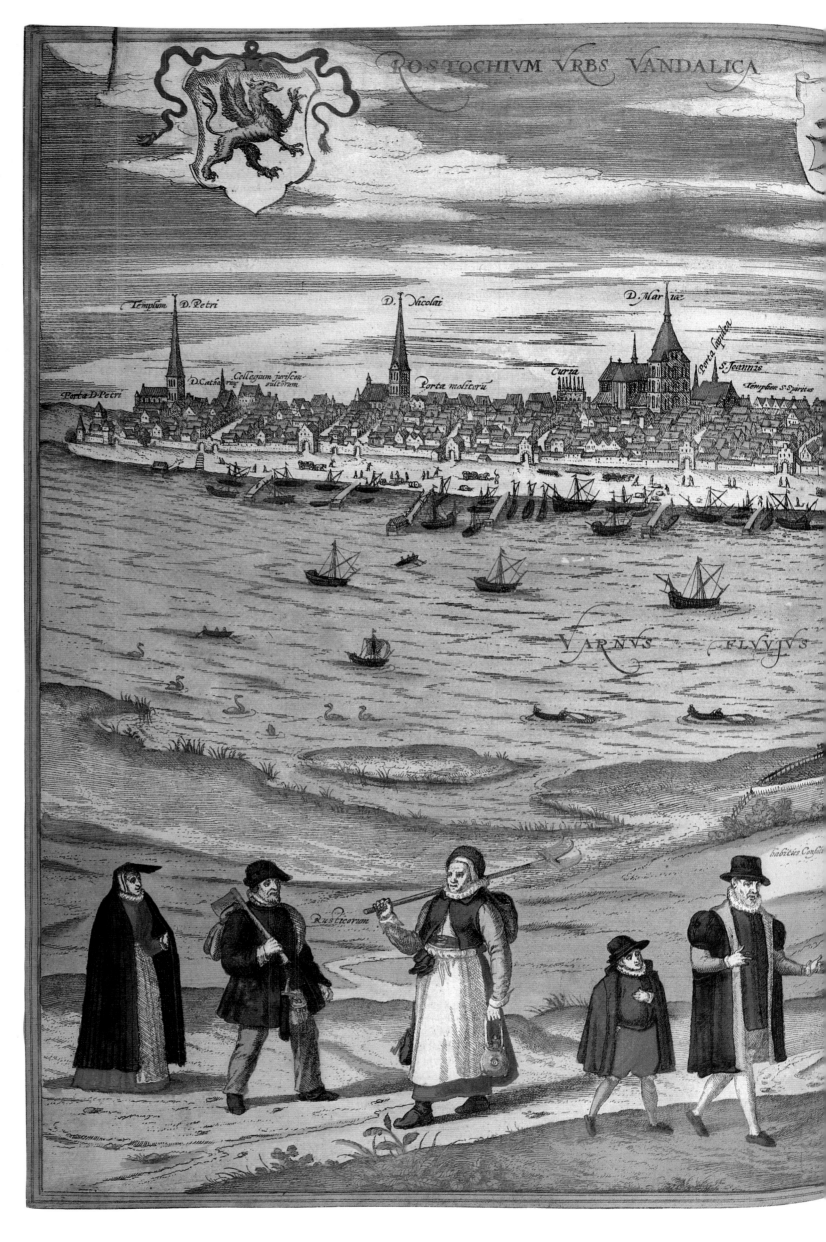

PLATE 47

ROSTOCK

Rostochium urbs Vandalica Anseatica et Megapolitana. 1598. *Volume V, number 47. 355 × 486mm.*

Probably after Heinrich von Rantzau, before 1598. Although it has often been claimed that a settlement existed here as early as the fourth century, the oldest municipal records appear to date from 1218, and the earliest signs of municipal prosperity from around 1260. For a time, from 1314 to 1319, Rostock was in the hands of the King of Denmark, but was soon returned to the protection of Mecklenburg, and joined the Hanseatic League under the jurisdiction of Lübeck. Rostock was one of the original members of the powerful Wendish Hansa in which it had an influence second only to Lübeck itself. A university, one of the earliest established in the Baltic region, was established here in 1419.

Rostock enjoyed its greatest prosperity from the late fifteenth century, just as its political influence began to decline. However, the city never completely lost the independence that it had enjoyed during the Hansa era. Something of the commercial bustle and activity of the place may be seen from the ships moored at the quayside on the left bank of the Warnow river and the prosperous-looking inhabitants standing on the east bank in the foreground of the engraving.

Dominating the city is the *Marienkirche*, which had seven doors. The city wall had seven gates, the quayside seven wharves, and the *Rathaus* – the *curia* adjacent to the *Marienkirche* – seven turrets with seven bells.

100

ANSEATICA ET MEGALOLITANA

S. Jacobi

D. Michaelis
Collegium philosophi-
cum
Auditorium magnum
S. Crucis
Porta Kroepelineasis
Porta Bramoreasis
mons Cathariua

Cius
Mulieris
Virginis
Ancillæ

PLATE 48

ROTTERDAM

Roterodamum, Hollandiae in ostio Roteri flu. Opp. Magni illius Desiderii Erasmi Patria. 1588.
Volume IV, number 13. 286 × 400mm.

After Jacob van Deventer, 1558–72. Rotterdam, literally the dam on the Rotte river, was founded by Wolfert van Borselen, *voogd*, or guardian, of Holland, in about 1420. It was sited in a low-lying, marshy tract of land in the area of Crooswijk, to the northeast of the city as it is seen here, and the *Hoogstraat*, seen running west to east (left to right) in the engraving. The oldest streets in the heart of the old city, which remained largely intact until the Second World War, were the *Oppert* and the *Lombardstraat*, not far from the *Bulgersteyn*, in the west of the town.

Up until the sixteenth century, Rotterdam was but a minor fishing harbour; Dordrecht (*q.v.*) was still the chief port of the *graafschap* of Holland. Between 1340 and 1348, Rotterdam improved its connections to the inland reaches of the Rotte and Schie rivers by building a canal linking it to Overschie. This speeded the transport of raw wool for the draperies at 's-Gravenhage (*q.v.*) and Leiden (*q.v.*), to the advantage of Rotterdam as an entrepôt. In 1389, Delft, to the northwest, built a small port at nearby Delfshaven, which is now part of Rotterdam. Although this threatened to compete with Rotterdam as a port, the town already possessed a thriving fishery and enjoyed good trading relations with England, supplier of the bulk of the raw wool trans-shipped here. A significant trade in wine and grain from France also began.

The greatest stimulus to the development of Rotterdam as a port came when, in the

ROTERODAMVM, Hollandiæ in oſtio Roteri flu. Opp.Magni il: lius Deſiderij Eraſmi Patria

late sixteenth century, it was granted the status of staple port, a distinction previously held by Dordrecht. New docks, such as the *Blaak* on the south side, on the Maas bank, were laid out. Much foreign trade passed through Rotterdam at this time, for Amsterdam had not yet fully developed as an international port, although a scheduled barge service, regulated in 1588, operated between the two towns.

Following the collapse of Antwerp (*q.v.*) in 1585, many immigrants, including Flemish weavers, came to settle in Rotterdam. The town prospered, and this prosperity began to manifest itself in the building of the *St Laurenskerk* (seen in the centre of the engraving), which began at the end of the fourteenth century and was much extended as the town grew. The large tower was begun in 1449.

Rotterdam prospered still further when the harbour at Delfshaven began to silt up. By 1600, it was the foremost port of Holland. Although its herring trade was lost to Vlaardingen and Schiedan to the west, the town continued to prosper, expanding outside the main dyked area, shown in the engraving, into the area called *Oost-* and *West-Nieuwland*, on the Maas side, between 1576 and 1600. While most towns in Holland grew but little after 1650–70, this did not apply to Rotterdam; while in the mid–sixteenth century it had counted 7,000 inhabitants, a century later, somewhat after this engraving was published, the figure had risen to some 50,000.

PLATE 49

ROUEN, NÎMES AND BORDEAUX

Rotomagus, vulgo Roan, Normandiae Metropolis [with] ***Nemausus, Nismes Civitas Narbonensis Galliae vetustissima*** [with] ***Civitatis Bordegalensis in Aquitanea genuina descriptio.*** 1572. *Volume I, number 9. Three subjects on one plates, in total 325 × 465mm.*

Rouen after Georg Hoefnagel; Nîmes after Sebastian Münster, 1569; and Bordeaux after Antoine du Pinet (*Plantz, pourtraits et descriptions de plusieurs villes et forteresses,* Lyon 1564). Rouen, ancient capital of Normandy, was a Celtic settlement called *Rotomagus* by the Romans. It was made the centre of Lugdunensis Secunda in the third century and later became an archbishopric. Although the town prospered under its early bishops, it was sacked several times by the Normans, who made it their capital in 912, and the principal residence of the dukes. Trade treaties were made with the merchants of Paris and later with London (*q.v.*), the Hanseatic League and Flanders.

During the English period Rouen continued as a prosperous merchant town, and at this time much of the great cathedral of St Ouen was built, Here also, Joan of Arc (*q.v.*) was tried and executed in 1431. Thereafter the French kings made several attempts to recapture Rouen, but were unsuccessful until 1449, when the English surrendered the fortified places in Normandy. During the fifteenth and sixteenth centuries, Rouen was a centre of art and culture in France, and one of the first towns to reflect the growing influence of the Renaissance.

Nîmes, ancient *Nemausus* in south-western France, was

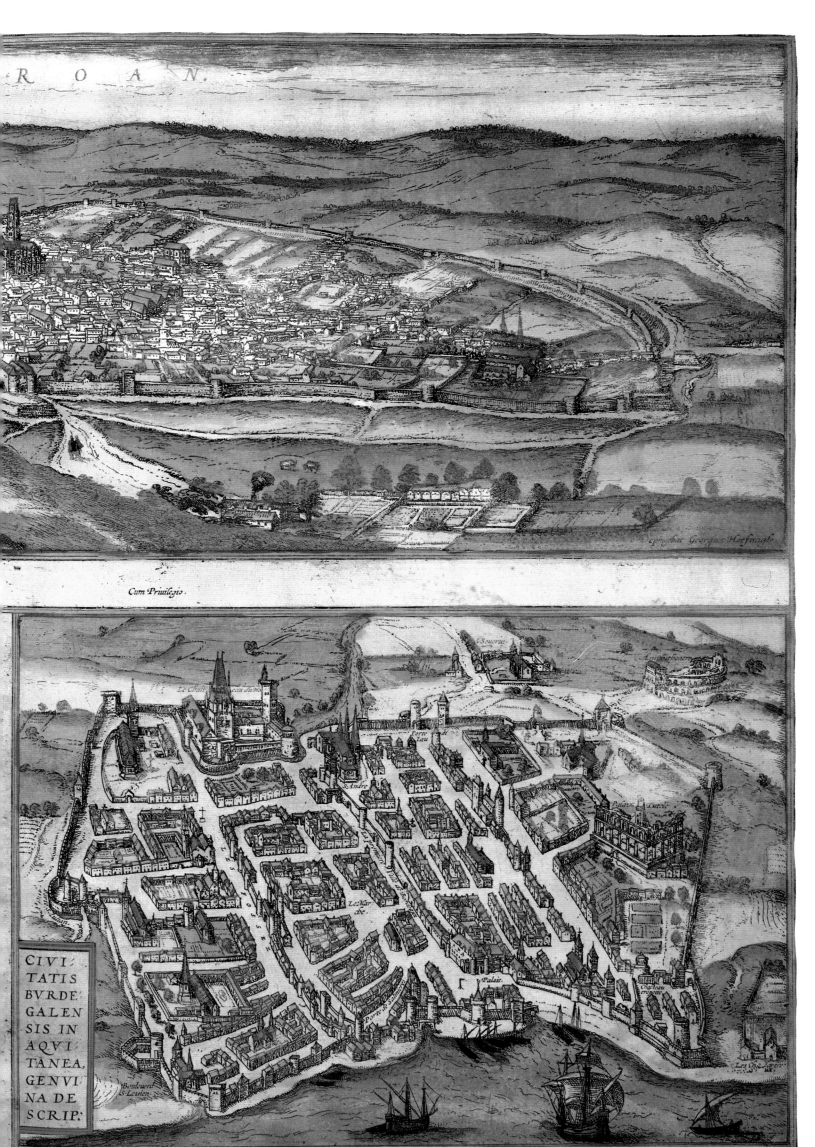

a large and important town in the Roman period. Agrippa built the baths, a temple to Diana and the *Pont du Gard*, the celebrated aqueduct seen near the right-hand edge of one of the smaller views in this engraving. Traces of the walls erected by Augustus may also be seen, as well as the amphitheatre, converted into a citadel by the Vandals.

Silk manufacture formed a major part of the prosperity of the town in the late Middle Ages, following the influx of silk weavers from Lombardy and Tuscany. It is estimated that some 10,000 inhabitants were engaged in the silk and related industries when this engraving was published.

Bordeaux, on the left bank of the Garonne, in south-western France, was the *Burdigala* of the Romans described by the geographer Strabo. It was made the capital of the province of Aquitania Secunda in the fourth century BC and has been the commercial capital of the region ever since.

Following the sacking by the Vandals in AD276, an enclosing wall – *enceinte* – was built; it can be seen clearly in the engraving, with the beginnings of suburbs visible. The wall, enclosing 300 hectares, protected the town for about 800 years. During the English period (1154–1453), Edward I wrote from Bordeaux in 1298, asking for persons competent to lay out new towns. While Bordeaux was not a new town, it was the centre of a region in which some thirty new towns, or *bastides* as they were called, were laid out by Edward I on a rectangular plan. They acted as frontier posts in Gascony, and helped the colonization of the region. A flourishing wine trade developed between Bordeaux and England: the annual departure of the wine fleet was the great event in the life of the population.

PLATE 50

SEVILLA
(Seville)

Sevilla. 1588.
*Volume IV, number 2. 355 ×
475mm.*

After Georg Hoefnagel.
Under the Romans,
Hispalis, as it was then
known, was a favourite
resort of wealthy Romans.
The emperors Hadrian,
Trajan and Theodosius
were born nearby. In the
fifth century, the Silingian
Vandals made their capital
here until 531, when it was
superseded by Toledo (*q.v.*)
under the Visigoths.

Under the Moors, who
took possession of the city
in 712, Seville prospered,
especially from trade in
olive oil. Arabs from
Emesa, in Syria, settled
here in large numbers.
Emesan families ruled the
town for several
generations, until Seville
was taken by the
Almoravids, puritanical
Saharan berbers who built a
military empire in Spain
and northwestern Africa
during the eleventh and
twelfth centuries. After
holding the Christian
Castilian forces near
Badajóz in 1086, their
oppressive regime in
Andalusia was broken by
the Almohads, who
captured Seville in 1147 and
made it their capital.

Seville prospered under
their rule, the dynasty
declined and by 1248 the
city was easily restored to
Christendom by Ferdinand
III. Following a short
recession, Seville once more
flourished during the
fifteenth century as a result
of the voyages of
Christopher Columbus and
discoveries in the Americas.

The lively activity of Seville
has been celebrated in art,
literature and music;
Mozart's *Le Nozze di Figaro*
and *Don Giovanni*, and
Rossini's *Barbiere di Siviglia*
are set here. Dominating
the centre of the engraving
is the *Santa María de la Sede*,
one of the largest cathedrals
in the world, begun in 1402
and completed by 1519. Its
belltower, the *Giralda*, is of
twelfth-century Moorish

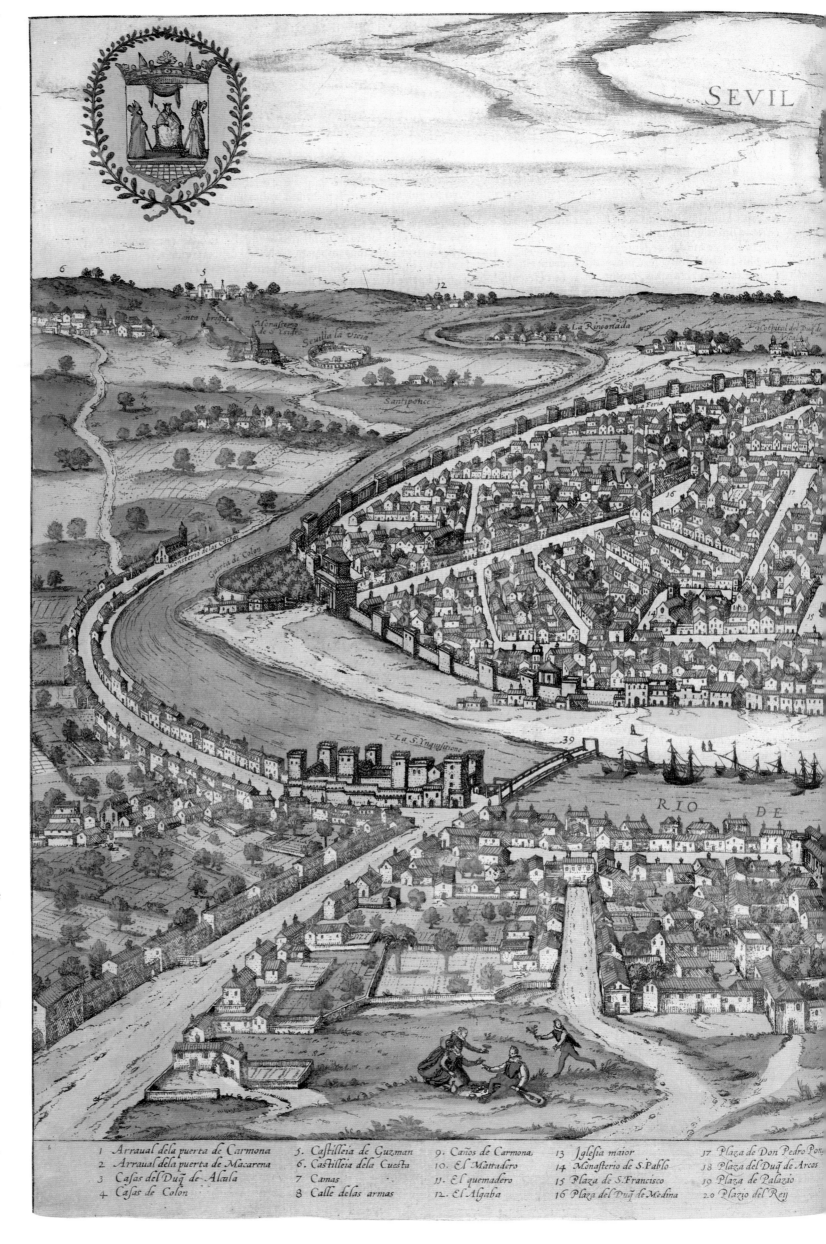

1 *Arraual de la puerta de Carmona*
2 *Arraual de la puerta de Macarena*
3 *Casas del Duq de Alcala*
4 *Casas de Colon*
5 *Castilleia de Guzman*
6 *Castilleia dela Cuesta*
7 *Camas*
8 *Calle delas armas*
9 *Caños de Carmona*
10 *El Mattadero*
11 *El quemadero*
12 *El Algaba*
13 *Iglesia maior*
14 *Monasterio de S. Pablo*
15 *Plaza de S. Francisco*
16 *Plaza del Duq de Medina*
17 *Plaza de Don Pedro Pon*
18 *Plaza del Duq de Arcos*
19 *Plaza de Palazio*
20 *Plazio del Rey*

LA

La Cruz

Monasterio dela trinitad

ta de S. Iusta y Rufina

Monasterio Agustin

Querta del Rei

S anbernardo

GVADALQVEVIR

origin. The main relic of the Moors in the city is the *Alcázar*, comparable with the *Alhambra* in Granada (*q.v.*) It was begun in 1181 by the Almohads; the *Torre del Oro* by the river, built in 1220, is the main visible part. The school, founded by Alfonso I in 1256, was raised to university status in 1502. Also seen in the view are the aqueduct, built by the Romans on 410 arches, and the city walls, with a circumference of 16 kilometres, twelve gateways and 166 towers.

The engraving shows many sailing vessels at the quayside, testimony to the mercantile activity of the town. The main export activities, governed by the *consulado* – a guild of merchants with a subsidiary at Cádiz – held a trading monopoly for Spanish merchants. In practice, however, this monopoly was broken by Genoese merchants trading cloth, foodstuffs and manufactured goods to the New World, particularly since 1529.

New World shipping was organized in 1537 in the form of the annual treasure fleets sailing between Cádiz, Seville and the Americas. Seville prospered from trade in wines, salt, grain, pottery and silks. Its population increased from 15,000 in the early sixteenth century to some 90,000 by 1594.

Madalena	25 Puerta de Triana	29 Puerta de Macarena	33 Puerta de Carmona	37 Torre dela Plata
Alameda	26 Puerta de Goles	30 Puerta de Cordoba	34 Puerta de la Carne	38 Torre dellas Muelle
asterio del Carmen	27 Puerta de S. Juan	31 Puerta del Sol	35 Puerta de Gerez	39 Puente de Triana
rta del Arenal	28 Puert dela almenilla	32 Puerta del Osario	36 Torre del Oro	40 Las Ataracanas

PLATE 51

's-GRAVENHAGE
(The Hague)

Hagae Comitis celeberrimi totius Europae municipii typus. 1617.
Volume VI, number 9. 381 × 460mm.

After Cornelis Bos and Joris van Hurn, 1616. In the thirteenth century, The Hague was nothing more than a hunting-lodge built between ducal estates at Leiden (*q.v.*) and 's-Gravezande. To this day it remains the seat of the Netherlands' court, while Amsterdam (*q.v*) is the capital city of the Netherlands.

The siting of the future town was governed to a large extent by such physical barriers as the nearby sand dunes, adjacent farmland, a few farm houses, grassland and a country lane. Nearby ran an old Roman road, connecting the former mouths of the Rijn and Maas rivers. On this site, then, Floris IV purchased the ruins of a fortified farmstead, or *hoeve*, in 1229, the spot where the *Binnenhof* (seen right of centre, adjacent to the *Hofvijver*, the artificial lake) would be established. Floris's successors extended these buildings to include a residence for Willem III (1227–56) and the *Ridderzaal* of Floris V (*c*.1254–96).

Taking up residence in The Hague, the counts, *graven*, of Holland ushered in a period of growth for the town, especially between the second half of the fourteenth and early fifteenth centuries. The early agricultural hamlet, *op de Geest*, became a mere appendage to the court, and was elevated officially to the rank of *dorp*, or village, in 1370. This status still holds today.

The parish church the *St Jacobus* (left of centre at number 4 on the plan) was established sometime

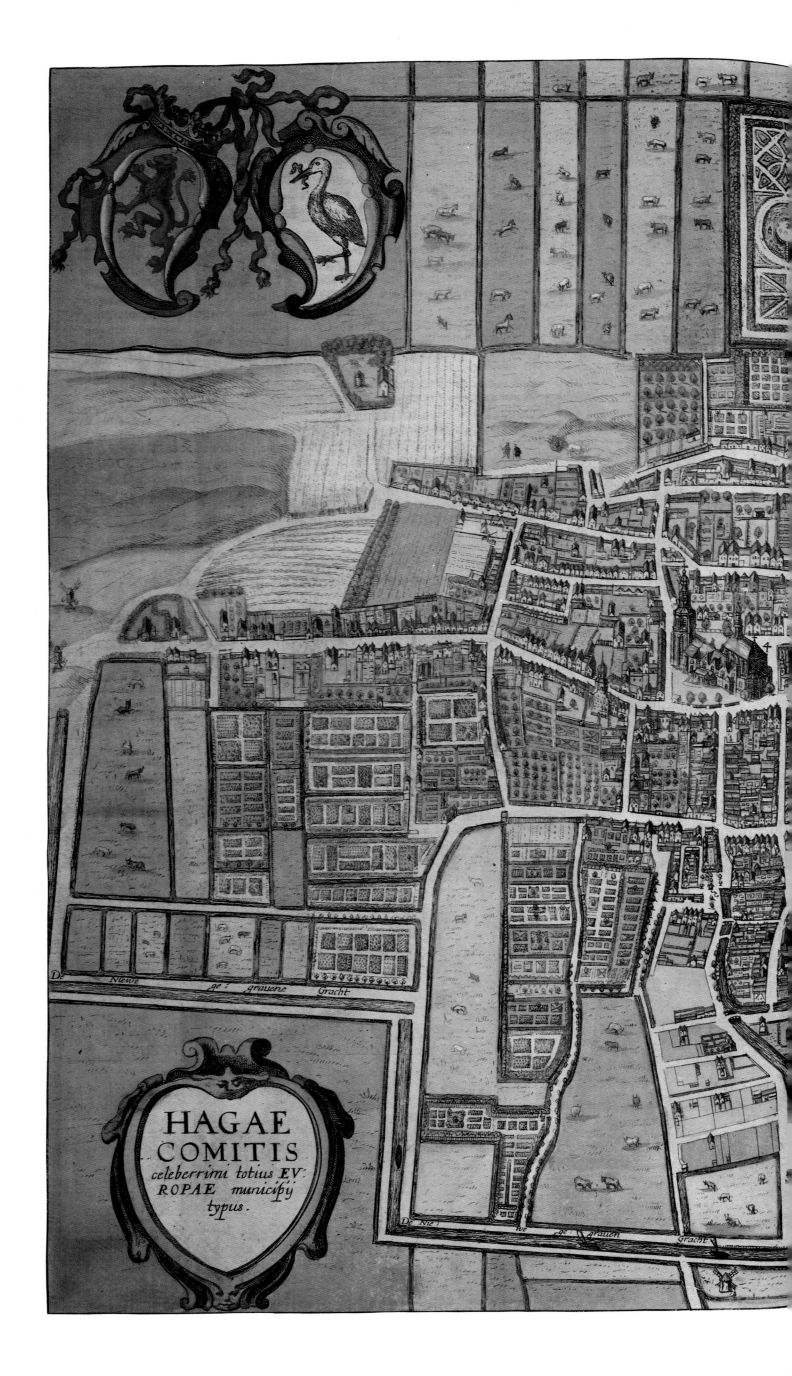

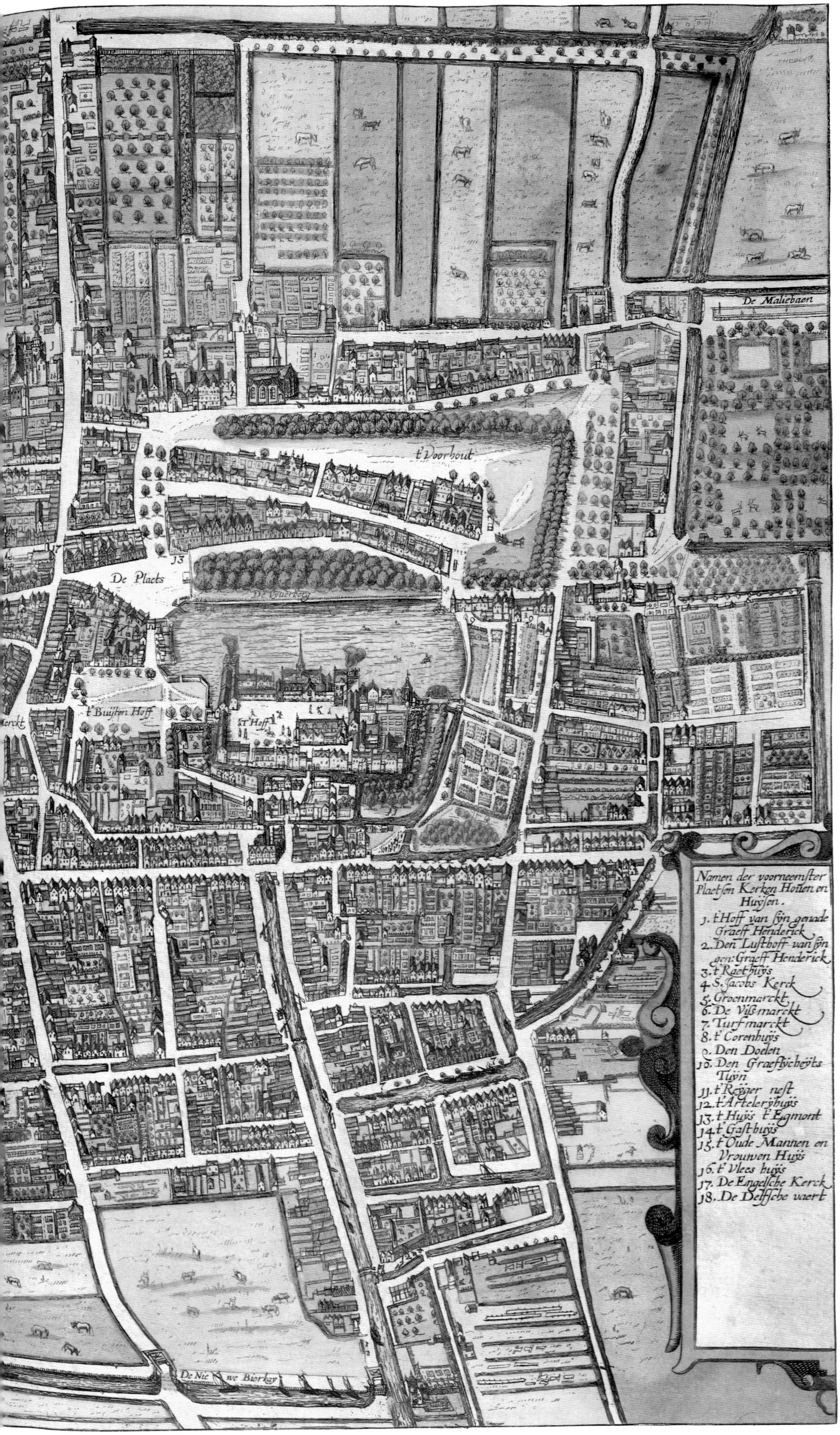

between 1370 and 1470, the first Golden Age of The Hague. It was replaced by a Gothic building of the fifteenth century, and five cloisters were established, of which the *Dominicanenklooster* is the only one remaining. A dozen chapels and numerous other religious foundations were also built. Along the *Voorhout* is the *Vijverberg*, made out of the earth excavated when the *Hofvijver* was cut. On the *Kneuterdijk* stood the palaces and houses of the nobility.

Although it is true that The Hague still does not officially possess city rights, in the fifteenth century it was accepted as such without a charter. Strife and unrest did not ignore the town: the changing fortunes in the cloth industry, civil unrest following the death of Charles the Bold in 1477; epidemics; fires and religious rivalries. The nadir came at the beginning of the Eighty Years' War when in 1575 the Spaniards arrived and dug themselves in, despite fierce opposition on the part of the inhabitants. Soon after, various offices of governments returned, including the *Staten Generaal* and the court of the *Stadhouder*. The second Golden Age of The Hague then began, continuing until the end of the seventeenth century.

Between 1594 and 1610, new inland quays were cut so that barges and other craft could moor in the *Spuikwartier*. During the Twelve Years' Truce with Spain, from 1609 to 1621, defences enclosing an area of 200 hectares were constructed, more than half of which remained as open land. The population of The Hague grew at a steady rate, from 7,000 in 1585 to 16,000 in 1622, just after this engraving was first published. As before, industry continued to be based on the cloth trade.

PLATE 52

STOCKHOLM

Stockholm. *1588.*
Volume IV, number 38. 161
× 487mm. and 156 ×
487mm.

After Hieronymus Schol.
Like that of Copenhagen
(*q.v.*), this view of
Stockholm is presented in
two panoramas to give a
complete picture of the
town as it appeared towards
the end of the sixteenth
century. Like the view of
Bergen (*q.v.*) they are based
on views by Hieronymus
Schol. Then, as now,
Stockholm was justly
famed for the beauty of its
situation on the east coast of
Sweden, between Mälaren
and Saltsjö. It was founded,
according to tradition, in
1255 on the island of
Stadholmen, by Birger Jarl,
long after the decline of the
earlier royal settlements at
Björkö (which had trading
links with Dordrecht
(*q.v.*)), and Sigtuna (site of
the first royal mint of Olaf
in the eleventh century).

Stadholmen bisects the
waterway from Mälaren, in
the west: Norrström flows
to the north, with
Norrmalm on its northern
shore, and Söderström
flows to the south, with
Södermalm on its southern
shore. Both views clearly
show the crowded nature of
the old settlement on the
small island; in the 1580s, it
was essentially a provincial
town of about 10,000
inhabitants, not yet
officially recognised as the
capital of Sweden.
Although Stockholm had
served as a fairly regular
residence for the king and
his government since the
fourteenth century, official
recognition of that
permanent status was not
conferred until 1634.

The city was concentrated
in and around the *Gamla
Stan*. The upper view
shows the massive
thirteenth-century royal
castle, *Tre Kronor Slott*, at
the northern extremity of

STOCK

*Donabat huic operi,
Hieronymus Scholeus.*

the island; the building was largely destroyed by fire in 1697. Nearby is the *Storkyrka* dedicated to St Nicholas; dating from 1264, it is the city's oldest church. In the area of the island where stands the palace, are the palisaded shipping quays, the *Skeppsbro*, with causeways, watermills and merchants' warehouses.

On *Riddarholmen* (the nobles' island) to the west of Stadholmen, may be seen the thirteenth-century *Riddarholmskyrka*, formerly a Fransciscan monastery church and now the burial place of the Swedish royal family. It houses relics of the many campaigns fought by Sweden in Europe. At the northern end of the island stands the fifteenth-century *Birger Jarls Torn*.

The lower view is taken from the Södermalm shore, a point diagonally opposite the upper view. The old town is shown connected to the mainland by a substantial bridge guarded by gates at both ends, and there is a particularly good view of the *Skeppsbro* at the right-hand side of the engraving.

PLATE 53

STRASBOURG

Argentoratum.
Straßburg. 1572.
Volume I, number 33. 338 ×
420mm.

After Abraham Hogenberg.
Like many other cities in
France with a Roman
history, Strasbourg was
originally a Celtic
settlement, which became
the fortified headquarters of
Argentoratum. Situated on
the Rhine plain near the
confluence of the Ill,
Strasbourg has, throughout
its long history, been a
frontier town; it has also
been fought over on several
occasions since 357, when
the town saw the battle
between Justinian and the
Alemanni, which held this
part of the frontier of the
Roman Empire. Its present
name dates from the
Frankish occupation in the
fifth century.

The strong links with
Germany began in the ninth
century with the homage
paid by the Duke of
Lorraine to Henry I.
Struggles between the
bishop and the citizens
characterize the early
history of the city; these
were finally resolved in the
thirteenth century, when
Philip of Swabia conferred

Steinstraſſer thor.

Straßburg

Burg S.Peter

Roßmarckt

Predigern

Schieſſerouen thor

Anno Christi M.XV. Epiſcopatus Bernnardi ſeptimo quorum fuit in fundamento dodicemium templi. tri genſis
Anno M.CCLXX VII ſub Epiſcopo Conrado à Lichtenberg Erckenius à Stinbar architectus, turrim exeruere cœpit, & per ducta fuit ſtructura uſq ad quatuor æſtudines gałea vel veſtigi turris, circa anni de M.CCC LXXXIIII. Reliquum 1439, ad Coronam beneficio Iunckberoram Pragenſium perfectum fuit.

Braler hof

Fronhoff

S.Clar auf dem

Abraham Hogenberg excudit Coloniæ.

the rank of Imperial Free City on Strasbourg in 1262. The history of Strasbourg also has its darker episodes, such as the burning of 2,000 Jews in 1349 on a fraudulent charge of poisoning the wells. In 1382, Strasbourg joined the Swabian *Städtebund* and was later able to aid the fledgling Swiss Confederation. The inhabitants early embraced the Reformation and even managed to remain neutral during the Thirty Years' War, thereby avoiding much physical damage.

The view shows Strasbourg in the mid–sixteenth century. It is dominated by the great cathedral, its west façade built to a design by Erwin von Steinbach, who died in 1318. The spire on the north tower was added in 1435–39; rising to a height of 142 metres, it is the tallest to have been completed during the Middle Ages. It was on the strength of this magnificent tower, coloured here in a vivid red, that the master-masons of the Holy Roman Empire conferred the title of Grand-Master on the master of the Strasbourg Lodge; the city itself was dubbed the Grand Chapter of the Order in perpetuity.

PLATE 54

TOLEDO

Toletum . . . 1566. 1598.
*Volume V, number 15. 372 ×
496mm.*

After Georg Hoefnagel,
1566. Spanish legend
ascribes the foundation of
Toledo to Hercules, to
Tubal, grandson of Noah,
to Iberia, daughter of
Hispanus, and to the Jews
who, having been expelled
by Nebuchadnezzar, are
supposed to have settled
here, naming their city
Toledoth, or City of
Generation.

Toledo, a stronghold of the
Carpetani, was taken by the
Romans in 193BC. Under
the Romans, it became a
colonia and capital of
Carpetania. Its ecclesiastical
importance was linked to
the arrival of Christianity in
Spain. From the reign of
Athanagild (534–547) until
the Moors arrived in 712
with a force led by Musa,
Toledo was the capital of
Visigothic Spain.

Under the Moors,
Tolaitola, as they called it,
prospered as a provincial
capital in the caliphate of
Cordova (*q.v.*) from 712 to
1035, and as an independent
state from 1035 to 1085. Its
rulers protected a large
Jewish colony, founded silk
and woollen industries and
made Toledo a centre of
Arab and Sephardic Jewish
culture. The Jews adopted
the language of the Moors,
becoming Mozarabs,
though retaining their
religion. In 1085, Alfonso
VI of Léon and Castille,
aided by El Cid, captured
Toledo making it his capital
in 1087. For a time, the
Jews were tolerated as they
had been under the Moors;
there were inevitable
disturbances, however,
such as the massacre of
12,000 in 1355 and the final
explusion of the Jews, along
with the Moors, in 1492.
From 1580, Arabic, except
that used in certain church
services, was forbidden. Up
until 1560, Toledo was
wealthy and powerful. In
that year, Philip II made
Madrid his capital and
Toledo then went into
political and commercial
decline.

VM

Oriens

El Ingenio

Palatium Regium Toletanum

Hoefnagel's view from across the Tagus shows a city built around the *Alcázar* and the cathedral, protected by a steep hillside and the river. The river is crossed by two Moorish bridges, the thirteenth-century *Puente del Alcántara* and the *Puente de San Martín*, first built in 1212 and rebuilt in 1390. The inner wall is alleged to have been built by the Visigothic king, Wamba, in the seventh century, the outer wall, seen here, being added by Alfonso VI in 1109. The *Alcázar* itself, a huge square building, called *Palatium Regium Toletanum* in the lower right-hand inset, occupies the highest ground, the site of a Roman fort and the citadel of the Moors. It was converted into a palace by Ferdinand (1200–52) and enlarged during the fifteenth and sixteenth centuries. The cathedral, seen in the lower left-hand inset, was founded in 589 by the Visigoth Reccared, and was used as a mosque by the Moors from 712 to 1227. It was razed by Ferdinand and refounded as a cathedral in 1227, completion not taking place until 1493, much of the work overseen by Hanequin de Bruselas, *maestro de la obra* from 1448. Also visible is the great Gothic church of *San Juan de los Reyes* (1476).

Toledo was especially famed for its swordsmiths. Toledo blades have been prized for 2,000 years, the *culter toletanus* being mentioned by Grattius in the first century BC. The industry thrived under the Moors, who produced blades of remarkable flexibility and strength, tempered as it has been asserted by some, with the blood of infidels.

PLATE 55

VENEZIA
(Venice)

Venetia. *1572.*
Volume 1, number 43. 335 ×
485mm.

After Bolognino Zaltieri,
1565. Venice was founded
by refugees from the
mainland at some time after
the invasions of northern
Italy led by Attila the Hun.
The previous inhabitants of
many Italian towns settled
along the coast and on the
islands in the lagoon at the
northern extremity of the
Adriatic, uniting
themselves as a naval
confederacy in 697. One of
these settlements, Rivoalto
– later Venice – became the
seat of government in 811.

In time, Venice assumed a
central role in the trade
between East and West,
reaching the zenith of its
prosperity in the fifteenth
century. It was Byzantium
that first granted the
Venetians recognition as a
community. Venetian
maritime aid had already
been sought by Byzantine
naval commanders against
Dalmatian pirates, whom
Pietro Orseolo II, Doge of
Venice, succeeded in
defeating in the year 1000.

Suffering raids into the
Lido, the Venetians
organized and armed their
vessels, thus forming the
nucleus of a great fleet.
Later, commanding the
major sea route to the
Levant, the city was able to
provide much-needed
transport at the time of the
Crusades, deriving from it
considerable profit.

Venice, a city of canals,
bridges, palaces, squares
and churches, is bisected by
the Grand Canal, which
follows the winding course
of the ancient Alto river.
The city is divided into six
ancient segments, once
distinct islands but now
unified. The engraving
gives an excellent
impression of this. Each
segment has its own *piazza*,
the greatest of which is, of
course, the *Piazza San*

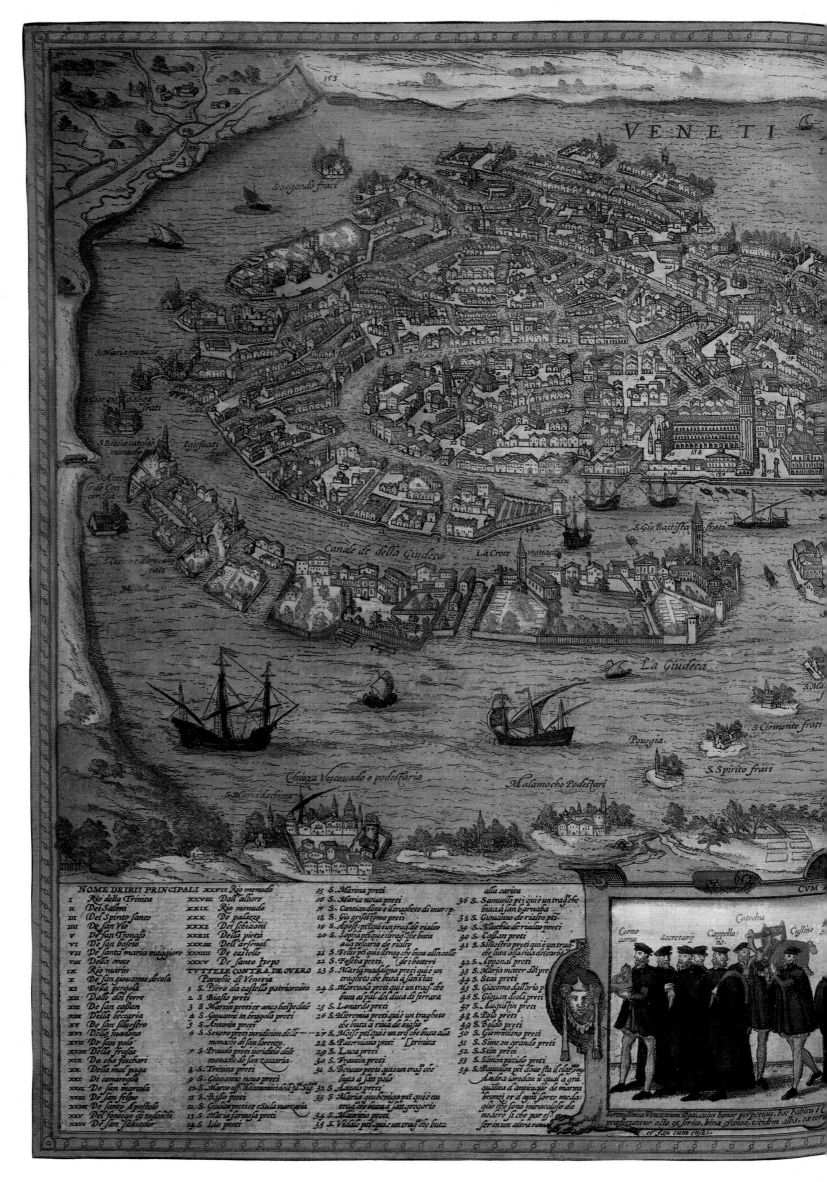

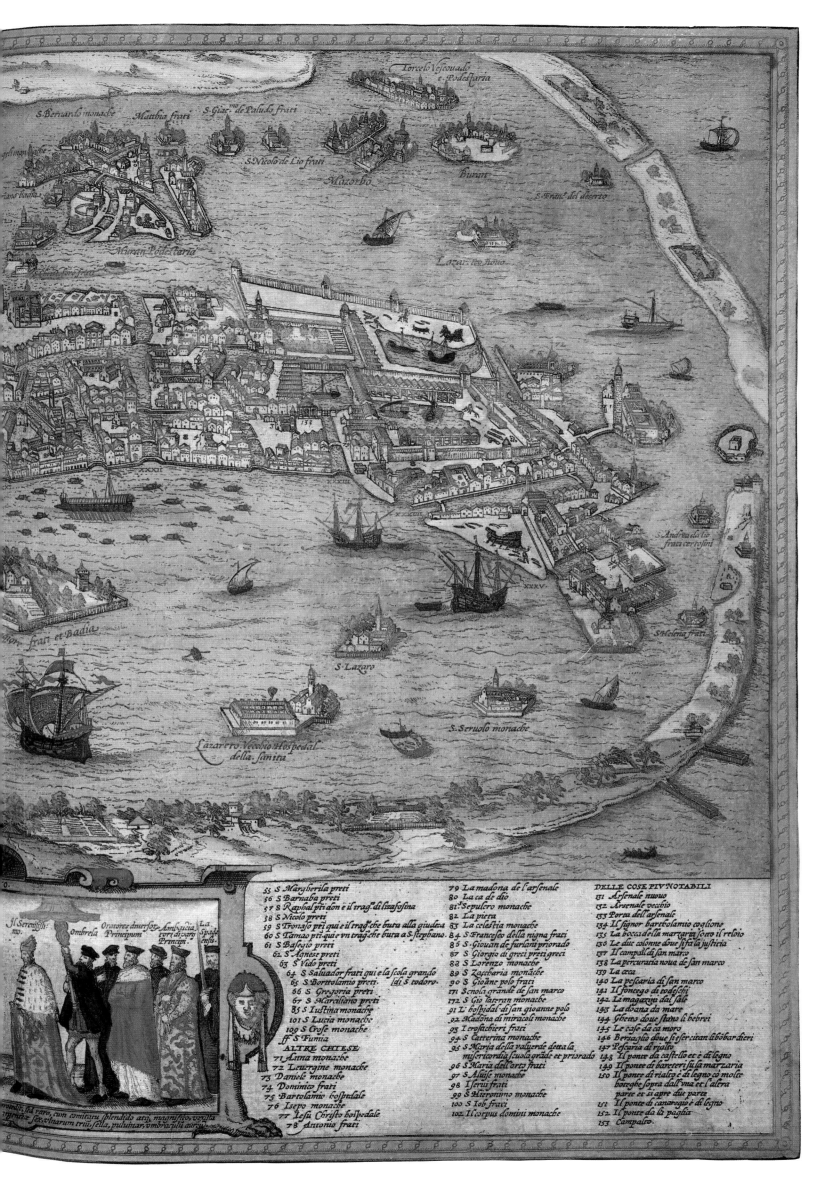

Marco. The Basilica of *San Marco* and the Doge's Palace adjoin it. This part of the city was originally a market place. It started to evolve into the focal point of Venice in about 827, when a small chapel, later the great Basilica, began to be built. The original Doge's Palace was built in the eighth century as a fortress outside the settlement walls; the palace as we know it today was built between 1309 and 1424.

The *Piazza San Marco* dates from 1480–1517. The vignette of the procession at the foot of the engraving serves to remind us that this *piazza* was, as it remains, a square expressly for people and for public functions, an open space around which the life of the city revolved. Just as tourists throng the *piazza* today, so merchants, seamen and visitors from near and far flocked to the city state, the Serene Republic, while it was a powerful maritime empire, the fulcrum between East and West.

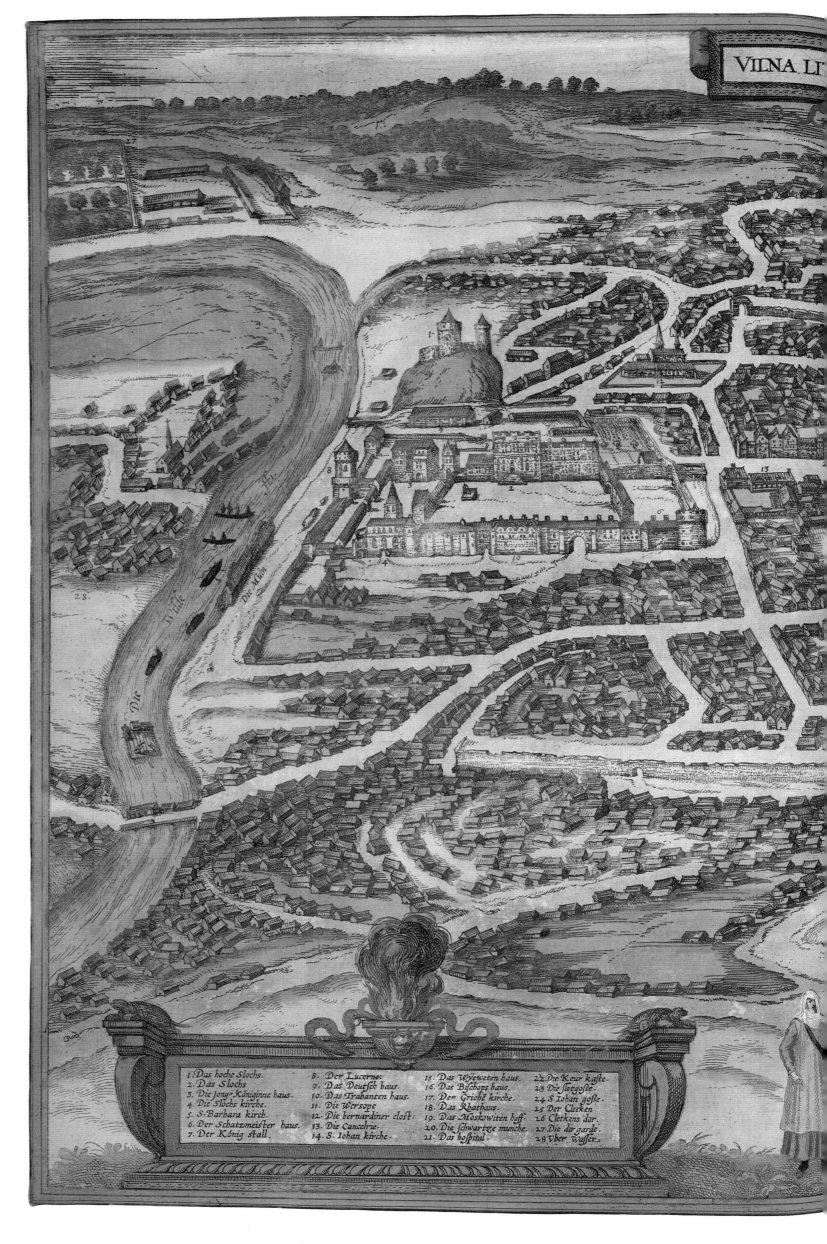

PLATE 56

VILNIUS

Vilna Lituaniae metropolis. 1581.
Volume III, number 59. 369 × 495mm.

From an unknown source. For centuries, the settlement at Vilnius commanded a river crossing on an ancient east-west trading route. In the tenth century, it was used particularly by Viking traders as a stopping place on their routes deep into Russia.

Vilnius is mentioned as a fortified location belonging to the Lithuanians as early as 1128. It became the capital of Lithuania in 1323 when Gediminas, Grand Duke of Lithuania (1316–41), moved his capital there from Trakai, at which time the fortifications shown here were built.

Lithunania became a united kingdom in the mid-thirteenth century, under Mindaugas. His successors, Gediminas, Algirdas and Kęstutis, recovered lost lands to the east and acquired vast tracts in Russia, but they were unable to recover lands lost to the Teutonic Order south of the Nemunas, in Prussia, and to the north, in Livonia. Under Vytautas the Great, Vilnius became the capital of a kingdom extending almost from the Baltic, near Klaipéda, in Samogitia, to the Black Sea.

In 1410, after two centuries of war, the Teutonic Order was defeated at Tannenberg and the Livonian Order overcome at Pabaiskas in 1435, halting the eastward march of German settlers. Vilnius was united with Poland in 1447, when the town's prince, Casimir IV, was elected to the Polish throne. Vilnius nevertheless adhered to Madgeburg law, introduced in 1387. It was also the site of a *hof* of the Hanseatic League, shown as *Deutsche haus* (number 9 in the key), the long, single-storey warehouse with a wooden jetty on the banks of the Neris (Viliya) river, near the ancient castle, *Das*

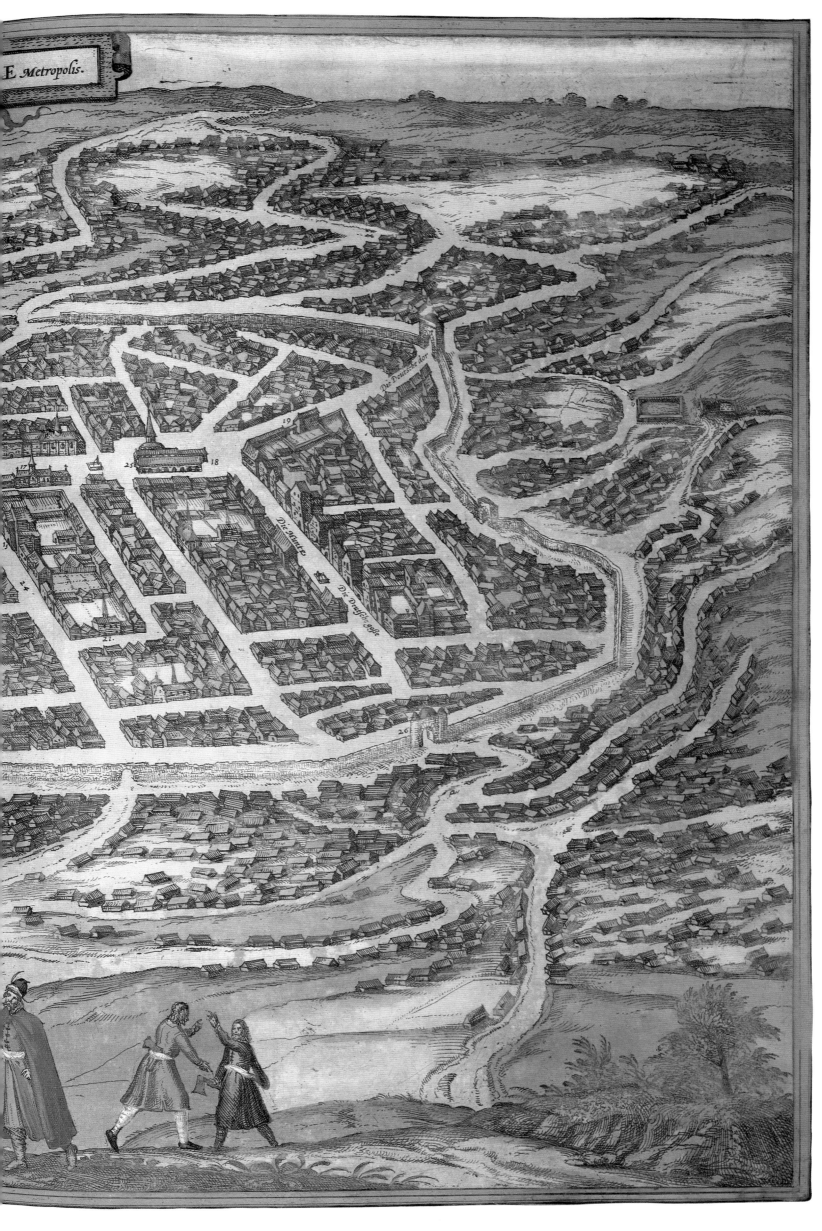

hoche Schlochs (number 1 in the key). Merchants from Moscow traded from *Das Moskowiten hof* (19 in the key).

Among the buildings visible in the wooden built city, as depicted here in the late sixteenth century, are the imperial palace and the Stanislas cathedral of 1387 (4 in the key), and several other churches and religious foundations dating from the fourteenth to the sixteenth centuries, indicating the status of Vilnius as an orthodox see of the Greek Orthodox Church and episcopal see of the Roman Catholic Church. The old city is completely enclosed by a heavily fortified masonry wall (coloured in greyish white in the view, like the castle buildings). The great Gothic cathedral of St John was built between 1327 and 1427 (14 in the key, shown as *S Iohan Kirche*). One of the most extraordinary monuments of German Gothic architecture was the St Anna and St Bernhard complex (12 in the key, shown as *Die bernardiner clost*); its remarkable west front in the late German Gothic style dates from about 1501 and was built in brick.

In general, Braun and Hogenberg's view of Vilnius records a city of wooden houses possibly as depicted by the Flemish artist, Guillebert de Lannoy, who visited it in 1414. In the intervening century and a half, however, much of the town was rebuilt in stone or brick by German merchants and settlers. Their *Deutsche Gasse* or the area around the *Rathaus* (18 in the key) exemplify this rebuilding. Much of the brick was imported from the west by the merchants themselves.

PLATE 57

VISBY

Visbia Gothorum. Wisbu Gotlandiae metropolis, antiquitus amplissima negotiatione celebris, et navigantium schola.
1598.
*Volume V, number 39. 362 ×
487mm.*

After Heinrich von Rantzau. Visby, on the island of Gotland, is the oldest city in Sweden. Although evidence of early trading activity on Gotland exists, Visby itself does not seem to be mentioned until the eleventh century. It was a meeting place for German merchants trading with northern and eastern Baltic. Arab, Anglo-Saxon and other coins have been found here, indicating wide-ranging trading activity. German merchants are mentioned as early as 1161, for Visby was also a staging post for German trade with Novgorod, Pskov, Plotsk, Kiev and Smolensk, in Russia.

During the thirteenth century, Visby, a flourishing town with some 10,000 to 20,000 inhabitants, was the second city of the Hanseatic League, after Lübeck. So powerful was Visby at this early period that it sent 500 merchants to Livonia in 1199 to join the Teutonic crusade and protect commercial interests in the eastern Baltic.

In 1361 Visby was captured by the Danes, under Valdemar Atterdag. In 1392 merchants of the Hanseatic League attempted to regain the town, sacking it in the process. From 1398 to 1407–08, the Teutonic Order defended Visby and Gotland against the *Vitalienbrüder*, pirates loyal to the deposed Swedish king, Albert of Mecklenburg. In 1408, the town was restored to Denmark, remaining under Danish control until the Treaty of Brömsebrö of 1645, which ceded Gotland to Sweden.

The engraving shows Visby somewhat in a state of

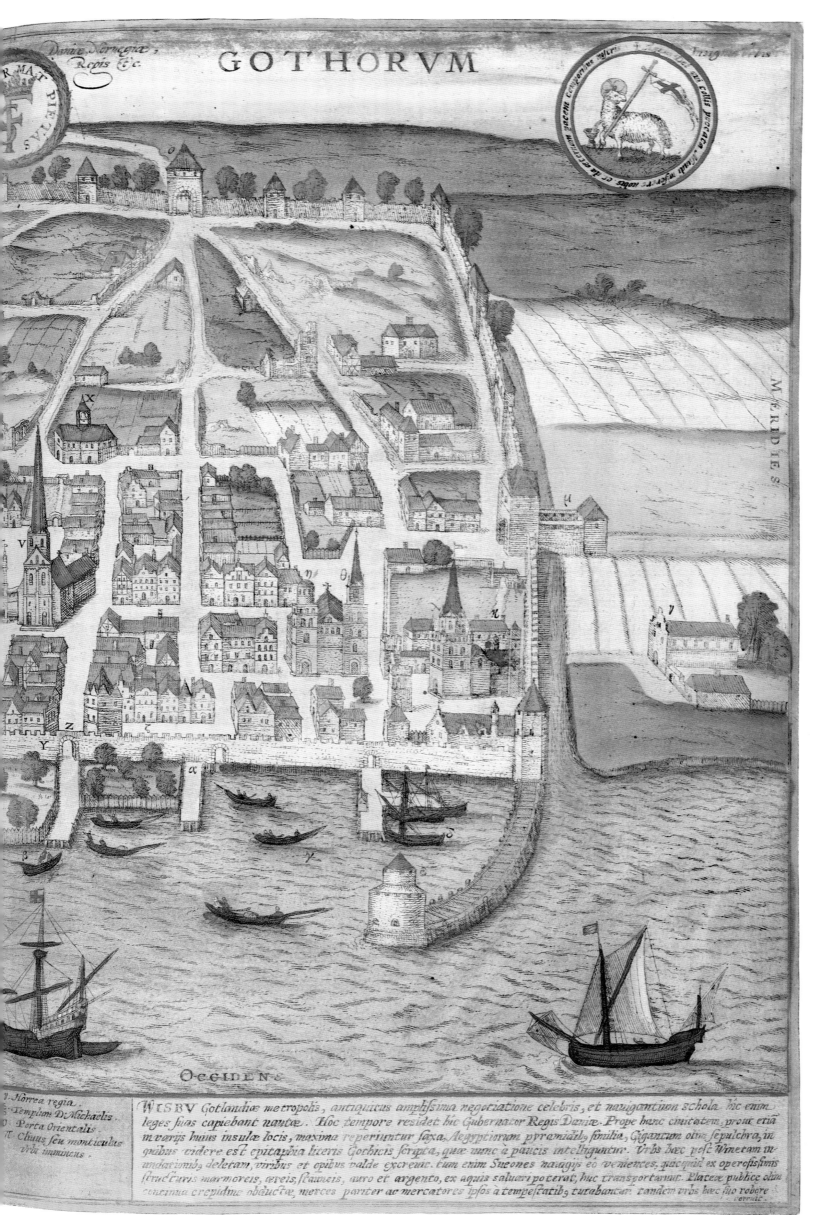

decay. The thirteenth-century walls enclose an area far larger than that built up near the harbour. A closer examination of the area of *Klinten*, inland, reveals several buildings left in ruin since the end of the fourteenth century, when the Danes and counter-attacks by the Hanseatic League damaged the fabric of the town. The western part, closest to the harbour, shows many of the great buildings of Visby's past: the church of St Mary, dating from 1190–1225, with its twin towers (Q in the key); ten other churches, among which are the Trinity, the St Olav, the St Nicolas, dating from the early thirteenth century (F in the key) and once part of a Dominican monastery, the late Romanesque *Helgeandskyrka*, of *c.*1250 (I in the key), the St Clement (G) and the twelfth-century St Lars (S), notable for its huge tower. The St Catherina (V), dominating the centre of the engraving, is a thirteenth-century Gothic building which once formed part of a Franciscan house.

The engraving shows both the old harbour – the *Portus vetus* (β), which had silted up – and the new harbour – the *Portus novus* (γ), to the south, protected by fortified towers and lighthouses. All of these attest to the city's extraordinary prosperity during the eleventh to fourteenth centuries. The engraving also shows the Valdemar cross, the monument to 1,800 of Visby's citizens who perished in the battle against Valdemar of Denmark on 27 July 1361.

PLATE 58

WARSZAWA
(Warsaw)

Varsovia. 1617.
Volume VI, number 47. 320 × 476mm.

After an unidentified source. In 1285, a charter was granted to a small settlement on the site of present-day Warsaw's Old Town (*Stare Miasto*). This was probably rebuilt from the old town of Jazdow which had been destroyed by fire in 1262. The foundations of a ducal castle were laid in 1289, immediately to the south of the old town.

The site of the Old Town was on the edge of a steep embankment, clearly seen in this view, which looks west across the Wisła river. The embankment, some 21.3 metres high, formed a natural rampart in the fortifications; these were built in 1339, with a double wall on the landward side and a single wall on the river side. Tributary streams of the Wisła formed natural moats on the town's northern and southern flanks.

In the fourteenth century, Warsaw was a small town comprising only some 150 building plots, about 30 metres long and 10 metres wide. The street pattern was a loose gridiron, with a market place in the central square. By 1408, the area within the walls had become built up, making expansion necessary. The New Town (*Nowe Miasto*) was then built on the north side of the old. After a fire in 1431, the ruling council decreed that no new timber buildings be permitted and

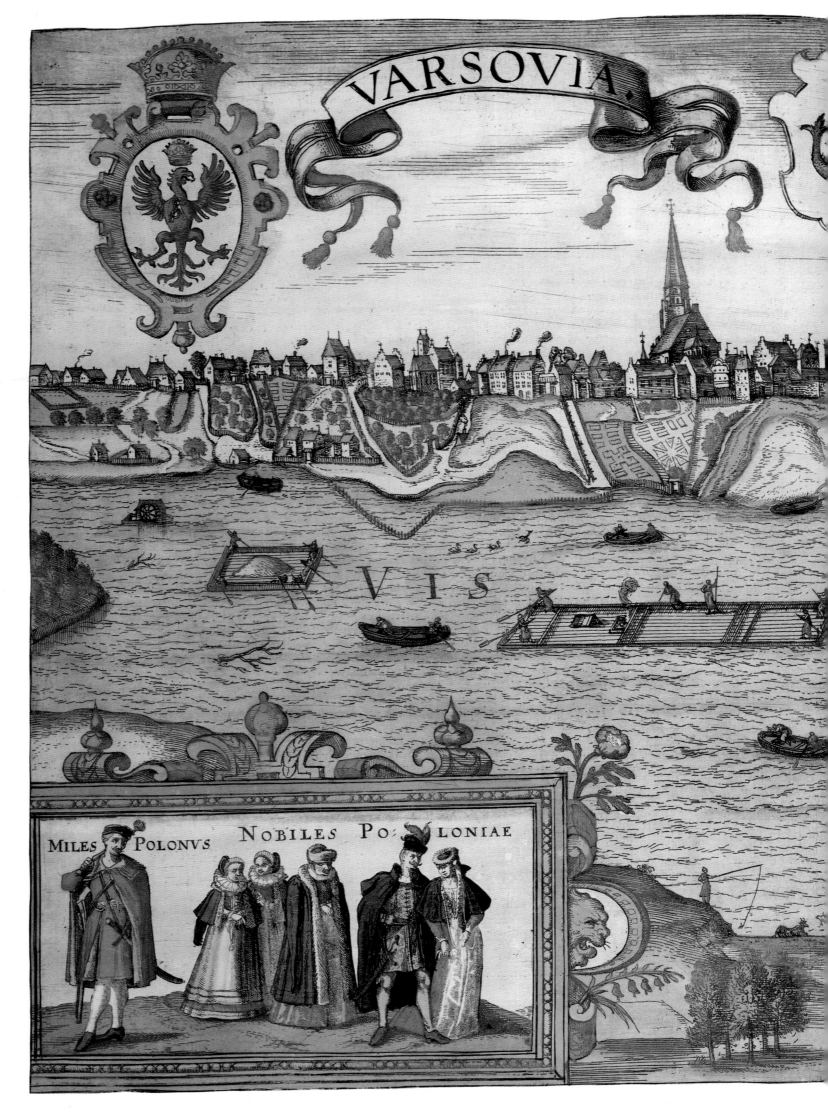

VLA FLV VIVS

that brick or stone were henceforth to be the only building materials allowed. From the fifteenth century, therefore, Warsaw became a city of brick.

The notable and highly favourable location of the city at the meeting point of the east-to-west and north-to-south trading routes had already made for steady growth. Warsaw's geographical position also had political advantages. Standing in the territory of Mazovia, which belonged neither to Poland nor Lithuania, Warsaw, in mediaeval times, was capital of both, remaining neutral between the two rival powers. Warsaw's position at the geographical centre of what was then the united kingdom was also more advantageous than that of Vilnius (q.v.), in Lithuania, and Kraków, in southern Poland.

In 1596, the kings of Poland abandoned Kraków as their capital and moved to Warsaw, thus ensuring the town's future growth and status. From 1572 onwards, the election of the kings of Poland were held at the Field of Wola, on the western outskirts of the city, to which all members of the *szlacht* or aristocracy were invited. The city's royal connections are marked in the engraving by the royal crests of the Polish kings included in the view.

Some indication of the importance of the river in the life of Warsaw may be gauged from the barges and timber rafts floating downstream to Danzig (q.v.) to be exported to western Europe. Note also the raft carrying salt.

123

PLATE 59

WIEN
(Vienna)

Vienna Austriae. 1617.
*Volume VI, number 21. 316
× 490mm.*

After Jakob Hoefnagel.
Vienna began as a Celtic
settlement called *Vindobona*
by the Romans, who
established a small fortified
camp on the site. From
here, they could command
the Donau and protect the
northern fringes of their
empire.

Vienna's geographical
location, at the meeting
point between Western and
Eastern Europe, shaped
both the city's history and
its physical appearance.
During the years of the
Crusades, Vienna grew
rapidly as a kind of transit
town or staging post,
especially after 1247, when
the charter granted by
Frederick II in 1237 was
fully confirmed.

The city's strategic
importance grew further
when it became the seat of
the Habsburg Dynasty in
1276. Vienna then grew to
become the capital of a
great central European
empire. It was one of the
most advanced cities in
western Europe and a
bulwark of Christianity; in
1529 and 1683, the invading
forces of the Muslim Turks
were turned back despite
the long sieges that they laid
to the city.

Urban defences were
therefore crucial to Vienna.
The Roman and Mediaeval

1. Templum D. Stephani.
2. Templum S. Michaelis.
3. Templum S. Petri.
4. Ad littus S. Mariæ.
5. Ad S. Crucem.
6. Ad Scotenses.
7. Ad S. Augustine.
8. Ad Prædicatores.
9. S. Dorothea.
10. S. Hieronymi.
11. S. Mariæ ad Angelos.
12. S. Iacobi.
13. S. Laurentij.

14. Ad Portum Cœli.
15. Hospitale Vrbanum S. Claræ.
16. S. Iobannis Baptista.
17. S. Nicolaus.
18. S. Mariæ Magdalenæ.
19. Templum Soc. Iesu.
20. Ad S. Saluatorem.
21. S. Georgij.
22. S. Ruberti.
23. S. Annæ.
24. Rubra Turris.
25. Propugnaculum Castoreum.
26. Antiquum Arsenale.

27. Propugnaculum Ciuile.
28. Porta Stubensis.
29. Pro: Braunianum.
30. Pro: Carinthium.
31. Pro: Excubitorum.
32. Pro: Cattiense.
33. Pro: Melicensæ.
34. Porta Scotensis.
35. Pro: Scotense.
36. Portæ Nouæ.
37. Pro: Porta Nouæ.
38. Arx Cæsarea.
39. Arx Noua.

40. Hospitale
41. Equile Cæs
42. Domus Pr
43. Vniuersita
44. Domus S
45. Aula Epis
46. Arsenale.
47. Arsenale
48. Carcer M
49. Domus I
50. Domus I
51. Domus P
52. Porta Peʒ

STRIÆ

83

walls were extended during the fifteenth and sixteenth centuries; those enclosing the city as shown in the engraving date from the Renaissance period and enclose buildings dating largely from the fourteenth and fifteenth centuries. In 1485, unable to hold out against Matthias Corvinus of Hungary, the city was partly sacked. Though unsuccessful, the Turkish sieges of 1529 and 1683 destroyed much of the suburbs beyond the walls; of necessity, these were hastily rebuilt.

As Vienna grew, housing was needed for the inhabitants of the crowded inner city. Owing to the destruction wrought by the succession of sieges that it suffered, the city's centre had almost constantly to be rebuilt. Many dwellings had to be built up to eight, or sometimes even ten, storeys high so as to accommodate Vienna's citizens and offer shelter to those flocking to safety during times of war.

The area of the city enclosed by the walls in the engraving corresponds to that known today as the *Alstadt*, centered on the *Stephansdom*, whose great south spire was completed in 1433. A university was established in 1365. A large number of fine buildings remain in the old centre of the city, recalling the former power of the religious houses – the *Schottenhof* and *Mölkerhof* – each a small town in itself.

125

PLATE 60

ZÜRICH

Zurych. Tigurum, sive Turegum, Caesari, ut plerique existimant, Tigurinis Pagus, vulgo Zurych. 1581.
Volume III, number 44. 365 × 476mm.

After Jost Maurer, 1576. This striking view of Zürich shows a closely built-up town sited on the banks of the Limmat, near the confluence with the Sihl. The right bank is known as the *Grosse Stadt*, and the left bank as the *Kleine Stadt*. The town was first mentioned in 807 as *Turigis*, and as *Tigurum*, the false latinised form as seen in the title, from about 1512.

The Teutonic town of Zürich arose in the ninth century from the union of the castle on the *Lindenhof*, the *Gross Münster (Propstei)*, the *Frau Münster*, and the community of free men on the *Zürichberg*. In 1336 craft guilds were admitted to share in the government of the town. One of the most important was the guild of the silk weavers, who flourished here in the twelfth and thirteenth centuries and were revived once more by Huguenot refugees arriving from France in the 1680s.

As a result of the efforts of the *burgemeister* Hanns Waldmann (1483–89), who attempted to create a great centre of commerce here during his lifetime, certain principles were embodied in the constitution of 1498 which remained in force until 1798, creating a wealthy and prosperous city of fine buildings, many of which are preserved today.

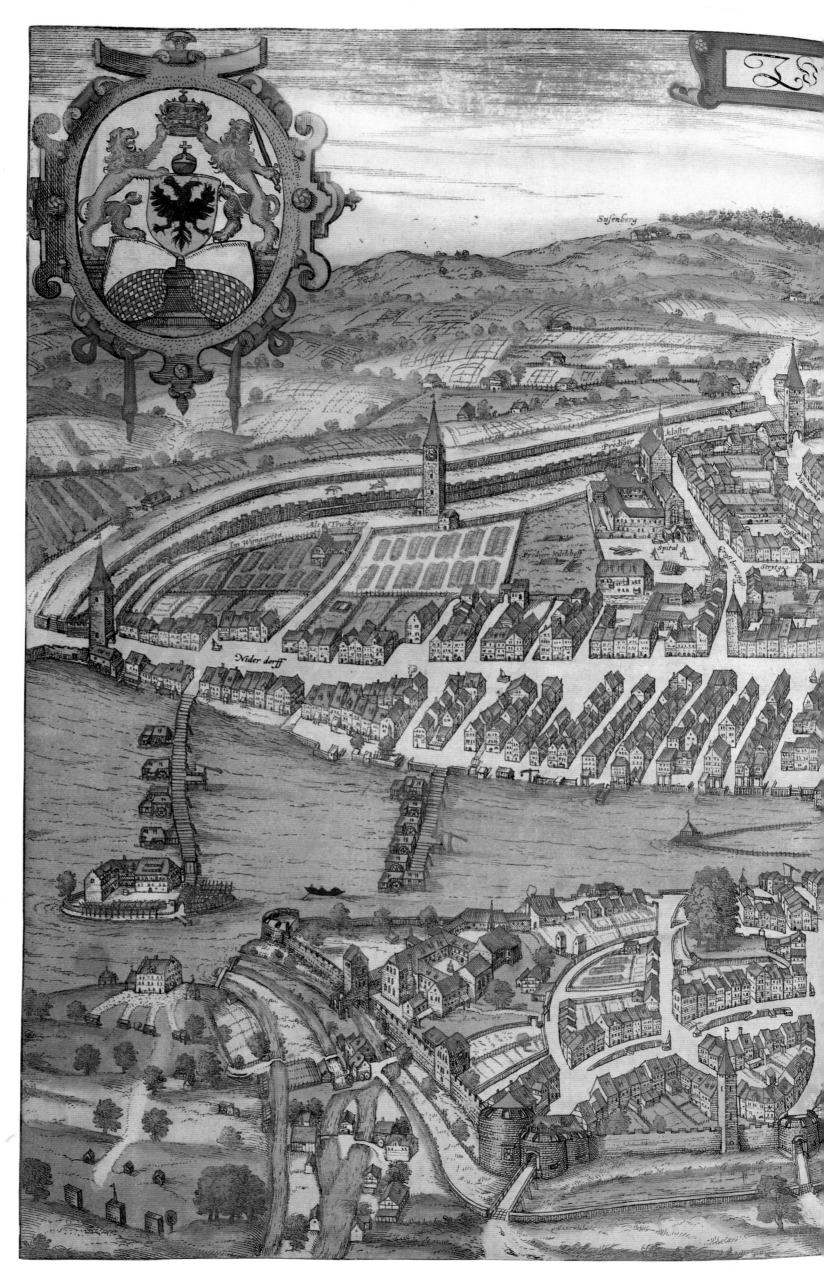

TIGVRVM, siue Tu
regum, Caesari, vt
plerique existimant,
Tigurinus Pagus, vul:
go Zurych; vrbs in
Heluetijs vt vetustissi:
ma, ita maxima, et
omnium celeberrima.

Wolffthurn

Hinder den oberen Thor

Lindenhor

Nüwstat

Stadelhofen

Münster gaß

Hinder munster gaß

Vff Dorff

Zum Rüden

Koufhuß

Wedinger hoff

Rathuß

Wasserkilch

Wellenberg

Kornhuß

S. Peter

Frouwen münster

Werckhof

Im Krats

Zug huß

Am Spit